GW01281541

"*Never* in the history of wine
has so much *useful*
cramme
The attention to detail is
mind-boggling."

"Decidedly *hip*."

"Gone is the *stuffiness*,
the *snobbishness* and the
air of *superiority*
common to *so many* wine guides."

"Brings wine to the *people*."

"*Fun,* quirky
but *informative* approach
to food and wine matching
in Australia."

TASTE
FOOD
& WINE
2009

choose the right wine every time

MATTHEW JUKES
TYSON STELZER

for Patricia Jukes and Lis Stelzer

WINE PRESS

Brisbane, Australia
www.tastefoodandwine.com.au
taste@winepress.com.au

First published in Australia by Wine Press 2008

Jukes, Matthew, 1967-.
Stelzer, Tyson, 1975-.

Taste Food & Wine: Choose the right wine every time

ISBN 978 0 9775548 8 1
ISSN 1833-7716

Design, typesetting, artwork and layout by Wine Press.
Proudly printed in Australia by Openbook Howden Design & Print, Adelaide.

contents

The **biggest** Taste yet –
50% larger than last year
making room for **more Taste** than ever

Featuring **more than eighty**
2008 vintage wines
Taste 2009 is again the **most up-to-date**
wine guide on the shelves

Announcing the **Best Wines** of 2009

All your **favourite** foods and their *perfect* wine partners

Announcing the winners of
The **Great Australian Red** 2008

The **Great New Zealand**
Pinot Noir Classification 2009

Emergency Wine List for those tricky moments
when you need to **nail** the *perfect* bottle in no time

Removable dust jacket becomes a
quick-reference **pocket guide**

Download The Best Wines of 2009
to your **mobile**
and never again be caught unprepared

An *updated* **Who's Who**
of Australian & New Zealand wine producers

New **wine retailers** in Australia and New Zealand

highlights of TASTE 2009

welcome to the third year of **Taste Food & Wine** – the biggest and best yet! If you're a season ticket holder you won't have missed the massive new format – 50% larger to make room for more **Taste** than ever!

If you're new to **Taste**, welcome along! We're here to help you eat and drink better, and we've got a lot in store to broaden your wine horizons and amaze your taste buds. If you're returning for a re-**Taste**, welcome back – do we have another great year lined up for you!

We've spent this year travelling around Australia and the world and you'll find all of our discoveries packed into the following pages – wine, food, wine shops, places to visit and people to meet. There's a lot of fun tucked in along the way, so invite your friends and get set for another journey of **Taste**!

authors' note

We've worked overtime this year to make **The Best Wines of 2009** the finest list of wines that either of us has ever put together. But after tasting more wines than we have in any other year, our final list is shorter than last year. Before you get into this list of superstars, we'd like to fill you in on a few realities regarding the wines that didn't make the cut, because the significance of this book is as much in what you don't see in it as in what you do.

> The **finest** list of wines that either of us has ever put together.

We've never been ones for mission statements before, but there are currently some serious issues concerning the subject of wine and the standing of Australia and New Zealand in the wine world. While it might annoy a few people to hear this, we feel that these are valid issues that have to be tabled in the hope that some good will come from their discussion.

Over the course of this year we tasted 10 000 wines between us for this book (and a further 30 000 on our travels), and the great news for the consumer is that the quality of wine worldwide is on the rise. Having said this, there are an awful lot more wines out there, and new labels and wineries are appearing on the scene every day. So, despite the fact that we taste through this monumental quantity of bottles on your behalf, we see more rubbish than ever. Our hit rate for this book is just 3%. Sadly, this is less than it was last year and the year before. This means that 97 out of

> There are currently some serious issues concerning the subject of wine and the standing of Australia and New Zealand in the wine world.

How to use this book

1 Look up your
menu, dish or style of cuisine
in **Food and Wine** to discover the types
of wine that make for a brilliant match

2 Choose your exact wine
in **The Best Wines of 2009** or
use **The Who's Who of Wine Producers**
to choose a bottle yourself from the best
regions, producers and vintages

3 Track down your bottle
using our **Directory of Wine Retailers**

4 Before your finish,
get the low-down on
**Serving Wine,
Wine Language,
The Great Australian Red 2008** and
The Great New Zealand Pinot Noir 2009.

every 100 wines that we open are mind-numbingly boring, extraordinarily bad value for money or should never have been put in the bottle in the first place.

Ten bullet points to help you to understand a little more about how we came to our conclusions.

So this year it is our sad duty to report that while Australia and New Zealand are making more and better wine, these countries are also making more bad wine, too. To this end, we have created ten bullet points for you to discuss with your friends to help you to understand a little more about how we came to our conclusions in **Taste Food & Wine 2009**.

- 2007 was an extremely **troublesome vintage** across Australia, and Pinot Noir, the barometer of grape varieties, is the first to complain when the weather turns bad. Of course other grapes suffer, too, so you will not see as many red 2007s in this book as you might expect. This strengthens the position of very well made 2004s, 2005s and 2006s and we advise that you buy speedily and accurately to stock up, following our advice in this book as well as **Taste Food & Wine 2008**.

- **Sauvignon Blanc** is performing better than ever at the top end in Australia, even though much of the wine industry pooh-poohs the variety. Credit must go to New Zealand for embedding Sauvignon in our psyche, but Australians should be more aware of the efforts that are made within their own shores to provide keen consumers with great value versions of this grape. Don't be snobby about Sauvignon Blanc – this is one of the "foodiest" of all white varieties – see our **Food and Wine** chapter.

- **Chardonnay**, **Riesling** and **Semillon** are Australia's strongest white grapes. New Zealand has its Sauvignons in poll position. But behind these **Pinot Gris** is still a mess; **Viognier** is, at best, unreliable; **Gewürztraminer** is, more often than not, a bit of a joke; and the "also rans" including **Verdelho**, **Albariño**, **Arneis**, **Chenin Blanc** and others generally have NFI. We have done our best to find as wide a variety of white wines as possible for you this year, but there is a lot of work to be done with these grapes. We urge you to stick to our hard-fought recommendations and not to gamble, for fear of disappointment.

- Having dealt with the whites, **Cabernet**, **Shiraz**, **Pinot Noir** and **Grenache** stand tall, but the real laugh comes with the rest of the red family. **Merlot**, despite a recent industry call to arms, and the random other misfits are a shocking disgrace. This is a strong statement, and one that we will back up with a very simple fact.

Merlot and the random other misfits of the red family are a shocking disgrace.

10   introduction

how to read wine and food entries

We've gone to great lengths to research what the wine is really selling for this year – not simply the RRP

Wines are listed in order of price

Regions from which the fruit is sourced

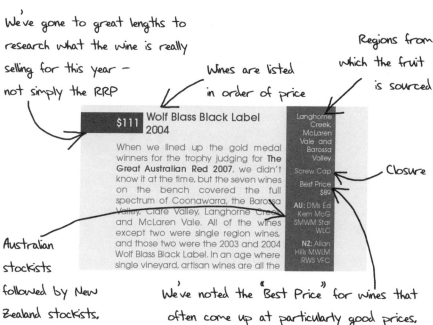

$111 **Wolf Blass Black Label 2004**

Langhorne Creek, McLaren Vale and Barossa Valley

Screw Cap

Best Price $89

AU: DMs Ed Kem McG SMWM Star WLC

NZ: Allan Hills MWLM RWS VFC

When we lined up the gold medal winners for the trophy judging for **The Great Australian Red 2007**, we didn't know it at the time, but the seven wines on the bench covered the full spectrum of Coonawarra, the Barossa Valley, Clare Valley, Langhorne Creek and McLaren Vale. All of the wines except two were single region wines, and those two were the 2003 and 2004 Wolf Blass Black Label. In an age where single vineyard, artisan wines are all the

Closure

Australian stockists followed by New Zealand stockists. See back page for key to abbreviations.

We've noted the "Best Price" for wines that often come up at particularly good prices. Decent shops will offer a further 10% off on 6-pack buys and 20% on dozens.

Variations on the dish or ingredient are highlighted in each entry and wines to match are listed.

Duck *Roast* or *pan-fried* duck is often served with fruit or fruity sauces, so you need to be prepared to balance this with a fruity wine. Reds are the call of the day here – Australian and New Zealand Pinot Noir is hard to go past (loads to choose from in **The Best 365 Wines of 2008**), good quality Beaujolais, Italian Barbera or Negroamaro, Australian Chambourcin (OK, this is rare, but what a challenge!), lighter

Pinot Noir
Chambourcin
Zinfandel
Riesling
Pinot Gris
Viognier
Cab Shiraz
Durif

The quick-reference wine box lists the most important white wines (white text) and red wines (dark text) in the same order that they appear in the entry, so it's easy to flick across to look up more detail.

In our final short list of "alternative" reds, we tasted more than 250 wines and only three made it into this book. Would you believe it, even Merlot had barely a three percent hit rate. STOP paying good money for bad wine. This might stop bad wines from being made. Remember, these dreadful creations are only still in production because you continue to buy them. Too many winemakers pretend to listen to us wine writers but do nothing to improve these shockers because their order books are still full. As Michael Jackson memorably sang, "I'm gonna make a change for once in my life!"

- **Shiraz** undoubtedly remains Australia's strongest suit. We are delighted to report that Cabernet has finally started to enjoy somewhat of a renaissance – about bloody time too, after screaming, pleading and cheerleading every winemaker to do better with this vital and noble grape variety. Welcome back, Cabernet, you have been in the wilderness for far too long and it's great to have you back.

- Australia now stands shoulder-to-shoulder with New Zealand in terms of quality **Pinot Noir** production. Both countries are to be applauded for the way in which they have tackled this extremely sensitive grape variety. But prices seem to have escalated far too quickly. The desire to make wines that rival the finest red Burgundies is yet to be realised. So, while we tinker with our vineyards and wait for time to age our vines, we should continue to spread the word globally about these delicious wines but not prevent people from embracing our collective passion for Pinot by pricing ourselves out of the market.

- **Over-oaked reds** are the bane of our existence. How many times do we have to tell winemakers to taste their wines during their production and reign in these oppressive flavours before they get too pungent and ghastly? Save money as well, for goodness' sake (new French barrels equate to an additional two to three dollars per bottle, at cost). The continued, deluded insistence that serious red wine cannot exist without turbo-charged oak is, frankly, preposterous. Top quality oak barrels should only be used for top quality wines where the fruit complexity and potential are matched with quality carpentry. Our desire is to see more wines made where the flavours of the grapes and their vineyards shine through with clarity and expression, allowing us to enjoy these wines sooner rather than never.

- **Sparkling wines** looked good, both white, red and in between, but there is an alarming trend emerging where the "better" wines are sold at inflated prices, often exceeding those of Champagnes. Australia and New Zealand make bloody good sparking wines, but surely we should be encouraging drinkers to celebrate with these fine wines instead of drinking Champagne at all times? The way to achieve this is to continue to uphold the already impressive standards but price these wines fairly. By all means, drink Champagne if you can afford it (sticking to our recommendations, of course, because there is a load of crap made in this famous region, too), but if you can't, or if you charge through the bubbles at breakneck speed, stick with great Aussie or Kiwi fizz.

- Everybody these days plays from a level winemaking playing field and, to a certain extent, history and past trophies are meaningless in this modern day. So approach each wine in this list with an open mind, whether they have a legendary name or are a first time producer, because we celebrate **excellence in the glass** and not irrelevant track records or glossy marketing hype.

> We celebrate **excellence in the glass** and not irrelevant track records or glossy marketing hype.

- As you know, we don't **score** wines in this book, and there is no number one winery, wine or winemaker. This is because each and every wine is of an exemplary standard in the first place and they all represent tremendous value for money, even those at three-figures. It is easy to be led into buying a 90+ point wine without understanding the subtle nuances of what it tastes like, what it will go with and when, how and with whom you should drink it. We prefer to let our words do the talking so that you understand exactly the flavour and the style of each of our wines, and how to get the most from every single glass. This is what we love about wine. Wine is not about numbers, it's all about **Taste** and taste is subjective, not something you can attach a percentage to. It is something that changes with your mood, your cooking and your company.

If you feel as revved up about these points as we do and want to make a difference, there is something very simple that you must do. Don't let yourself down. Make a commitment to drink only good wine this year. We believe very strongly in this cause, and this is the reason that we have written this book. The wines in it this year may be fewer than last year, but they are better than ever before.

> Make a commitment to drink only good wine this year.

Download
The Best Wines of 2009
to your mobile phone
and *never again* be caught unprepared.

Our goal every year is not only to
set you up with the most *amazing*
selection of wines *possible,* but to make them
accessible *wherever* you are.

We invented the dust jacket
that folds into a quick-reference
pocket guide
so you can keep **The Best Wines of 2009**
on hand at *all times.*

Now all you need is a mobile phone
with internet download capabilities
and you can have Taste at your *fingertips*
wherever you are.

Download the complete list or
customise your selection
to suit your **Taste.**

download   15

by the same authors

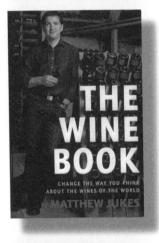

The Great Australian Red

Shiraz Cabernet is **The Great Australian Red**. First championed in Australia in the late 1800s as generic "claret", the blend of Shiraz and Cabernet was resurrected in the 1950s. By 1962, Max Schubert, the creator of Grange, had made what he himself named the best wine of his illustrious career. A blend of Coonawarra Cabernet and Barossa Shiraz, 1962 Penfolds Bin 60A is now Penfolds' most successful show wine of all time, and has on countless occasions been heralded as the greatest Australian red wine ever made.

Over the ensuing decades, the direction of red winemaking in this country was changed forever by the profound impact of this wine and hundreds of others which shared a similar formula. Schubert and his contemporaries were convinced of the potential of Cabernet, both on its own and as a blending partner for Shiraz. By the mid-1970s, the blend was rife across the landscape of the Australian wine industry.

But that was thirty years ago, and a long way from the frenetic pace of the industry today. Australia now churns out tens of thousands of labels every year. How many of these represent blends of Shiraz and Cabernet? Merely a few hundred.

If many of the greatest wines that this country has ever produced are Shiraz Cabernet blends, why don't we see more made today? It seems that the blend has slipped out of the limelight, in the wake of the rise of Shiraz Viognier and an entourage of alternative red varietals. We have created **The Great Australian Red** competition to shift this focus back to our unique icon.

The Shiraz Cabernet blend is an Australian institution. This country championed it, refined it, and still does it better than anyone else on the planet. It's our only unique, definitive red. This is Australia's national treasure of the red wine world, and it deserves to be recognised and celebrated as our greatest red wine.

The future of Australia's wine industry depends on it just as much as has its past. Tapping into the strength of our past and framing it as the unique draw-card of the future, which rival winemaking countries simply cannot replicate, the Shiraz Cabernet blend is the secret weapon to take the Australian wine industry into its next era. In the current climate of drought at home, financial turmoil abroad and rising international competition, this has never been more pertinent. The present Australian wine industry is in need of a trigger to bring its attention back to the blend so crucial to its history and future.

The Great Australian Red is an innovative wine competition to encourage, identify and promote Shiraz Cabernet blends. The competition is free of the constraints of region, price and style, drawing together great examples of all styles, at all price points, from almost every Australian state.

> In the current climate of drought at home, financial turmoil abroad and rising international competition, Australia's unique draw-card, the Shiraz Cabernet blend, has never been more important.

Again this year, we assembled a formidable team of judges to work alongside us to find the greatest examples of the blend made today. **The Great Australian Red** has put the Shiraz Cabernet blend back into the focus of Australia – and the world.

the judging

When we started The Great Australian Red competition, we were amazed that no one had ever done it before. Three years down the line, the wines that have emerged from this competition, both in terms of sheer quality and value for money, are exactly what we wanted them to be when we coined the expression "the blend that defines Australia". This year we feel that every one of the wineries that submitted samples raised their game by yet another notch, and we applaud this commitment to the one true, iconic Australian wine style.

the judges

The judging panel for **The Great Australian Red 2008**:

Brian Croser —	Tapanappa (Chair of Judges)
Matthew Jukes —	Wine Writer, UK
Tyson Stelzer —	Wine Writer, Australia
Tom Carson —	Winemaker, Yabby Lake
Stephen Pannell —	Winemaker, S.C. Pannell
Bill Downie —	Winemaker, William Downie
Tash Mooney —	Winemaker, Fox Gordon
Amelia Pinsent —	Wine Writer, UK
Stuart Knox —	Fix St James, Sydney
Paul Diamond —	Selector
Scott Farraway —	Wineaway, Brisbane
Travis Watson —	The Wine Emporium, Brisbane

We spend a lot of time putting together the list of judges each year, trying to find a balance between winemaker, retailer, restaurateur, journalist and buyer. This year's team was our most highly-experienced yet, encompassing every wine discipline you could wish for, and we believe that the results are our finest to date.

At our pre-tasting briefing, chairman Brian Croser set the scene for the coming two days with a masterful speech about seamless balance between the two varietals, integrity of fruit, perfumed aromatics, fine tannins, perfectly balanced alcohol levels and controlled oak. While all of us had respectfully turned our mobile phones off, Matt Cartwright, our legendary logistics expert, received a call from one of his friends and the ring tone which ensued left us all in fits of giggles. Brian was about to begin another heartfelt diatribe when *Raiders of the Lost Ark* filled the room at full volume. It could not have been better timed, such is the legendary status of this pioneering winemaker. We are very grateful to him and to all of the judges for taking time out of their busy schedules to join us, which speaks volumes for the passion that they, too, possess for this unique style of wine.

Ever the gentleman, Brian presented us with a gift to thank us for his opportunity to Chair this prestigious event. 1979 Petaluma Coonawarra was the first vintage that Brian made and he told us that this was one of his very last bottles, so we carefully set it aside and opened it two weeks later. It had to be the wine to drink to celebrate the completion of writing this book.

With guests joining us for dinner and wine enthusiasm high on the agenda I (TS) decided to serve this wine blind. Hovering over the decanter and pouring carefully, I checked the details of the back label to ensure that my forthcoming options would be factually correct. Assuming that Petaluma Coonawarra was a Cabernet Merlot blend, as it is today, imagine my shock (I bloody nearly dropped the bottle!) when I read that this wine was a 60/40 Shiraz/Cabernet blend made from Coonawarra and Clare Valley fruit. Suddenly everything slotted into place. This wasn't just a generous gift of an ancient and famous red wine, it was something far greater: Brian's Great Australian Red. When the wine was poured the colour, aroma and flavour were nothing short of breathtaking. As we raised our glasses to Brian Croser and to the completion of **Taste 2009**, we did so with the perfect wine.

the trophy winners

The Great Australian Red 2008: **Penfolds Bin 389 Cabernet Shiraz 2005**

VINTAGE CELLARS™

AUSTRALIA'S FINE WINE SPECIALIST

The Vintage Cellars Trophy for the Best Wine over $50:
Penfolds Bin 389 Cabernet Shiraz 2005

The Mercure Hotel Trophy for the Best Cabernet-dominant Blend:
Wolf Blass Black Label Cabernet Shiraz 2005

The Openbook Howden Trophy for the Best Shiraz-dominant Blend:
Geoff Hardy K1 Tzimmukin Shiraz Cabernet 2005

The Alcan Stelvin Trophy for the Best Wine under $20:
Yalumba "The Scribbler" Cabernet Shiraz 2006

the great australian red

pull the rabbit out of the hat

judge's comments

With forty-eight consecutive vintages under its belt the winner this year has clearly refined the Cabernet Shiraz style. However, in the current climate and with its enormous corporate owners, Penfolds still manages to pull the rabbit out of the hat and this is testament to the passion and talent of Peter Gago who, virtually single-handedly, keeps this winery's reputation at the forefront of everybody's minds, acting as ambassador, winemaker, font of all knowledge and downright good bloke. It is as much a trophy for 389 as it is for him. There is, thankfully, a lot of this wine produced this year so everyone should have a chance to have a decent go at this extraordinary 389.

South Australia clearly has a stranglehold on the Shiraz Cabernet style because of the depth of plantings of both varieties, but Western Australia, Victoria and Queensland all joined in with medals this year, so there is clearly a desire throughout the nation to embrace this phenomenal style of wine.

With large amounts of vineyards at their disposal, it's not surprising that we see a large number of wines from big producers taking out the top gongs, although it is good to see Geoff Hardy's new super-premium appearing for the first time. Just outside of the trophy zone were a host of other small wineries making brilliant wines, and we should support them all.

With medals being awarded to every vintage from 2001 to 2007, with a particular focus on 2005 and 2006, it is clear to see that even in the weaker vintages great examples of this style can be made. This further reinforces that this is Australia's most important style, irrespective of vintage.

taste on tour

Here's your chance to taste the winners of **The Great Australian Red** with us. Join us for dinner during our national book launch of **Taste Food & Wine 2009.** Each dinner will feature medal winners from the competition alongside local produce, brought to you by the two biggest supporters of **The Great Australian Red,** *Mercure Hotels* and *Vintage Cellars.*

These events always sell out fast, so contact your local *Vintage Cellars* store or one of the following *Mercure Hotels* to secure your place.

Mercure Melbourne – 13 Spring St – Friday 14 November 2008

Mercure Sydney – 818 George St – Saturday 15 November 2008

Mercure Brisbane – 85 North Quay – Tuesday 18 November 2008

Mercure Perth – 10 Irwin St – Thursday 20 November 2008

trophy presentations

We invite you to join us for the trophy presentation and tasting of the winning wines at the Mercure Grosvenor in Adelaide on Saturday November 8, 2008. Please email us for details (stelzer@winepress.com.au).

The Gold Medal winners are:

Aramis White Label Shiraz Cabernet Sauvignon 2006

Geoff Hardy K1 Tzimmukin Shiraz Cabernet 2005

Penfolds Bin 389 Cabernet Shiraz 2005

Ulithorne Paternus Cabernet Shiraz 2006

Wolf Blass Black Label Cabernet Shiraz 2004

Wolf Blass Black Label Cabernet Shiraz 2005

Yalumba "The Scribbler" Cabernet Shiraz 2006

The Silver Medal winners are:

Anvers Razorback Road 2005

Ferngrove The Stirlings 2005

Jacob's Creek Johann Shiraz Cabernet 2001

Kaesler W.O.M.S 2006

Neagles Rock 'One Black Dog' Reserve Cabernet Shiraz 2005

Penfolds Bin 389 Cabernet Shiraz 2006

Penfolds Cellar Reserve Cabernet Shiraz 2005

Penley Estate Condor Shiraz Cabernet 2006

Scarpatoni Estate Reserve 2006

Summerfield Wines Tradition 2005

Taltarni Reserve Shiraz Cabernet 2004

The Lane Vineyard JC 2007

Willunga 100 Cabernet Shiraz 2006

Wyndham Estate George Wyndham Shiraz Cabernet 2005

Yalumba The Reserve 2002

The Bronze Medal winners are:

Amicus Shiraz Cabernet 2005

Ballandean Estate Generation 3 2005

Bremerton 'Best of Vintage' 2005

Brothers In Arms No. 6 Shiraz Cabernet 2005

Dividing Range 2006

Dominique Portet 'Andre' 2006

Elderton Barossa Ode to Lorraine CSM 2005

Flaxman The Stranger 2006

the great australian red

Glaetzer Anaperenna 2006

Grant Burge Wines Nebuchadnezzar Shiraz Cabernet 2003

Harewood Estate Shiraz Cabernet 2007

Henry's Drive Parson's Flat 2006

Hollick Wines Shiraz Cabernet 2005

Hollick Wines Shiraz Cabernet 2006

Jacob's Creek Johann Shiraz Cabernet 2002

Jim Barry PB Shiraz Cabernet Sauvignon 2006

Kangarilla Road Hellbent 2006

Lady Bay Vineyard 2006

Lake Breeze 'Bernoota' 2006

Lindemans Limestone Ridge Shiraz Cabernet 2006

Longview Vineyard 'Red Bucket' 2007

Macaw Creek Reserve Shiraz Cabernet 2003

Macaw Creek Wines Reserve Shiraz Cabernet 2005

Malleea by Majella 2005

McGuigan Handmade Cabernet Shiraz 2007

Metala Shiraz Cabernet Sauvignon 2006

Mildara Coonawarra Cabernet Shiraz 2005

Mildara Coonawarra Cabernet Shiraz 2006

Mitchelton Imprint 2007

Musician by Majella 2007

Neagles Rock 'Mr Duncan' Cabernet Shiraz 2006

Oddfellows 2005 'Svengali' 2005

Penfolds Koonunga Hill Seventy Six Shiraz Cabernet 2006

Penfolds Koonunga Hill Seventy Six Shiraz Cabernet 2007

Scarpatoni Estate School Block 2005

Soul Growers Shiraz Cabernet 2006

Summerfield Wines Reserve Cabernet Shiraz 2003

Taltarni Reserve Shiraz Cabernet 2005

Wolf Blass Black Label 2006

Woodstock Shiraz Cabernet 2005

Wyndham Estate George Wyndam Shiraz Cabernet 2006

Wynns Coonawarra Estate Johnsons Block Shiraz Cabernet 2004

Yalumba FDR1A 2004

All trophy winners will be presented with limited edition framed prints of
Dr Cameron Stelzer's oil on canvas, the third in **The Great Australian Red** series.

THE GREAT
NEW ZEALAND

PINOT NOIR
CLASSIFICATION

the great new zealand pinot noir classification

The Great New Zealand Pinot Noir Classification is based on an average rating across the five most recent vintages of Pinot Noir that we have tasted. We both keep detailed notes and scores from all of our tastings as well as impressions of the total performance of every estate listed. We collaborate on these to develop a list of rolling averages. Any estate can move up or down on each and every release, as a number have this year – this is a rolling classification that enables everyone to improve if they so desire.

A classification of **5** is awarded to the top estates and **0** to the lowest, although we do not publish the 0s. Inclusion, even at level 1, is a commendable performance as the majority of estates have not yet achieved this level.

5

Ata Rangi
Felton Road
Mt Difficulty

4

Dry River
Peregrine
Bell Hill
Escarpment
Pyramid Valley

3

Cloudy Bay
Martinborough Vineyard
Pegasus Bay
Rippon
Wither Hills
Bald Hills
Craggy Range
Dog Point
Hinton Estate
Mountford
Mt Edward
Two Paddocks
Valli

Each estate is graded on its **estate wine**. No single vineyard or special cuvée wines are taken into consideration.

2

Chard Farm
Gibbston Valley
Olssens
Palliser Estate
Villa Maria
Auntsfield
Kumeu River
TerraVin
Voss

1

Carrick
Huia
Nautilus
Quartz Reef
Amisfield
Foxes Island
Gravitas
Murdoch James
Neudorf Vineyards
Pisa Range
Rockburn
Spy Valley
Te Kairanga

With five vintages in the tank the **bold** rating is awarded. The producers not in bold are tentative inclusions for whom we have not yet seen five consecutive vintages – these will be 'bolded' and firmly positioned on the fifth vintage.

There is no ranking *within* each tier (estates are ordered alphabetically).

We have travelled the length and breadth of New Zealand, sent out exhaustive requests for samples, fronted up for every tasting and tasted every New Zealand Pinot Noir that has come anywhere near us. Thank you to the many estates who responded to our requests this year. If an estate is not included, it is either because the wines don't stack up in our minds or that we have not yet come across them. We apologise if we have missed anyone. We do, of course, welcome the opportunity to taste your wines.

2009

the great new zealand pinot noir classification

2009

Last year saw the start of our New Zealand Pinot Noir initiative when we launched **The Great New Zealand Pinot Noir Classification**. We always knew that this would cause a stir, pleasing those winemakers who got a mention and ruffling the feathers of those who didn't. Our desire to explain to the consumer our complicated thoughts on this globally important wine style in the end manifested itself in a relatively simple tabular form which we believe works really well and, we are delighted to say, has received the support of the New Zealand wine industry and the opinion-formers within.

Please forgive us for dropping this quote in, but it has spurred us on to work even harder this year in order to finesse this classification further:

"This is one of the most intelligent assessments on the state of New Zealand Pinot Noir." – Wine NZ

There is movement in the classification this year but the net effect is of a slight downward trend, with only three estates joining our hall of greats for the first time. One estate made the unprecedented leap of two levels, and is to be congratulated for this. Craggy Range's portfolio has grown significantly both in range and quality and we are delighted to bring this incredible improvement to your attention.

Congratulations to all of those estates who have made this table this year. It is worth emphasising that the difference between the levels is slight and while upward and downward movements are inevitable, inclusion in this list at any level is commendable. Maintaining a position is a reflection of continued excellence.

We predicted last year that the New Zealand Pinots set to hit the shelves in 2008 would represent the largest collective improvement in lower-tier New Zealand Pinot Noir that we have seen in any single year. The wines that we have tasted this year have certainly reflected this. The new kids on the NZ block are no longer so new. Their vines are starting to mature nicely, and they've clearly been listening to people like us who keep banging on about wine quality, balance and value.

The Great New Zealand Pinot Noir Classification reflects the ups and downs of New Zealand Pinot Noir this year, for the "ups" to be celebrated and the "downs" to set about working harder to reach the next level.

the great new zealand pinot noir

THE BEST
WINES
OF 2009

sparkling wines

$8	**Pepperton Estate Goodwyn Brut Cuvée NV**

Here's a real surprise start to our list because this wine is as far removed as you can imagine from the recipe on the tin. The Riverina is categorically not the source for top-flight sparkling wine fruit and Semillon has never, to our knowledge, made its way into a bottle of Champagne. But, blimey, this wine is astoundingly attractive, and for this reason it stands shoulder to shoulder with wines of much higher pedigree. At the end of the day this book is called "Taste" and not "Label Shagger," and this is why it has earned its place.

Riverina

Cork

www.pepper tonestate. com.au

$13	**Jacob's Creek Sparkling Rosé NV**

The team at JC has impeccable taste because this is a difficult style of wine to get right and they have nailed this, and the Orlando Trilogy Rosé, in a competitive class. It's fine and tight with a delightful crisp finish (acidity is crucial in sparklers and far too many are chubby and sweet these days – yuk!). The theme is red cherries and fresh-picked strawberries, so this is party fizz personified. Pick it up on special for ten bucks.

Australia

Cork

AU: 1st DMs DW Lland SMWM VCs WLC

NZ: Mill

See back page for key to stockists

Jacob's Creek Sparkling Shiraz NV

$14

Australia

Cork

AU: 1st DMs
DW Lland
SMWM VCs

This finely-tuned leviathan of a company has done it again, this time with a wine that every maker seems to have a go at, but so few companies can truly make well. Over the last few years we have always managed to find a handful of JC wines worthy of inclusion in this imperial list and this inexpensive red sprinted into place without so much as a glance over its shoulder at the flagging competition. The stunning, briary, beautifully balanced, dry-but-not-tannic themes work so well here. We have virtually no other sparkling reds in our list this year and this wine is one of the reasons why. When you can buy JCSS for fourteen bucks, why would you spend twice as much on a wine that's half as good? Black plums, pepper and spice abound and the juiciness is cut with savoury spice – WOW.

Wolf Blass Red Label Chardonnay Pinot Noir NV

$14

South-Eastern Australia

Cork

Best Price: $9

AU: 1st DMs
DW Lland
WLC

There are so many wines at twice the price that do not come close to the balance, smoothness, build and professional quality of this wine. When people phone us up and say that they're organising a big party on a tight budget, this is the first wine that we recommend. You can buy it for well under $10 in bulk and it's a proven party-pleaser. Even if a few wine bores sneak into the crowd, you can still pour this for them without fear that they will turn into complete wine snobs and turn up their noses.

$15 Orlando Trilogy Cuvée Brut Pinot Noir Chardonnay Pinot Meunier NV

Effortless and with superb balance, it's not what Trilogy's got, but what it hasn't that's remarkable, because most of the other sparklers at this price taste like cardboard, fish heads, detergent or paprika BBQ shapes. Seriously! This is a real winner with its clean apple, lemon and a touch of spice.

South-Eastern Australia

Cork

Best Price: $12

AU: 1st Boc Chalk DMs DW Nicks Lland Sixty Sum VCs WLC

NZ: HWC Mill

$16 Orlando Trilogy Sparkling Rosé NV

We've never seen this little beauty before, and it's a shame, because this is a delicious, proper, sparkling rosé at a tidy little price point. All you need are a pack of plastic cups, a busload of giddy chicks, some spangly handbags and Gloria Gaynor on the screech. Us blokes can lean back and watch as the entire annual allocation of Trilogy Rosé disappears from sight in one beautifully choreographed evening. This wine is clean, it tastes like liquidised rose petals and plump strawberries and it has a fresh, long finish. What more do you want for $16? Apart from the DJ to change the track right NOW.

South-Eastern Australia

Cork

AU: 1st Chalk DMs DW Lland VCs

Victoria and Tasmania

Cork

Best Price: $15

$20 Taltarni Brut 2006

It's unlikely that a bargain bubbles could compete with the big boys when it's made by a small, boutique producer more famous for big, robust red wines. But Taltarni is fast becoming the bubbles to be seen with. This clean, fresh, citrus-

AU: 1st Boc Chalk DW Ed Lland PWS Rand Sixty SMWM Sum VCs WLC

accented style is just the thing as an aperitif and it will also see you right through the night when you're out on the razz.

Bleasdale Sparkling Shiraz NV
$21

Australia's most consistently brilliant Sparkling Shiraz? We think so. There is no need to build massive biceps and huge quadriceps into this style of wine. What is crucial, though, is to make it as slippery, curvy and succulent as possible. Think Beyoncé, not Mr T. Spicy, ripe, dark chocolate and rich plums load the nose and front palate and black cherries steam into view on the rear, with a veritable wiggle in its fabulous toosh.

Katnook Founder's Block Sparkling Shiraz 2005
$21

A more masculine wine than the other two sparkling reds this year, this is a foodier proposition. It's not a wine that is more tannic than the others, it's just a little more structured and a little dryer. Fat black plums and dark cherry fruits make up the battering ram of flavours here and there is ample pepper and spice to make it the perfect companion to a meat feast. A savoury finish with yet more spice means that you could even stretch to top flight Indian lamb dishes and really impress your mates.

Jansz Tasmania Premium Non Vintage Cuvée
$24

You would expect a company that makes such

Sidebar:

NZ: Glen WFW

Langhorne Creek

Cork

AU: 1st Aus Chalk DMs DW EEC Ed Nicks Lland Sum VCs WLC

NZ: SC

Coonawarra

Cork

AU: 1st Sel DMs DW SMWM Sum VCs

Tasmania

Cork

Best Price: $20

brilliant rosé bubbles as Jansz to be able to nail the white, too. And, guess what, they did! While many of its rivals are blends from everywhere, this wine is made purely from Tasmanian fruit, giving it a zest that edges it ever further into consummate elegance.

$26 Jansz Tasmania Premium Non Vintage Rosé NV

Jansz is one of the best producers of sparkling wines outside of Champagne itself. Trying to nail the rosé style is always going to be a challenge – even the big boys in Champs struggle, save for a few true experts (see below). So when this firm, buttock-tighteningly fresh, yet ever so elegant pink elixir hit our glasses we did a treble-take and proceeded not to spit it out (unlike several thousand other samples!). Go Tassie! What a superb wine – it even has space for some cracking sweet spice notes and an uncommon length to add to its alluring red flavours.

$37 Croser Piccadilly Valley 2005

Wincingly tight and yet somehow impressively rich and involved on the palate, Croser Brut raises the bar as every vintage passes. At this rate it could soon glide past all comers, making it the best value Antipodean fizz on the market. With its ball-stamping acidity it is likely to live for five years with ease, so perhaps we should start putting some cases away for a rainy day? After all, you won't see this region's boundaries getting any larger in the near future – pity we can't say that about dear old Champagne.

AU: 1st Boc Chalk DMs DW Ed EEC Nicks PWS SMWM Sum TWC VCs WLC

NZ: HWC SC WFW

Tasmania

Cork

AU: 1st Chalk DMs DW Ed PWS SMWM Sum TWC VCs WLC

NZ: HWC

Adelaide Hills

Cork

AU: 1st Aus Boc Chalk DMs DW Ed GPO Nicks Lland PWS Rand Sixty SMWM Sum VCs WLC

NZ: HWC

Chandon Blanc de Blancs 2005 $38

South-Eastern Australia

Cork

AU: 1st Chalk DMs DW Ed Nicks PWS Rand SMWM Sum VCs WLC

This is the only Chandon wine to make our list this year, which shows two things. That the competition is catching up – and there's nothing like a little heat to force you to raise your game. And also that the recommended retail price of these wines seems to have crept northward, as it did last year, and we don't want to see it going any further. So, hopefully not for the last time, this delicious lemon-zest-accented wine with a creamy palate has won its way into our list.

J. Dumangin Fils à Chigny-les-Roses Brut 17 NV $45

Champagne, France

Cork

AU: 1st VCs

Before the big Champagne houses arrive in a cavalcade of splendour in our list, the two small houses of Dumangin and Gimonnet have again strutted to the front of the pack. They come in at the same price as last year – good news, and more than what we can say for many Aussie sparklers, whose prices creep ever closer to Champagne levels. This is another reason why you should reach for Dumangin's honey and spice flavoured stunner as your party partner. Jacky Dumangin's son Gilles travels so prolifically that there are more international flags on the front page of his web site than there were in the Olympic opening ceremony. Click on the next page of the site and a flashing cork will tell you that they even do personal labels for weddings. What more could you want? Jacky and Gilles went up the hill to fetch a pail of Brut 17. Beats Brut 33 any day.

$50 Pierre Gimonnet & Fils Cuis 1er Cru Cuis Brut NV

Champagne, France

Cork

AU: 1st DMs VCs

While Dumangin is made of equal thirds of Chardonnay, Pinot Noir and Pinot Meunier (the classic Champagne recipe), it's great to see a pure Chardonnay wine in the shape of this Blanc de Blancs from the village of Cuis. There are no red grapes in the Gimonnet building, and this means that the style of wine here is rapier sharp, nervy, cleansing, and epic with posh canapés.

$57 Bay of Fires Arras 2002

Tasmania

Cork

Best Price: $50

AU: 1st DMs EEC Ed GPO Nicks PWS SMWM Sum VCs WLC

As elegant as Jean-Claude Van Damme in a nightie, this is a massive mouthful of seriously decadent fruit and there is staggering power here, too. The only reason that this wine works is that there is sensational acidity, tightly coiled, Cobra-like, at its core. In the same way that Krug is as subtle as a brass band, but somehow manages to captivate your entire olfactory system, Arras pulls off the same trick, but at an earlier moment in its timeline. This is a truly world class sparkler – that successfully turns the world upside down.

$72 Pol Roger Reserve Brut NV

Champagne, France

Cork

AU: 1st Aus Chalk DW Ed EEC Lland PWS Rand SMWM Sum VCs WLC

NZ: Glen HWC WFW

In a world where most of the big Champagne houses are owned by international handbag companies and insurance brokers it is so refreshing (no pun intended) to drink a wine that is made by a family-owned company. Classic in every way, even Winston Churchill used to drink a tankard every day before starting work – and he was no shrinking violet! What are you waiting for?

Louis Roederer Brut 2002 $77

2002 vintage Roederer is not a heavy style of wine and it is unusually ready to drink, making it a deliciously flashy gift for someone you fancy. Explain that this is not a wine to cellar, that they should open it on the spot, and Egyptian physical training will surely follow.

Billecart-Salmon Brut Réserve NV $80

François Roland-Billecart is one of the most highly respected figureheads of any Champagne house. He also happens to be one of the nicest blokes to have dinner with, because of his insatiable appetite and staggering thirst for fine wine. Always the last man standing, with a cigar in one hand and a digestif in the other, we have enjoyed sensational evenings with him, both out on the town and with him cooking in his own kitchen. It is his magical *joi de vivre* which makes its way into Billecart's wines and we adore it. Is this the best non-vintage Champagne in the world in terms of sheer beauty and value-for-money? The answer is unequivocally in the affirmative.

Laurent Perrier Ultra Brut NV $80

With its distinctive, ever so slightly terrifying blue and silver label, you know you are in for a bit of mild sado-masochism when you pop the cork on this wine. Ultra Brut, meaning jolly dry, is one of the most thrilling Champagnes around. It obliterates your palate in a moment and then kindly allows

---

Champagne, France

Cork

Best Price: $70

AU: 1st Boc Chalk DMs DOr DW Nicks PWS SMWM Sum VCs

NZ: HWC SC WFW

Champagne, France

Cork

Best Price: $70

AU: 1st Aus Chalk DMs DOr DW EEC Ed GPO Nicks PWS Rand SMWM Sum VCs WLC

NZ: Glen HWC WFW

Champagne, France

Cork

AU: DMs SMWM Sum

NZ: SC

---

you to rebuild it again, piece by piece with every sip. Awesome with sushi and even better with oysters, there is a warning on the back label to remove all garments before drinking this wine, so follow this advice to the letter and you will find that life improves beyond your wildest dreams.

$81 Louis Roederer Brut Premier NV

Champagne, France

Cork

Best Price: $70

AU: 1st DOr DW Ed EEC GPO PWS Rand SMWM VCs WLC

NZ: Glen

So highly sought after are the wines of Louis Roederer that even this non-vintage cuvée is on limited allocation to retailers worldwide. Ripe, creamy, succulent and sexy, Brut Premier is a hedonistic NV which delivers an enormous amount of flavour at a reasonable price. One glimpse of this label before a dinner party and you know that your host has impeccable taste and you are set for a superb evening.

$84 Jacquesson Cuvée No 732 NV

Champagne, France

Cork

Best Price: $75

AU: 1st DMs DOr EEC Nicks PWS Rand SMWM VCs

NZ: SC

This is an intellectual offering from a very small Champagne house where each and every cuvée is given its own consecutive number, making this the 732nd blend ever made since their centenary wine in 1898. The attention to detail here is extraordinary. M. Jacquesson quite rightly believes that no two NV blends are the same, so you will see both 731 and 732 on the shelves this year. The great majority of Jacquesson wines are vinified in oak and they have minimal dosage (hence are relatively dry in style). Cuvée number 732 was produced from a blend based on the 2004 harvest. If you know anyone who is 732 years old this year, this is the perfect present.

Gosset Grande Réserve Brut NV $86

Champagne, France

Cork

AU: 1st DMs DW Ed EEC GPO PWS Rand SMWM Sum VCs

NZ: Sel Glen

Non-vintage wine, as the name suggests, is made from a blend of different years' harvests. Vintage wine, by contrast, is made from just one. Gosset takes exactly the same model as Krug and blends vintage wines together to make this very special Grande Resérve. It has the power and majesty of an aged vintage Champagne but the price point of an NV. This is the wine that really smart connoisseurs choose when they want to impress their mates but not appear to be too vulgar.

Bollinger Special Cuvée NV $92

Champagne, France

Cork

Best Price: $75

AU: 1st Aus Boc Chalk DMs DW Ed Nicks Lland PWS Sixty SMWM Sum VCs WLC

NZ: Glen HWC Mill RWM SC WFW

You've got to be in the mood for Bolly, because it is one of the biggest and most impactful styles of Champagne around. It takes no prisoners on the palate, it is not kind to little old ladies and it does not favour those with weaker constitutions. The reason for this is that Bollinger is based around a core of Pinot Noir fruit from the village of Aÿ – the finest in the entire region – which gives structure and intensity to Champagne. There is no greater proponent of this style than Bolly. Even this non-vintage is a blockbuster of its kind, so don't pour it as an aperitif unless you have sufficiently robust canapés and friends to cope!

Bollinger Rosé NV $175

Madame Lily Bollinger, the old battleaxe who, eons ago, made this formidable House a staple part of every Champagne lover's wine diet, said that she would never allow a rosé to be made at

Bolly. Just before she died she relented and allowed a vintage wine to be made – La Grande Année Rosé. But she never witnessed the production of a non-vintage rosé during her incredible time at Bollinger. Just a few months ago, however, an N.V. Bollinger Rosé was made for the very first time. Drinking La Grande Année Rosé is like having Rachmaninov himself play his Piano Concerto No.2 in a private performance for you on a Steinway. We suppose the only question is – how does this non-vintage wine differ from this outlandish image? It is very simple, Rachmaninov becomes Chris Martin (the Steinway stays). And, oh, the price more than halves.

Champagne, France

Cork

AU: DW PWS Rand SMWM

NZ: HWC

$185 Billecart-Salmon Cuvée Nicolas-François 2000

Champagne, France

Cork

Best Price: $170

AU: DMs DOr EEC Ed PWS SMWM VCs

NZ: Sel Glen HWC

2000 NF is an extraordinarily bombastic wine by comparison to the usual breathtaking beauties that emerge from this famous cellar. With great swathes of flavour, suggesting the drama and precipitous nature of Burgundy's hillside of Corton-Charlemagne rather than the hills of Champagne, it is important to remember that even though this is a brand new release (and at the time of writing, is not even in Australia) it is already 8 years old. In white wine terms this would be a fabulous innings, but with this hypnotic millennial offering, it is but a mere pup. Make sure that all of those who are lucky enough to take part in the performance which surrounds opening a bottle like this are of Oscar-winning standard because the facial expressions, gasps and expletives will surely have critics reaching for their notepads.

Billecart-Salmon Cuvée Elisabeth Rosé 2000

Champagne, France

Cork

AU: DOr DW Ed Nicks PWS SMWM VCs

NZ: Sel Glen HWC WFW

$250

In the past, Elisabeth has been a pretty, elegant, demure girl who, as the years tick by, blossoms into a very polished and stunningly attractive lady. 2000 Elisabeth, however, bears no relation to her siblings because from the outset she looks like Lara Croft. It's hard to believe that she could get any sexier than this – but she will. The impact on the nose and palate of this explosive rosé are hard to put into words but pyrotechnics are involved somewhere along the line and you are left feeling completely ravished. Despite the bubbles, drink it as you would a top-flight Pinot Noir and get hold of some of the most beautiful, glistening breasts you can (duck preferably, but any fit bird will do).

Dom Pérignon 2000

Champagne, France

Cork

Best Price: $220

AU: 1st Aus Boc Chalk DMs DW EEC Ed GPO Nicks PWS Rand SMWM Sum VCs WLC

NZ: Glen HWC Mill SC WFW

$270

After the elegance and immediacy of the 1998 vintage Dom, it was inevitable that we would return to what made this brand so famous, and that is a big, structured vintage like this 2000. The flavour waltzes around your palate like the 'talent' on *So You Think You Can Dance* and the aromas cover every single example of patisserie from the finest French bakers. Once again, this is a huge style of sparkling wine, but unlike Krug, it is more suited to main course fish dishes. So drop the anchor and get those lines out.

$295 Krug Grande Cuvée NV

Champagne, France

Cork

Best Price: $265

AU: 1st Boc Chalk DW Ed EEC GPO Nicks PWS Rand SMWM VCs WLC

NZ: Sel Glen HWC Mill SC

For those of you familiar with Krug, skip this tasting note and go to the next wine, because you do not need a note on this iconic creation. If you are new to this mighty Champagne house, then let us first say congratulations on your lottery win. You cannot spend it anywhere else as wisely as you can here. The baffling thing about Krug is that it is very much a sparkling wine but it has the intensity and length of a red. Celebratory and desperately exciting, this wine transcends its type and lives in a world of its own. Please drink it with main course food rather than as an aperitif because, in spite of its bubbles, this is more vinous than any other Champagne. Pray you don't get hooked (resistance is futile) because this wine is the lowest rung on the Krug ladder. And with the vintage and Clos du Mesnil above it you will need another win on the scratch cards immediately to finance this passion.

Throughout this chapter, look out for **green boxes** with comments on the most important white and red **grape varieties** in the world. These notes are your first step to unlocking the mysteries of the vast array of aromas and flavours that you'll find in **The Best Wines of 2009**. Pay close attention and you'll also pick up some fascinating facts to spout next time you crack a bottle.

Chardonnay (Shar-dunn-ay) is the chameleon of white grapes, effortlessly adapting itself to hundreds of different guises throughout the wine world. It ranges in style from pale, neutral and characterless to wildly exotic, rich and golden – you should be able to detect anything from peach, melon and lemon fruit to honey, butter, freshly baked patisserie, hazelnuts, vanilla, butterscotch, orange blossom and fresh meadow flowers in full-on Chardonnays. While this creature is forever slipping in and out of vogue, it remains responsible for the most revered and expensive dry white wines in the world, and should not be ignored.

white wines

Oxford Landing Sauvignon Blanc 2008 $8

South
Australia

Screw Cap

Best Price: $6

AU: 1st Boc
DMs DW
Lland Sum
VCs WLC

NZ: HWC WFW

*See back
page for key
to stockists*

Our cheapest white wine this year is absolutely bloody amazing, bearing in mind that it's made from a grape variety that Australia ought not to be this good at. If you did a blind tasting of this variety with a Frog and a Kiwi it would take on all-comers with its spicy lemon and lime fruit flavours and if you mention the price, the frog and the kiwi would keel over, giving us the ideal opportunity to cook up a storm. Anyone for frogs legs and kiwi à l'orange? Food and wine matching at its best!

Hardys Nottage Hill Chardonnay 2007 $10

South
Australia

Screw Cap

AU: DMs WLC

NZ: Mill

Notty has done it again and takes the honour of leading the way in our Chardonnay list for the third year running. It has honeyed, crème brûlée flavours and a surprising amount of sexy oak for this little money, making it one of the best value wines on the market.

Jacob's Creek Classic Sauvignon Blanc 2008 $10

Australia

Screw Cap

Best Price: $8

AU: Boc DW
SMWM

With less tropical fruit and more pointy citrus than the Oxford Landing, this wine draws its energy from its herbal minerality as opposed to its exotic fruitiness. With this in mind, it's a more European-shaped Sauvignon Blanc which will appeal to a more classically-shaped set of taste buds. The highlight here is the beautiful mineral acidity on the finish. Fine and textured, the fruit is subtle and elegant. The **Jacob's Creek Reserve Sauvignon Blanc 2008** ($15) is more serious with great length and zesty lime fruit. It has the same texture but the volume is turned up on its minerality.

$10 Lindemans Bin 65 Chardonnay 2007

It's always a hotly contested competition and we're only seconds away from round one. The first match in the white wine section this year and the two wines are Notty and Lindy. In the blue corner is Notty and in the red is Lindy. Matthew with his spit bucket and white towel is championing Lindy. Tyson in his close-fitting kimono is backing Notty. Go boys! Fosters and Hardys are Australia's two biggest wine companies and they go head to head with these two wines. We do, too, and so should you. Put them both on the table and you be the referee. Will the honesty of this creamy, lush, pineapple-chunk flavoured wine bring it up trumps?

$10 McWilliam's Hanwood Estate Chardonnay 2008

What's remarkable about Hanwood is its lightness. Made from twenty percent cool climate fruit, it is perfect for those of you who drink elegant wines. For the more sensitive souls out there, this wine isn't going to bring you to tears. With fresh baby mandarin segments and an ethereal air to the palate, it's totally opposite

Reserve

South-Eastern Australia

Screw Cap

AU: 1st DMs DW Lland SMWM VCs

Australia

Screw Cap

AU: 1st Sel DMs DW Lland VCs WLC

NZ: Mill

Australia

Screw Cap

Best Price: $8

AU: 1st Boc DMs Ed Lland Sum VCs WLC

in style to the two Chardonnays before it.

Mike Press Wines Adelaide Hills Sauvignon Blanc 2008

$11

Adelaide Hills

Screw Cap

Best Price: $8.50

www.topdrop wines.com.au

AU: Aus WLC

Just when we had firmly placed Mike Press into a red winemaker's box, he came bursting forth with a bottle of Sauvignon in his hand and a cheeky grin on his face and promptly poured a large glass for everyone in attendance. All were amazed at the sheer class of the wine, erupting with vibrant grapefruit flavours and spicy lemons. This unlikely hero has pulled a delightfully lively Sauvignon from his ever-expanding box of tricks. And who knows what might emerge from it next year?

De Bortoli Windy Peak Sauvignon Blanc Semillon 2008

$13

South-Eastern Australia

Screw Cap

Best Price: $12

AU: 1st Boc DMs DW Lland Sum VCs

It's lovely to taste an SBS where you can't tell what the exact percentages of the blend are because the synergy between the two grapes is so exact. Here, the Semillon doesn't add any of its trademark waxiness to the Sauvignon. The overall impression is one of a fresh, zesty, citrus cocktail underpinned with fine, minerally acid and a whisper of alluring, wistful herbaceousness. This is the perfect marriage and it's all done for a mini price tag.

De Bortoli Windy Peak Chardonnay 2007

$13.50

Victoria

Screw Cap

Best Price: $12

As you progress through this book the name

white wines 45

Windy Peak appears a hell of a lot, as it did last year. In fact, there are so many wines here from this extraordinary producer that you could buy a mixed case, which makes Windy Pants the only true all-rounder in **Taste 2009**. This Chardy is bloody lovely – 'nuff said.

$13.50 Peter Lehmann Barossa Riesling 2008

AU: 1st Boc Chalk DMs DW Nicks Lland Sum VCs

Barossa

Screw Cap

The best value whites in this book are Rieslings, which should come as no surprise to you, because this has been true for years. Those of you who are not drinking this grape variety are missing out on drama and excellence in every glass. Most wines have an energy about them that can propel them forward for many, many years. But one or two drink superbly young, and this is the style that we have searched for in our sub-$15 Rieslings this year. When you're going to a BYO evening and you haven't done your shopping, this is about as safe a style as you can get because it goes with all styles of cooking, and it will probably only set you back $10.

AU: 1st Aus Boc DMs DW Nicks Lland PWS VCs WLC

$13.50 Possums The Springs Unwooded Chardonnay 2008

McLaren Vale

Screw Cap

www.possums wines.com.au

A brand new name to the book, and it's nice to see an original Aussie name on a bottle of wine! However, it is not made from what it says on the label. We can assure you it is made from grapes. Although, having said this, there is an unmistakable tang to this unoaked Chardonnay that certainly snaps you to attention. A perfect food and wine match would be stunning goat's cheese salad or you could really push the boat out and make some gougères – then wash these snazzy cheese puffs down with a glass of the possum.

Bleasdale Langhorne Creek Chardonnay 2008

Langhorne Creek

Screw Cap

www.bleas dale.com.au

AU: DW

$14

Langhorne Creek is hardly famous for its Chardonnay, so it's a massive credit to Bleasdale that, despite having their eye on their more famous red grapes, they can make a white as fresh and tight as this. Its fresh citrus blossom bouquet is like an icy breeze through an open window.

Leasingham Magnus Riesling 2008

Clare Valley

Screw Cap

www.leasing ham-wines. com.au

AU: WLC

$14

With news that Leasingham is up for grabs from its owners Constellation, let's all hope that the most historic winery in Clare doesn't become extinct, because life would be very dull without wines like this. The best Magnus to date has very fine white peach and lemon fruit with layers of perfumed white blossoms. Magnus maximus.

St Hallett Poacher's Blend Semillon Sauvignon Blanc 2008

Barossa

Screw Cap

Best Price: $10

$14

Blimey, this is a wonderful Poacher's and it is a far cry from the early vintages – which were trailblazers in themselves. Gosh, this business moves fast, and with superstars like St Hallett in to bat for Aussie it's no surprise that we are doing

SO well across the globe. This wine is not meant to have texture as sumptuous as this and it certainly isn't meant to last for minutes on the finish. There is one hell of a lot of wine here for the money and if you are into ice cold, zesty, citrus and stone fruits then get hold of this brilliant quaffer. Have it on hand when you need a white with the unlikely combo of zing and depth.

$14.50 Tahbilk Marsanne 2008

Oh my goodness me....thump....I have dropped to my knees (MJ). How can a wine that costs less than a snazzy sandwich taste this sensational? We have done vertical tastings of this beauty back to the late seventies, and it still looks fit and tidy despite its age (YEAH). Get on board with this '08 the very second it hits the shelf. Why, we hear you sing out in perfect harmony like the Qantas choir? Because this is the brightest and bubbliest young Tahbilk Marsanne we have ever seen! It's got that 'sugar cube' pineapple nose and totally tight line that never once blossoms into the fat schoolgirl who can't climb the steps onto the school bus and needs a kick up the arse from her Ma. This '08 has walked to school for weeks and is trim and brimming with flavour. Fit, smily and gorgeous, with honeysuckle, green melon and lemon balm notes, this is the most definitive, youthful Marsanne on the planet.

AU: 1st Aus Boc Chalk DMs DW Ed Lland Rand Sixty VCs WLC

NZ: SC

Nagambie Lakes

Screw Cap

AU: 1st Boc Chalk DMs DW Ed GPO Nicks Lland PWS Rand Sixty SMWM VCs

NZ: HWC WFW

*Plump, rich, vaguely floral, peachy and always oily, **Marsanne** (Marce-ann) makes rather hefty, foody wines. Flying solo, it tends toward waxy, honey and mildly tropical nuances, but likes to be blended with a co-pilot like the more elegant grape Roussanne or the trendy Viognier.*

Tyrrell's Wines Verdelho 2008

$15

Hunter Valley

Screw Cap

AU: 1st DW Sixty VCs

NZ: Sel Glen

We have waded through bucketloads of Verdelhos this year and only four wines made the grade. It's a shame that this grape is still seen as being a slightly goofy sort, because we love really smart, spanky, crunchy Verdelho and reckon it has a worthy place in our full-on dining repertoire. As a BYO white, Verdelho treads the boards in every department. Get your laughing gear around this little imp and then feel a magical, spritzy, pear and apple time bomb go off on your palate when you least expect it. It's bloody cheap, too, so book a table now and bring your Esky with you.

Willow Bridge Estate Sauvignon Blanc Semillon 2008

$15.50

Geographe

Screw Cap

www.willowbridge.com.au

AU: 1st VCs

You certainly know you are in WA when you dunk your hooter into this wine. Yee hah, there is an entire plantation of green capsicum that fills the air and it is chased along by ten thousand limes goose-stepping in metronomic precision across your tongue. If you need a white to pick you up and give you a jolly good shaking then this is it. Oh, by the way, it is wicked with oysters, mussels and clams.

Alkoomi Wines Unwooded Chardonnay 2008

$16

Frankland River

Screw Cap

While most of Australia's best cheapie Chardys tend to hail from South Australia and Victoria,

Western Australia deserves your attention when it comes up with wines as fresh and zesty as this. It's a contrasting style, made from cool Frankland fruit, giving it Asian pear and fresh ginger purity and it performs exactly as it should – unwooded and uncomplicated.

$16 Jim Barry Wines Watervale Riesling 2008

Already drinking beautifully, this wine is tight and fresh with lemon and lime flavours in a very grown up style. It's staggering for the price, and yet this is exactly what Jim Barry's wines do so well. Only three Rieslings snuck in under the $16 barrier this year because we are ruthless in eliminating wines that lack precision or deliciousness.

$16 Wirra Wirra Scrubby Rise Sauvignon Blanc Semillon Viognier 2008

Wirra Wirra is one of those companies that, given the opportunity, will blend for complexity rather than leaving a single varietal to fend for itself. They're also not afraid to throw the rule book of classic white blends out the window of the winery and instead come up with something quirky and original. In this inexpensive white they achieve an enormous amount of tonal variation by utilising three cracking white grapes. Viognier adds flesh and richness to its brittle Semillon and Sauvignon shell.

www.alkoomi
wines.com.au

AU: 1st DW
SMWM

Clare Valley

Screw Cap

Best Price: $12

AU: 1st Aus
Boc Chalk
DW Ed Nicks
Lland VCs

South
Australia

Screw Cap

AU: 1st Chalk
DMs DW Ed
Lland SMWM
VCs WLC

Fleurieu

Screw Cap

AU: 1st Aus
Chalk DW
Lland Sixty
SMWM VCs
WLC

Chapel Hill Verdelho 2008

$17

One of Michael Fragos' best wines, year in year out, is his unwooded Chardonnay, but even this punchy wine lost out this year to the crunchy, fresh, zesty and lively Verdelho. Who'd have thought that this ultra-cool hairball could make a wine this uplifting and wincingly acidic?! He is a horizontally laid back dude so it must hurt him hard every time he tastes juice as vertical as this drink. It's like biting into a crunchy green apple with some pear blossom on the side. The back label says that it has a "feisty" palate, but feisty doesn't come close. This is DIY shock therapy without the electrodes.

Yarra Valley

Screw Cap

Best Price: $15

AU: 1st Boc
Chalk DMs
DW Lland VCs

NZ: Sel Glen

De Bortoli Yarra Valley Gulf Station Chardonnay 2007

$17

The only problem with this wine, as you will see when you reach the Gulf Pinot Noir as well, is that it will take six more months to reach its ideal drinking period. Far from a problem, you'll just have to drink something else in the meantime. That's why we're here! You have much to look forward to in this very restrained, textured style, made to a much more serious specification than any Gulf Station that has gone before it.

Hunter Valley

Screw Cap

Best Price: $14

McWilliams Mount Pleasant Elizabeth Hunter Valley Semillon 2008

$17

"Lizzie" transforms from a delightful charmer in her youth to an elegant lady in her later years,

white wines 51

but it seems to us that in between she tends to fall into a grumpy Avril Lavigne teenage sulk. It is a privilege to enjoy her company before she takes off in a huff, and this opportunity is available through McWilliam's cellar door. Her young guise this year is one of a core of lemon juice acidity, on to which are hung glistening green herb and asparagus notes.

AU: (earlier vintages) 1st Boc Chalk DMs GPO Nicks Lland Sixty SMWM Sum VCs WLC

$18 Ad Hoc "Hen and Chicken" Chardonnay 2007

Pemberton

Screw Cap

www.larry cherubino. com.au

When we set out to tackle the three-and-a-half thousand wines that we short-list for this book, there is no need for us to fulfil the duty of ticking every regional box in Australia. But no sooner did we find a beautiful Frankland Chardonnay than a Pemberton one turned up as well! Well done WA, for making great Chardonnay outside of the stronghold of Margaret River. The flavour profiles that we enjoy from these diverse regions allow so many more recipes to come into play, rather than the same old style of wines being made everywhere. Keep 'em coming – we'll never get thirsty when we have these wines to hand. Thanks Larry!

AU: DW Ed SMWM

$18 Ad Hoc Wall Flower Riesling 2008

Western Australia

Screw Cap

www.larry cherubino. com.au

A wall flower Larry Cherubino is certainly not, preferring to be centre of attention or otherwise nearest the bar. Ad hoc he is, because you never know what is coming next from his winery. This is a very precise Riesling for this money, with fine apple fruit and a seamlessly integrated palate.

AU: DW Rand

De Iuliis Show Reserve Hunter Valley Verdelho 2008

Hunter Valley

Screw Cap

www.dewine.com.au

AU: Sel DMs Sixty

$18

De Iuliis is a fresh style with heavenly mandarin flavours and a little more fruit density than our other three Verdelhos in this list. We're not sure which show this is a "Reserve" wine from, bearing in mind that it had barely been bottled when we saw it, but Jukesy will judge in the Hunter Show the week that this book goes to print, so we'll see if it stands up to its name!

Devil's Corner Tasmania Sauvignon Blanc 2008

Tasmania

Screw Cap

AU: 1st DMs DW Sum TWC VCs

$18

Take a chisel to a lime ice pop and work away until you get the most evil-looking point on the end and you will have exactly the shape and flavour of this extraordinary wine. Thank goodness that the palate fills out with gooseberries and poached pear juiciness, otherwise that ice pop would slice clean through the top of your head, leaving you looking like a human unicorn with the mother of all ice headaches.

Peter Lehmann Eden Valley Riesling 2008

Eden Valley

Screw Cap

Best Price: $15

AU: 1st Aus Boc Chalk DMs DW Ed Nicks Lland VCs WLC

$18

PL's EV Riesling is two or three belt holes tighter than his straight offering, loading minerality and rapier sharp fruit into the mix. By all means crack on now, because it's an intense lime-juice-scented wine, but we are sure you will be able to sense that there is so much more to come behind the scenes as this wine ages gracefully.

$19 Bremerton Verdelho 2008

Fresh, floral aromatics lead the way here, with guava notes making a welcome appearance. The palate is zesty and tight, balancing the fruit cocktail onslaught, making this a great value quaffer for Asian cuisine banquets.

$19 Leo Buring Eden Valley Riesling 2008

Massive statement coming! The Buring 2008 Riesling foursome is as impressive an outfit as we have seen from anywhere this year. Make sure you don't cut your tongue on this wine, it is that sharp. And be sure also that you have enough fresh red chillies to throw into whatever you're cooking tonight, because this wine can handle it.

$19 Nepenthe Sauvignon Blanc 2008

Andre Bondar showed us a very sneak preview of this fantastic wine and it is intricately detailed and lusciously layered, without for a moment losing the classic Nepenthe hallmarks of lemongrass and gooseberries. This is the finest Nepenthe Sauvignon we have seen in years, and it is the ideal wine for fusion feasts and goats' cheese frenzies.

$19 Penfolds Thomas Hyland Chardonnay 2007

In rally car driving, this wine is the equivalent of

Langhorne Creek

Screw Cap

AU: 1st DMs DW Lland Rand SMWM VCs

Eden Valley

Screw Cap

AU: 1st Aus Boc DW Nicks Lland PWS SMWM VCs WLC

NZ: Mill

Adelaide Hills

Screw Cap

AU: 1st DW Ed EEC Nicks Lland Sixty SMWM VCs WLC

Adelaide

Screw Cap

Best Price: $15

---

 the best wines of 2009

dropping a cog

AU: 1st Chalk DW Lland SMWM VCs WLC

NZ: Sel Glen HWC Mill

"dropping a cog", because Hyland Chardonnay is a total change of pace to those that precede it. Where the others have been made with dextrous hands and a "something from nothing mentality," we know where this wine has come from – the extraordinary sources of fruit that Penfolds has at its disposal. The remarkable thing about it is not how much we love 2007 Hyland but the price point that this company attaches to this degree of excellence. 2007 Hyland is the best ever, and yet the price is less than a six pack of Foster's. Taste-wise, if you've ever yearned for a slice of white Burgundy in your glass, but simply can't afford it (we know how this feels!), Hyland will keep you going until you can.

Eden Valley

Screw Cap

Best Price: $14

AU: 1st Boc Chalk DMs DW EEC Nicks Lland PWS SMWM Sum VCs WLC

NZ: HWC Mill SC WFW

Pewsey Vale Eden Valley Riesling 2008 $19

There is so much going for Pewsey Vale Eden Valley Riesling. Here are just some of the descriptors that we brainstormed in less than a second. World-class, historic, stylish, reliable, classic, racy, exciting, gripping, pure, beautiful, age-worthy but immediately enjoyable, bargain-priced... we could go on. The 2008 adds finesse, very fine, ethereal, delicate and exceedingly long and minerally to this list of notes, making this our favourite release in a decade.

Hunter Valley

Screw Cap

Audrey Wilkinson Semillon 2008 $20

This nimble wine is a super-dry, light, racy Semillon which rips the back of your palate off and leaves you gasping for more. Lemony, zesty, tight and spicy, this wine has an air of urgency about it

white wines 55

which gnaws away at your psyche until you finally unscrew the cap. Phew, you can now bathe your taste buds again and fix your skull back into place. Great value at this mark, load up for summer parties and keep the yabbies coming.

$20 Fox Gordon Princess Fiano 2008

Not to be confused in any way with Shrek's other half (Princess Fiona) unless, of course, she is not in ogre mode. All the exoticism is reined in on this Fiano, elevating it to the highest echelon of haute couture, which makes it all the more remarkable for such a new grape to this country. In Campania, in southern Italy, this is the most highly prized of all white grapes, capturing elements of Viognier, Riesling and Albariño in its clenched fist of acidity. Here, Tash Mooney loses nothing in translation and this wine at this price point is the finest value Fiano we have ever tasted. Flash Gordon.

$20 Linda Domas Vis à Vis Viognier 2008

Linda keeps her head well below the parapet when in all honesty she should stand up occasionally and soak up the applause from her legions of adoring fans. There are few people who work as hard as this lass does, and her wines show every bit of her talent to perfection. Vis à Vis uses a slug of Chardonnay to lubricate the Viognier-missile-shaped palate and the result is an orange, lemon and apple salad of a wine that is as fit and nervy as it gets. This is artisan

www.audrey wilkinson. com.au

AU: Sel DMs Sixty

Adelaide Hills

Screw Cap

www.fox gordon. com.au

AU: Aus DW VCs

McLaren Vale

Screw Cap

www.ldwines. com.au

AU: DMs

winemaking at a bargain price – sadly a rare breed these days.

Eden Valley

Screw Cap

Best Price: $17

AU: 1st Aus Boc DW Ed Rand Sixty VCs

NZ: Glen Mill WFW

St Hallett Eden Valley Riesling 2008 · $20

There is no other country on the planet that can make a line of Rieslings as pure and consistent as we have assembled for you again this year. St Hallett, better known for its reds, is a mainstay in this distinguished line with this delicious and pretty wine with pure pear and lime juice flavours.

Hunter Valley

Screw Cap

www.tempus twowinery. com.au

AU: DMs DW SMWM

Tempus Two Zenith Hunter Valley Semillon 2008 · $20

Lizzie Jackson is in the winemaking pilot's seat at Tempus Two and Zenith is indicative of the upward trajectory on which she is navigating this space station winery. It's perfumed with lemon blossom and flavoured with spicy grapefruit with fruit concentration that builds from start to finish.

Clare Valley

Screw Cap

AU: 1st Aus Chalk DW Ed Nicks PWS Rand SMWM Sum VCs WLC

Polish Hill River

Clare Valley

Screw Cap

AU: 1st Aus Chalk DMs DW Ed Nicks PWS Rand SMWM Sum VCs WLC

O'Leary Walker Watervale Riesling 2008 · $21

The difference between this and the Rieslings before it is that there is a lot more bracing acidity going on here. This is a serious wine, built to age. Its themes are zesty lemon, lime and spice with great length. The O'Leary Walker duo continue to push the boundaries of bargain Clare Riesling and you can partake in their joys in virtually every bottle shop across the country. **Polish Hill River 2008** ($21) is even tighter and finer still, with tart green apple and pear fruit and brilliant length.

$21 Skillogalee Single Vineyard Riesling 2008

Clare Valley

Screw Cap

AU: DW Nicks Sixty SMWM TWC WLC

In this book we don't make a fuss about wineries of the year, winemakers of the year and such like, but we are ever vigilant, keeping our fingers on the pulse of everything that moves in this industry. So it is worth pointing out that Skilly has improved its offering at a rate that is well ahead of the curve, making it one of the most exciting, fast-paced improvers on the Aussie scene, and we raise our glass to what must be an enormous effort made there every day. This wine is benchmark Skilly Riesling from a great vintage.

$21 Wirra Wirra Hiding Champion Adelaide Hills Sauvignon Blanc 2008

Adelaide Hills

Screw Cap

AU: DW Ed Rand SMWM

If you're going to be a champion at anything, then why not hone your hiding skills, because you're going to need them with this wine in order to prevent your other half from drinking the lot before you get a chance. Top tip – a spare bedroom wardrobe always works because it's dark, cool and unlikely to be investigated. At least then when you drink the wine you can do it bottle by bottle, although do cover your tracks and remember that you're a champion, not a beginner, at hiding your fine wines. This is a delightfully fresh and pure Sauvignon Blanc with very fine, minerally acidity and a great combination of subtle lemon fruit and passionfruit overtones.

Brokenwood Hunter Valley Semillon 2008

$22

Hunter Valley

Screw Cap

AU: 1st Chalk
DMs DW Ed
Nicks Rand
Sixty SMWM
Sum VCs

2008 was a rotten vintage in the Hunter with very little red wine being made at all, thanks to some insane rain at harvest time. But those canny Hunters have another trick up their sleeves, that of their world class Semillons, and you simply must investigate their superb '08s. Brokenwood offers two running themes in this wine and they criss cross and interweave as the wine glides over the palate. The first is a firm, straight-jacketed, zesty lemon thrust which is classically Hunter and it zooms around, realigning your mantra as it goes. The second is a fleshier, more generous pineapple note which appears succulent and malleable, but which, too, has a racy line of acidity skewered right through its heart. On the one hand it is drinking beautifully right now and on the other it seems reserved and raw – this is what we adore about Brokenwood's stylish wines. There is no guilt in knocking a load of bottles over tonight, because you know that it will always be drinking at its peak. And you can't say that about many HVSs.

Chapel Hill McLaren Vale Albariño 2008

$22

McLaren Vale

Screw Cap

www.chapel
hillwine.
com.au

AU: Aus DW
EEC SMWM

If you're new to this grape variety then pay attention because Albariño is not only Spain's finest white grape but it is Australia's hottest import and nobody yet has nailed it like Chapel Hill. Used to warm temperatures but unusually taut in its youth, this is a spot-on choice for McLaren Vale, but nothing will prepare you for its

white wines 59

fine, minerally, chalky texture and ripe white nectarine flavours. It's good with Mediterranean foods but better with South China Sea cuisine.

$22 Knappstein Three 2008

Clare Valley

Screw Cap

AU: 1st DMs DW Rand VCs

A Gewürz, Pinot Gris and Riesling combo that, for the first time, is exactly bang-on. As much as we have liked this wine in the past, at last the Riesling controls Gewürz's input, taming its peachiness such that there is no fat or exotic fruit on show, just stunningly 'green' Gewürz notes. Pinot Gris adds no flab either, just fruit, and the result is the first perfect Three (out of three).

$22 Kumeu River Village Chardonnay 2007

Kumeu, Auckland

Screw Cap

Best Price: $16

AU: 1st Aus Boc DW EEC GPO PWS Rand VCs

NZ: Glen Mill WFW

This is a serious "Grand Vin," but it has the word "Village" on its label! Kumeu alludes to the classic French Burgundies in the name of this wine and in the bottle it has loads of high tensile Puligny-Montrachet-like fruit. It's too young now, thank goodness, and perhaps a little too serious for some, so only drink this wine if you think you're remotely competent with this grape variety. Otherwise, you're not allowed. So there!

$22 Lawson's Dry Hills Sauvignon Blanc 2008

Marlborough

Screw Cap

AU: 1st DW Nicks Lland PWS Rand VCs

Our introductory Kiwi wine in the Sauvignon class comes after six Aussies, but plenty of wines were aiming for this spot and the majority of them were too confected or clumsy. By contrast, Lawson's snaps to attention, with wonderfully

NZ: Glen HWC
Mill WFW

Clare Valley

Screw Cap

www.leasingh
am-wines.
com.au

AU: DMs

Orange

Screw Cap

AU: 1st DMs
DW VCs

taut lemon and lime fruit with a seamless assemblage of passionfruit and spice. It's good to see Lawson's in our list again this year – a unique performance for a Kiwi Sauvignon.

Leasingham Wines Bin 8 Medium Sweet KS Riesling 2008 $22

We have stood in line with empty glasses for years awaiting the release of an Aussie wine in this style. We were excited last year to introduce you to Leasingham's first Kabinett Style Riesling – but it was only available at this illustrious estate's cellar door. Making its way to a Dan Murphy's near you for the first time, this is a sensational style with apple and pear fruit and layers of sweet spices. We hate the term "medium sweet" because it's neither particularly medium nor sweet. What it is, though, is extremely juicy in a crushed white grape sense. This is the perfect thing with creamy white cheeses, Thai curries involving coconut milk, tempura vegetables with sweet chilli dipping sauce, meat-based pâtés and terrines. Mmmm.

Logan Sauvignon Blanc 2008 $22

LSB is an extremely intellectual wine, very serious indeed, and many people won't understand it. It's loaded with Pouilly-Fumé-esque gun smoke characters, making it less fruity than most Sauvignons, but much more intriguing, in our opinion. The trick here is that Peter Logan, thinking woman's winemaker eye candy, does three picks of Sauvignon at three ripeness levels to create a complex panoply of green

white wines 61

> ***Sauvignon Blanc*** *(So-veen-yon Blon) is an up-front, brazen, aromatic, happy-go-lucky style, with an asparagus, gooseberry, fresh herb, lemon and elderflower scent, and refreshing, zesty, dry, citrusy fruit on the palate. 'Savvy' is the definitive apéritif grape variety and the saviour of oriental food and wine matching!*

capsicum, gooseberry and guava flavours. He then ferments a skerrick of it in Hungarian oak barrels, which broadens the mid-palate and gives it a touch of Eastern Bloc promise.

$22 Pikes Riesling 2008

The anticipation prior to opening a bottle of Pike's wine is palpable and in situations like this the worry is that the wine might disappoint. But this has never happened with a Riesling from Pikes, and we suspect it never will. This 2008 glided into our selection with effortless grace and paraded its precise balance and integrated flavours of green apples, pure lemon and concentrated lime in style.

Clare Valley

Screw Cap

Best Price: $18

AU: 1st Aus Boc Chalk DMs DW Ed Lland PWS Sixty VCs WLC

NZ: HWC

$22 Tim Adams Pinot Gris 2008

More Grigio in style than Gris, certainly at this very early stage of its life, Tim manages to cram so much energy into his wines it is amazing. There is minerality here, too, and it counterpoints the mildly tropical grapefruit and lemon fruit perfectly so that there is no way that this wine will ever become too fat and topple over. There are far too many pretenders jumping on the PG train and making a real mess of this style of wine. Tim, by contrast, has always hit the bull's eye with this variety and as every year passes he just gets

Clare Valley

Screw Cap

AU: Aus Chalk DW Ed SMWM

better and better.

Tim Adams Semillon 2007

Clare Valley

Screw Cap

AU: 1st Aus DW SMWM VCs

$22

Bonecrusher Adams is a legend and his entire range of wines is a joy to behold. For years this Semillon has been a scene-stealer in blind tastings and it is always one of the least expensive wines to trounce the big boys! With fresh-baked cake flavours, wild honey and butter notes and fine, zesty, citrus acidity on the finish, this is a super-smooth wine with brilliant length. It ages exceptionally well, too.

Fox Gordon Abby Viognier 2008

Adelaide Hills

Screw Cap

AU: Aus DW Ed VCs

$23

The thing about Abby is that she is really reigned in with a focus on acidity rather than ripe fruit, giving her a refreshing and controlled personality. Fine pear flavours and really tight minerality distance this wine from Yalumba's more succulent style. Who would you like to entertain tonight? Abby would be a great dinner date.

Esk Valley Hawke's Bay Sauvignon Blanc 2008

Hawkes Bay

Screw Cap

Best Price: $21

AU: PWS

NZ: Sel Glen HWC Mill WFW

$24

Esk Valley is part of the Villa Maria family, and you would normally expect one of their own raft of Sauvignons to occupy this position in our book. But, by golly, this Hawke's Bay Sauvignon has the ice pick minerality, pure lemon and pear fruit and guava-like texture to completely win us over.

$24 Ravenswood Lane Sauvignon Blanc 2008

Adelaide Hills

Screw Cap

www.thelane.com.au

AU: Aus WLC

Without a Semillon element to befriend it, a straight Sauvignon Blanc from the Adelaide Hills has to fend for itself against a vast number of competitors. This wine has nothing to worry about because of its taut minerality, zesty citrus fruit and laser-aligned direction. A decade ago the Adelaide Hills region had lost sight of just how good its Sauvignons should have been but there are a handful of players still striving every year for perfection. This means that Australia has a worthy armoury with which to repel foreign imposters.

$24 Stonier Mornington Peninsula Chardonnay 2007

Mornington Peninsula

Screw Cap

Best Price: $20

AU: 1st Boc Chalk DMs DW GPO Lland PWS Rand Sixty SMWM VCs

Stonier's Estate wine has always won its position over the Reserve wine because of its impeccable balance. Will Geraldine get her Reserve in this year? Read on! There is oak here, but it's so controlled and in perfect harmony with the lime juice notes of this Mornington Chardonnay.

$25 Auntsfield Estate Reserve Sauvignon Blanc 2007

Marlborough

Screw Cap

Best Price: $23

www.auntsfield.co.nz

If you thought that the use of oak in Peter Logan's Sauvignon was subtle and well-judged, then Auntsfield throws you into a doona cover and then has five minutes with a cricket bat, softening you up, before presenting you with one of the oakiest Sauvignons we've ever

NZ: Mill WFW

recommended. But it's a bloody good wine because the intensity of the fruit more than handles the exotic vanilla pod notes and the acidity is so punchy and mineral that it cuts right through the hazel nut cream spiciness and tropical fruit. Foolish? Maybe. Daring? Certainly. This wine is the exception to break the rule.

Jacob's Creek Steingarten Riesling 2007

$25

Barossa

Screw Cap

AU: 1st Aus Boc DW Nicks Lland SMWM VCs WLC

NZ: Sel Glen

This is a departure from style, showing a lot less stein and a lot more garten! With real richness and lime juice notes this is not as stony or mineral as usual but more drinkable, forward and attractive, with a delicious finish. Good news! It's one to shuffle to the front of the queue of your collection, ahead of the 2005 and 2006.

The Yard Channybearup Vineyard Sauvignon Blanc 2008

$25

Pemberton

Screw Cap

www.larry cherubino. com.au

AU: Aus SMWM

Channybearup is illegal in most countries and we don't want to involve the WWF in any way, shape or form, but so long as it's kept in Larry's Yard, well away from everybody, we'll all be fine. There is great, fine, minerally texture to this wine. It's tightly honed and fresh and more about river pebble texture than it is about fruit, and all the better for it. Really elegant, toned and honed, with all of Sauvignon's usual sticky-outy bits polished clean off. Ouch!

$25 Vasse Felix Semillon 2008

Margaret River

Screw Cap

AU: 1st DMs DW SMWM VCs

There is a style of Semillon in Australia that is so far removed from the lithe Hunter model it is incredible. With the presence and weight of a Chardy, but none of the associated flavours, this sensitively oaked Semillon is one hell of a bottle from the movers and shakers at Vasse Felix. With very fine, mineral notes carrying the spicy gooseberry and hazelnut cream palate, there is so much excitement and class in this wine it is hard to see it all in one snapshot. Use it to do the job of a top Chardonnay when you are menu planning, but expect a very linear, fit, exciting, lime juice theme and no flab whatsoever peeping over its waistband! Just like its ravishing winemaker Virginia Willcock!

$26 Pepper Tree Semillon 2008

Hunter Valley

Screw Cap

www.pepper treewines. com.au

AU: DW

This is one of the palest coloured wines of the year – in low light you might think that it's water (no shame then in taking a massive gulp!). But the nose and richness on the palate are incredibly taut, crisp and evocative for such a naïve looking thing. Offer us a glass of luminous, lolly-water Chilean Sauvignon Blanc in a bar instead of this wine and we will spit it back in your face, 'cos we want Hunter Semillon! It is the most fashionable accessory around for a decent night out on the town – someone should tell the droves of trendsetters this now. If you want to enjoy haute couture white wine, then drink this beauty – call the editor of Vogue NOW. What is it with Aussies and Hunter Semillon? It's light, dry, refreshing, made here, goes with everything and is

the best wines of 2009

exceedingly good value. What is everyone waiting for? Another container of South American wine to hit our shores? Spread the word, join the club, don't delay, be the coolest person you know.

Knappstein Ackland Single Vineyard Riesling 2008

$27

Clare Valley

Screw Cap

AU: 1st DW Rand Sixty SMWM VCs

Paul Smith's parting shot from this historic winery is as fine and detailed as any Riesling we have seen this year. It's precise and yet deceptively rich. Unlike many of the Rieslings in our book this year, which are so dramatically, searingly tight, Ackland has the knack of being balanced and genial, while still having enough acidity under the bonnet to carry it for a decade.

Leabrook Estate Gewürztraminer 2008

$27

Adelaide Hills

Screw Cap

AU: Sum WLC

This is a delicious wine with a bit o' flesh (ooh aah). It's an intricately honed Gewürz with high aromatic notes that shatter crystal chandeliers, but also the toned and honed decolletage of a supermodel. We have seen some pretty frightful Gewürztraminers this year and this is the only one to make our list, so give it the respect that it deserves and ship it in. Hoorah!

Palliser Estate Sauvignon Blanc 2008

$27

Martin-borough

Screw Cap

Best Price: $23

When people say "Kiwi Sauvignon," they are usually referring to the colloquial term for those black-shirted mutants who run rings around (and run over the top of) every other rugby player in the world. But on this occasion kiwi Sauvignon refers to the fruit aroma of this wine, and while we're at it, add passionfruit, grapefruit and lime zest, too, because this is one of the most aromatic Sauvignons of the vintage. However, this wine is not a party popper (that is, one bang and it's all over) because the palate and length are more like a drum roll which fades away softly without missing a beat. This is the twenty-second vintage that I (MJ) have tasted, loved and bought, which just goes to show you how professional and downright delicious wines from this influential estate are.

AU: 1st Chalk DMs DW PWS SMWM VCs

NZ: Sel Glen HWC Mill SC WFW

$27   Phil Ryan Signature Series Semillon 2007

We were the first people outside the McWilliams team to taste this wine while it was still a baby in the tank. It stunned us from day one. Finally, more than a year later, we are allowed to break our code of silence and scream about this wine. As guarantees of quality go, the name "Phil Ryan" on a bottle promises great excitement inside. The secret that you won't find on the label is that this is baby Lovedale (read on), sourced from young vines in the greatest Semillon vineyard in the world. It tastes like Lovedale stripped down to race spec.

Hunter Valley

Screw Cap

www.mc williams. com.au

$28   De Bortoli Estate Grown Yarra Valley Chardonnay 2007

One of Steve Webber's most incredible talents is that when he builds a wine of this quality, he doesn't spoil the movie by showing everything in

Yarra Valley

Screw Cap

Best Price: $24

AU: 1st Aus Boc Chalk DW PWS VCs

 the best wines of 2009

the trailer. So, you have to wait and the wine will take you through its story at its own pace. Keep your wits about you, though. It's got that Will Smith thing going. Tick, tick, tick, tick, boom!

Craggy Range Single Vineyard Kidnappers Vineyard Chardonnay 2007

$30

Hawkes Bay

Screw Cap

AU: Aus EEC PWS SMWM

NZ: Sel Glen HWC SC WFW

This is a really flashy wine with a Californian glossiness to it (in the best possible way, of course). Glistening hazelnut brioche and marmalade notes and very fine, minerally acidity swell to tropical fruit richness on the finish. Matthew ate two chocolates after this wine (to stay alive, he says) and he could still taste it! This wine has the texture and class of a very expensive bottle indeed.

Ravenswood Lane Chardonnay 2007

$30

Adelaide Hills

Screw Cap

www.thelane. com.au

AU: Aus EEC

It is just so exciting to come across a wine that confounds expectation so completely that you have to stop dead in your tracks, put the chicken down and take note. One might usually expect top Aussie Chardonnay to grow in all directions as you climb the price ladder and search for the best single vineyard fruit, but this wine has refined its flavour to the point where you simply scratch your head and wonder who changed the glasses on you for a bottle of Corton-Charlemagne. John Edwards has been banging on for ages about how special the dirt is at The Lane and this wine shows why.

$30 The Lane Vineyard Block 11 Semillon Sauvignon Blanc 2008

Adelaide Hills

Screw Cap

www.thelane.com.au

There were one hundred (that is not a typo) SSBs in our final taste-off between the glorious, zesty Willow Bridge and this utterly sensational The Lane SSB, and not one of them was up to our standard. We know that we are fussy buggers, but we have to be, because we are tasting for YOU and we know that you deserve the very best wines around. This brand new wine is as taut and nervy as it gets and when you puncture the surface it erupts in a mass of wild flowers, soaring minerality, gentle spice and shiny lemon notes. With brilliant line and length, this is a very grown up proposition indeed.

$30 The Lane Vineyard Gathering Sauvignon Blanc Semillon 2007

Adelaide Hills

Screw Cap

www.thelane.com.au

AU: EEC

This is one of the finest white blends in Australia and there is no style in New Zealand that competes with it, either. There's so much spice and drama going on in the glass, overlaying incredible hazelnut nuances and the faintest of orange blossom notes, that you literally have to remind yourself to breathe, such is the impact on your nervous system when you take a sip of this wine. Defined and refined, this is as good as it gets.

$30 The Lane Viognier 2007

Adelaide Hills

Screw Cap

www.thelane.com.au

The fascinating fact with this wine is that in 2007 The Lane did not have any old oak barrels whatsoever, because it was the first vintage carried out in the new winery on top of the hill, and so everything was new. The fact that this Viognier has been able to swallow gulps of freshly seasoned oak and still retain its beauty, curvaceous lines and heavenly aroma is testament to the impeccable vineyards and stunning mineral soils from whence they came.

Craggy Range Old Renwick Vineyard Sauvignon Blanc 2008

$32

Marlborough

Screw Cap

Best Price: $25

AU: Aus Chalk DMs PWS Rand SMWM

NZ: HWC WFW

With some grape varieties, shouting louder gets you heard. Shiraz is probably the best example of this. But others like Pinot and even Chardonnay can say so much more by lowering the volume and enunciating more precisely their message. Old Renwick SB 2008 is such a wine because there is no overt Sauvignon brashness, but a calmness that is arresting. It's ultra fine and controlled with lemon spice, hints of honey and brilliant, crystalline minerality. The trick with this wine is that it appears to be so light and fresh and yet it is so strong and long as it grows on the palate. How could something so light and so innocent grow to such magnitude?

Kooyong Estate Chardonnay 2006

$32

Mornington Peninsula

Diam cork

Best Price: $26

AU: 1st Aus Chalk DMs DW PWS Rand SMWM VCs WLC

All of the troops are on parade already in this white-peach flavoured wine, with minerality and savoury complexity joining in the fun. You can feel confident to pull the cork and drink it right away, because it's raring to go right now, with nothing to hide. The boundless energy here is infectious.

$32 Poole's Rock Hunter Valley Semillon 2005

At three-and-a-half or so years old, Poole's Semillon is just at the point where it still retains the primary zestiness of youth but starts to tip into the spice and toasty period of its life. The complexities of age build and the whole flavour game changes. This is often a strange period for a wine and many bottles shut down and go into a chrysalis for a while. There is no danger of this happening with '05 Poole's Rock, though, because it has a massive power pack of energy driving it forwards. So you, Taste Trooper, have a very easy ride with this wine because it is driving perfectly and will continue to do so for the next five years!

Hunter Valley

Screw Cap

www.pooles rock.com.au

AU: Chalk DW Sixty

$34 Dog Point Vineyard Section 94 2006

It is absolutely unheard of in the wine world that a tiny plot of vineyard, planted with Sauvignon, and sold with a company name that is only six years old, should command such unbelievable respect. You only have to say "Section 94" in top gastronomic circles for everyone to know that you are talking about a Marlborough Sauvignon Blanc made by a company called Dog Point. The reason that this wine sends a shiver down our collective spines is that it has an X-factor that even some of the greatest estates in the world cannot build into their wines, no matter how hard they try. The technical specifications of this wine make sense of the flavour which, simply put, should prepare you for a mildly oaked Sauvignon

Marlborough

Screw Cap

AU: 1st Aus Boc DMs Ed Nicks PWS Rand SMWM Sum VCs

NZ: Sel Glen HWC SC WFW

Blanc, but in reality no amount of documentation could ever explain the other-worldly nature of this wine. It unites spicy baked gooseberry fruit with hazelnut cream oak at levels of concentration and integration that defy comprehension. Every time you sip this wine you will spend several seconds paralysed in ecstasy, before returning to the conversation, which inevitably will be about this wine. It goes without saying that if you haven't ever drunk Section 94 then you are missing out on a unique vinous experience. At this price there are only a handful of wines on the planet that can deliver the joy that this wine brings.

Leeuwin Estate Margaret River Prelude Vineyards Chardonnay 2007 — $34

Margaret River

Screw Cap

AU: 1st Aus Chalk DMs DW PWS SMWM VCs

This wine has all sorts of flavours that we've been missing in our Chardonnay flight. It has a faint Norwegian wood smoke aroma, not that either of us have sauna-ed naked with the girl's Nordic ski team on manoeuvres. But imagine tromping through the snow and catching a whiff of a just lit cooking fire in the distance. Now forget that, and concentrate on the sauna! This is a true prelude to the Art Series (read on).

Felton Road Riesling 2007 — $35

Central Otago

Screw Cap

We reckon that Riesling is Otago's white grape, not Pinot Gris, and we are prepared to put a small wager on this statement. When wines like this come along, we are sure that you would join us in this belief. Felton Road owner Nigel

Greening (the only man who wears deck chair fabric on a daily basis in his natty jackets) is a Riesling devotee and his infectious enthusiasm has meant that there are now three in the range. This one is not only the cheapest but also the best. So, join us in absurd attire and raise your glass to one of the most eccentric and lovable visionaries in the Kiwi wine scene.

AU: Boc Sel DMs Ed EEC PWS Rand SMWM Sum VCs

NZ: HWC SC WFW

$35 KT & The Falcon Peglidis Vineyard Watervale Riesling 2008

Clare Valley

Screw Cap

www.ktand thefalcon. com.au

Kerri Thompson is KT on the label and she made her name making Leasingham's awesome Rieslings before breaking away with her own label. Her most exciting wine to date is this Peglidis, with its lemon-infused palate, hints of white peach and almond meal and a little of the fine fuzziness of the outside of a peach. With miniscule production, only 350 people will have the privilege of purchasing a case of this wine. Make sure you're one of them.

AU: Aus DMs WLC

$35 Tim Adams Reserve Riesling 2007

Clare Valley

Screw Cap

Double R is Tim's new secret weapon. MJ discovered this wine in a bar in McLaren Vale, of all places, and it seemed at the time that Tim Adams wanted to hide it from the UK market, but we put an abrupt stop to that plan. Unusually for Riesling, this is a more powerful and structured wine, rather than being tighter and more introverted, and this means that it can be used cleverly with food and wine matching, stepping up to Thai pork dishes with ease, and every serious Asian fish dish you could think of. If more

AU: 1st Aus Sel DMs DW Ed SMWM VCs

people drank this style of Riesling we are certain that Chardonnay consumption would be dented.

Dr Loosen Wehlener Sonnenuhr Kabinett 2007

$37

Mosel-Saar-Ruwer, Germany

Screw Cap

AU: DMs EEC PWS Rand SMWM VCs

"The sundial" of Wehlen is situated in the middle of the most precipitous blue-slate-scattered vineyards high above the Mosel River and its most evocative expression is made by Erni Loosen in this wine. 2007 was a superb vintage in Germany and this bargain-priced wine is already up to speed. If you want to know the way in which top German Riesling differs from the wines of Australia and New Zealand, then pick any bottles from this list and set them against this wine. In three glasses you will have the purest and most accurate expressions of this variety on the planet, and all three for less than $100. As you would expect, the German wine is the more luscious and juicy of the threesome, with its lower alcohol levels and fruit cocktail notes. Perhaps less versatile when it comes to food matching, it is, however, the only way to start the weekend – drinking a bottle on Friday night after work will be one of the most pleasurable experiences of the week.

Clare Valley

Screw Cap

Best Price: $32

AU: Boc DMs DW Ed Nicks PWS Rand SMWM Sum VCs

NZ: SC

Grosset Springvale Watervale Riesling 2008

$37

Jeffrey Grosset's Springvale Riesling is a veritable Dr Jekyll and Mr Hyde in the 2008 vintage, with its demure, innocent Dr Henry Jekyll exterior hiding a malevolent Edward Hyde attack on the palate,

white wines 75

which builds incredibly in the glass. It is at once perfumed and pretty and at the same time structured, forceful and linear. Scary and exciting!

$38 Cullen Mangan Vineyard Semillon Sauvignon Blanc 2007

Margaret River

Screw Cap

Best Price: $32

AU: DW PWS Rand SMWM TWC VCs

NZ: Sel Glen HWC

Cullen's straight-laced SSB is just starting to emerge from its gawky adolescence and it is a thing of beauty. The oak used here knits so well with the wine that it doesn't topple things over – which it could so easily happen with a clumsier winemaker at the helm. Cullen's SBS from the 'Cullen Vineyard' uses a tad more carpentry and while it might be a cleverer wine in the long run, we are championing Mangan SSB in 2007 because it is very nearly ready to pour. Vanya Cullen ensures that the join between these two raspingly delicious, lip-lickingly crisp varieties is starting to fade. The main event is finishing its sound check and checking its rigging in preparation for some full-on entertaining. The show starts mid-October in Australia and then tours the globe for five or six years. Don't miss it – it is sure to sell out fast.

$38 De Bortoli Yarra Valley Reserve Release EZ 2008

Yarra Valley

Screw Cap

www.de bortoli. com.au

AU: DW PWS

Absolutely wicked. Edelzwicker is the name in Alsace for a white blend. It's only really used for inexpensive wines because most producers prefer to bottle single varietals, commanding higher prices. By contrast, Steve Webber has used this for his ultimate blended creation of Gewürz, Pinot Gris and Riesling. So clever, so EaZy. It's assembled like an intricate piece of marquetry, beautifully textured, finely detailed and blessed with wisps of spice, hints of honey and curls of lemon pith.

*'Gewürz' is German for 'spice' and 'traminer' is German for 'dry' – **Gewürztraminer** (Guh-vurz-tram-inner) makes wines with the most distinctive, spicy aromas of any grape variety. Pungent lychee and rose petal abound on the nose, and the palate is usually exotically oily, rich and intense. The finish varies from bone dry to just off-dry, and it often has the unusual knack of smelling sweet but tasting dry.*

Clare Valley

Screw Cap

AU: 1st SMWM VCs WLC

Leasingham Classic Clare Riesling 2005

$38

This wine has only gone up by $8 since we wrote it up in our book two years ago. For some reason it is still available (get shopping, you lazy buggers!). This is, and always will be, one of the great wines to emerge from the Clare Valley. In the hierarchy of Aussie Riesling, this wine, code-named CCRHR is one of the "Grand Cru" creations. When you bear in mind that it's less than $40, it's a wine that you simply cannot afford to miss if you are remotely serious about this variety, the region or great Aussie wine. Let's all try to make sure there is no stock available next year! We have taken more than our share of responsibility for this noble pursuit already!

Adelaide Hills

Screw Cap

www.thelane. com.au

AU: EEC WLC

The Lane Pinot Grigio 2007

$39

This wine is as close as Australia gets to making styles of wine that Friuli is so famous for in North-Eastern Italy. While everybody else in Australia either makes undernourished, spritzy

white wines

supermarket PG on the one hand, or fourteen-stone bridesmaids in pink shantung on the other, this wine perfectly encapsulates all that is beautiful about the variety.

$39 The Lane Vineyard Beginning Chardonnay 2007

Adelaide Hills

Screw Cap

www.thelane.com.au

This wine is so good and so well made that we are struggling to find words to do it justice. I (MJ) was lucky enough to taste every single barrel in the cellar last year and in a blind tasting it was difficult to tell what variety it was, because it was so unbelievably focused and introverted. Over the last few months it has momentarily flashed out coded messages which, if you were not quick enough to grab them, disappeared straight back into its core. We are now being treated to a muted, slow motion, Tai Chi like dance of flavours that are Beginning to form the final elements of the wine. Mesmerising and fascinating, this incredible wine is set to realign every palate it comes into contact with. Make sure you are in the queue.

$40 Leo Buring Leonay DWL17 High Eden Riesling 2008

Eden Valley

Screw Cap

AU: Aus DW GPO PWS SMWM

This High Eden Riesling and its Clare Valley sibling (read on) are the most devastating duo of wines that we have seen this year. Who needs a wine atlas with the intricate details of Australian's wine Geographic Indicator Cartographies when you can simply unscrew these two wines and experience such a thrilling display in the glass, such that you will never again wonder about the difference between these two regions? The use of the word "high" in the label of this wine is very accurate, because this is the way we felt after partaking of its searingly pure lime juice flavours. It has so much energy and yet is so pretty. We are still gobsmacked at this wine!

Clare Valley

Screw Cap

AU: Aus DW PWS SMWM

Leo Buring Leonay DWL18 Watervale Riesling 2008

$40

We were so knocked back by these wines that we went back to them a day later for dinner and then again for lunch the day after – and they got better each time. We had a vote around our table of friends as to which was the preferred wine between them – there was an exact split down the middle. Very serious and very tense, this is one of the best Rieslings of what is shaping up to be a very impressive vintage. Its pure, ultra-honed palate has unwavering persistence.

Marlborough

Screw Cap

AU: Ed

NZ: SC WFW

Pyramid Valley Vineyards Growers Collection Hille Vineyard Marlborough Semillon 2007

$40

Made in a desperately introverted White Graves style, this is a wine that has as much going on in the nose and palate as our darling Dog Point Section 94. Super-intellectual and in need of more than monastic calm, at least for the first few sips, this is a toasty, spicy, gooseberry-imbued wine. It has a quarry-full of minerality and a vortex of acidity which leave you completely dumbfounded and searching around the room for your bearings. Once you become

white wines 79

accustomed to the shape and size of the Pyramid everything else pales into insignificance (at least for the length of time it takes to polish off a bottle).

$41 Dalwhinnie Moonambel Chardonnay 2006

Pyrenees

Cork

AU: Aus DMs DW Nicks Rand Sixty SMWM Sum VCs

This vineyard resembles a moonscape, such is its barren rockiness, and these awesome stony flavours are just what you want when you are building Chardonnay of this class and distinction. It has a coil of energy inside it, with huge power nestling there, but it doesn't reveal everything unless you ask really hard. The opposite of lusciousness, this wine has a different shape to every other style in our list. More thoughtful and contemplative, it permits you greater scope in partnering it with fish and chicken dishes.

$42 Cape Mentelle Chardonnay 2007

Margaret River

Screw Cap

Best Price: $33

AU: 1st Aus Boc Chalk DMs DW Ed Nicks Lland PWS Rand SMWM Sum VCs

This is the best Chardonnay from Cape Mentelle for years. Rob Mann is on fire right now, and he finally has something to drink with his mind-blowing 2005 Cabernet, so we know where the smartest dinner parties in Western Australia are… see you at Prevelly beach. His 2007 Chardonnay has the longest finish in the history of Cape Mentelle. It's very well-sprung and tight, with grapefruit spice and great minerality that will sustain it for a very long time indeed.

Yabby Lake Vineyard Mornington Peninsula Chardonnay 2006

$42

Mornington
Peninsula

Screw Cap

AU: Aus Chalk
DMs DW PWS
Rand SMWM
VCs

Don't overload your cooking with too much heat or spice, because this Concord-shaped wine needs to be enjoyed with the finest of simply-grilled fish or the most expensive organic roast chicken, allowing it to show every bit of its magnificent talent. Utterly restrained and understated, it's as if all of Yabby's efforts have been put into making it longer and longer so it doesn't stick out at any stage. Don't be tempted to unscrew the screw cap yet because it will grow and build incrementally for years.

De Bortoli Yarra Valley Reserve Release Yarra Valley Chardonnay 2007

$43

Yarra Valley

Screw Cap

AU: Boc DW
PWS Rand
VCs

The alarm has gone off but this wine hasn't even got out of bed yet. This is exceedingly serious Chardonnay and it's incredibly young. It's very compact and honed but with plenty of space in its folds for all manner of barrel- and vineyard-derived complexity. DB Reserve is so good because it's so restrained, unlike many other Chardys that are fat and ugly. It's a mega-good and mega-well-priced wine.

Skillogalee Trevarrick Clare Valley Riesling 2008

$43

Clare Valley

Screw Cap

AU: DW Ed
Sixty SMWM

Skilly's estate Riesling was a dead cert this year, but when we heard that Trevarrick was also available we thought that you ought to be the first to hear about it right here. This dramatic wine will demonstrate just how far and fast this estate is moving forward. It is simply a stunning creation. We tasted it alongside the top wines from Grosset, Leasingham, Pikes, Annie's Lane, Penfolds, Leo Buring and all of the other usual suspects, and it ranked among the best of them. It tastes like very pure green apple skin and lemon blossom and it will live for decades.

$46 Stonier Reserve Chardonnay 2007

Mornington Peninsula

Screw Cap

AU: 1st Chalk DMs DW PWS Rand Sixty SMWM VCs

This is a hell of a lot of wine – absolute super premium quality at a premium price. It's laced with Geraldine magic of gorgeously fine white peach flavours, freshly grated nutmeg oak and a very savoury, dry finish. Geraldine's talents have never before hit the heights that she has achieved this vintage. The Estate and Reserve wines take this winery to new levels. We have also been sent a very secret sample of **Stonier KBS Chardonnay 2007** and it's utterly fantastic!

$46 Yalumba the Virgilius Eden Valley Viognier 2007

Eden Valley

Screw Cap

AU: 1st Chalk DMs DW Ed Nicks Rand VCs

NZ: Sel Glen HWC Mill SC WFW

This is the first Virgilius to ever make our cut. It's big and rich with freshly baked cake, honey and spice elements but, crucially, it's got the minerality and tone to keep it all under control. How you reign in a variety as ebullient as this is beyond us. But the girdle of acidity is so bracing that this curvaceous wine is sculpted into breathtaking shape. The silhouette that it leaves on your palate is unforgettable.

In the best examples, **Viognier** *(Vee-yon-yay)* offers a mind-blowing perfume of peach kernels, wild honey and apricot blossom, followed by an ample, curvaceous body with plenty of charm and a lingering, dry aftertaste. Choose carefully – this grape can be both a divine, sensual, provocative temptress and a fashion victim's folly!

Clare Valley

Screw Cap

www.leasingham-wines.com.au

Leasingham I.V.R. Watervale Riesling 2008

$48

When this wine arrived at Stelzer Towers there was a mood of grape expectation and uncontrollable excitement. Simon Osicka is a softly spoken, very deep thinking winemaker. Over the past few years he has crafted some highly intellectual wines and I.V.R. is the peak of his performance to date. In Vino Relaxo is anything but. This is an exhausting wine, with a challenging nose, enormous presence and unnerving power. The acidity and energy coiled up in the core of this breathtaking Riesling are nothing short of terrifying. It may just about be ready to drink in ten years' time if all goes well. Compared to Classic Clare Riesling, which in itself is a work of art (Venus de Milo), I.V.R. is every bit as collectable but in a thoroughly modern way (like Maman, Louise Bourgeois' Giant Spider). Now we know the Clare Valley pretty well, but where and how does this wine get its stunning aura and elemental energy? An emergency call to Simon, a day before this book went off to the printers, gave us the incredible answer. It comes from a family-owned, contour-planted vineyard situated just north of the Watervale pub, planted mostly with 1967 vines (an awesome year in all respects – MJ!). There is

white wines

a very narrow strip of red soil through the middle of this vineyard. You can have a boot on each side of the divide and the fruit from the red soil tastes completely different to that of the black. This wine is made exclusively from red soil fruit and only three and a half tonnes of grapes were harvested and kept apart from the rest. Simon tried as he might to 'put it' into Classic Clare, but it just wouldn't fit and, not wanting to compromise its extraordinary integrity and exact sense of place, I.V.R. was born. We were the first to taste it and you are the first to read about it. This kind of privilege makes our job so very special and drives us on to find more and more wines like this every year. Dear reader, your task today is to try to find a bottle of this wine – only 150 dozen were made. When you do, you can Relaxo, too.

> **Riesling** *(Rees-ling) is one of the truly great white varieties, producing a vast array of wine styles, from aromatic, bone-dry apéritifs; through structured, limejuice-scented, foody beauties; via long-lived, complex, off-dry stunners, and ending up at heart-achingly beautiful sweeties. Lemon, tropical fruits, rhubarb, petrol, honey, honeysuckle and spice are there in varying degrees throughout this cornucopia of guises. Riesling seems to be perpetually out of fashion (why?!), but we are both head-over-heels besotted with this heavenly grape! Australian Riesling remains one of the most outrageous bargains of the wine world.*

$48 Umamu Estate Margaret River Chardonnay 2006

Margaret River

Screw Cap

www.umamu estate.com

We pronounce Umamu as if we are thirty-stone sumos, which provokes much mirth. Mr Dukes (no relation) came from Pierro to Umamu and his impeccable credentials are already falling into place. Brand new to us, Umamu has gone straight

Yarra Valley

Screw Cap

AU: Aus Ed
Rand Sixty
SMWM

PHI Lusatia Park Chardonnay 2007

$50

in to our hit list of Margaret River wines to covet, thanks to its spicy fig flavours and concentrated fruit and oak balance. It was very satisfying for Mr Jukes (yes, the one on the cover), all the way from London, to introduce this wine to Mr Stelzer. This foreign exchange very rarely happens.

So utterly coiled up was this wine when it landed on our tasting bench that we were initially in two minds as to whether it should make the selection this year. But we kept it on the table and tasted it at the end of the flight – between Art Series, Giaconda and Yattarna (at double the price). The initial concern was that its fruit austerity kicked the oak out of balance. But we shouldn't be afraid of youthfulness in top Aussie Chardonnay. We accept it in Burgundy, after all, so we should here as well! On second tasting it was every bit good enough to steam into this book. Phee, PHI, pho, phum. It stood shoulder to shoulder with the giants.

Hunter Valley

Cork

Best Price: $45

AU: 1st Aus
Chalk DW Ed
Lland Sixty
SMWM VCs
WLC

NZ: Sel Glen
SC

Tyrrell's Wines Vat 1 Hunter Semillon 2002

$51

2002 Vat 1 is now getting into its stride and this wine is cantering along like a thoroughbred. With flashing spurs of zesty, lemony fruit and powerful haunches of spice and toast developing, this is a wonderful wine which shows off all that is magnificent about Hunter Valley Semillon. With years ahead of it, Vat 1 will put on honeyed weight and silkiness, but we love it right now while

white wines 85

there is still a thrilling stampede of acidity on the finish.

$55 Bruno Colin Bourgogne Blanc 2006

Burgundy, France

Cork

AU: DMs Rand SMWM VCs

The super-cool and ultra-talented Bruno Colin has stonkingly good vineyards, thanks to his dad, Michel. From them he crafts this delightful, delicious Bourgogne Blanc. It has been made like a Grand Vin, so it's no wonder that it is several levels above the norm. This is a beautifully textured wine with ripe stone fruit flavours and a pretty, exotic finish – ooh lah lah!

We have estimated the prices of the Bourgogne Blancs and Bourgogne Rouges in our book this year as stock is yet to land in the country.

$55 Felton Road Chardonnay 2007

If you want to know just how well New Zealand and Australia are doing versus global competition, take this, and any of the Aussie Chardonnays on either side of it in this book and then ram-raid an ATM for enough cash to buy a French equivalent prior to doing a taste-off. We reckon you'd have to spend three times as much money to get anywhere near the level of skill and sheer deliciousness of this and your other wine.

Central Otago

Screw Cap

Best Price: $36

AU: Ed EEC GPO PWS SMWM Sum VCs

NZ: Sel Glen HWC SC WFW

$60 McWilliams Mount Pleasant Lovedale Hunter Valley Semillon 2008

Hunter Valley

Screw Cap

AU: 1st Chalk GPO Rand Sixty SMWM VCs

Lovedale has an electrical storm of acidity in its core, which powers the wine through glorious decades of life. In 2008 the voltage has been turned down a fraction, making it more

the best wines of 2009

The dominant aromas in dry **Semillon** (Sem-ee-yon) are honey, lemon and lime juice. Sometimes lanolin, creamy vanilla and toasty oak elements creep in, depending on the style. Semillon also makes drop-dead gorgeous, unctuous sweet wines, tasting of tropical fruit, honey, honey and more honey. Its perfect dance partner is Sauvignon Blanc.

approachable and drinkable right now. It has a swell of butter, lemon and spice that ripples through its outer layers, resonating with the power of this phenomenal vineyard.

Burgundy, France

Cork

AU: Rand

Patrick Javillier Cuvée Oligocène Bourgogne Blanc 2006 $60

Javillier's Bourgogne Blanc shouldn't really be considered along with other BBs, because it's made from his most mineral vineyards, in the same barrels and with the same treatment as his Meursaults. As a result, it's more masculine and mineral, with a more Grand Vin flavour than the other Bourgogne Blancs in this list. 2006 also happens to be his best vintage of Oligocène ever, with fine, fresh citrus fruits running helter skelter through the bouquet and palate.

Burgundy, France

Cork

AU: DOr Ed EEC PWS Rand SMWM

Etienne Sauzet Bourgogne Blanc 2006 $61

This is a brilliantly pure Bourgogne Blanc with a shy bouquet and a beautifully refined palate which showcases lifted, fresh and subtle citrus flavours, fine, minerally acidity and great length. Its three-quarters of a hectare of vines average thirty years of age and some are as old as fifty. This is a remarkable and breathtakingly elegant wine.

white wines 87

$63 Eileen Hardy Chardonnay 2006

Upper Yarra, Rokeby, Coal River, Tumbarumba

Screw Cap

AU: 1st Aus DMs GPO PWS SMWM VCs WLC

Eileen has gone from being a mumsy frump to being able to strut her stuff down a catwalk in five years. This makeover is the most extreme in the Australian wine world and we are loving it. There is some flamboyance and swagger in this wine that comes from its warmer elements, but its steely core will propel it forward, and it is this that captivates us. It is like Premier Cru Chassagne with its masculine minerality.

$68 Pierro Margaret River Chardonnay 2006

Margaret River

Screw Cap

Best Price: $60

AU: 1st Aus Boc Chalk DMs Ed Lland PWS Rand SMWM Sum VCs

With its veritable kaleidoscope of exuberant flavours, this is a slightly atypical Pierro in that it is quite rich and powerful. It's loaded with exotic spice, tight grapefruit and fine minerality. You really need to cook the right thing if you are to serve it – this is the definition of big, fat, roast chicken wine.

$80 Domaine Leflaive Bourgogne Blanc 2006

Puligny-Montrachet, Burgundy, France

Cork

AU: DOr Ed EEC PWS Rand SMWM VCs

NZ: Sel Glen RWM

Leflaive is the finest Bourgogne Blanc of the outstanding 2006 vintage made by, arguably, the finest producer of Chardonnay in the world. We would prefer to buy this than practically any other Puligny-Montrachet or any of the Premier Crus that everyone seems to get so excited about. When we visited this hallowed cellar, this was the first wine that Pierre Morey poured for us. It is brilliantly luminous, utterly fresh and finely crafted around a core of minerality. We looked at Pierre in gaping disbelief and garbled something about where you can go from here when the first wine you serve is so astonishing. With a wry grin he replied in impeccable English, "It's like a boxing match, it's the first punch that really counts because after that it doesn't really matter." You simply must track this wine down this year – and be prepared to be knocked out!

Adelaide Hills

Cork

AU: Aus DW Ed PWS Rand SMWM

Tapanappa Tiers Vineyard Piccadilly Valley Chardonnay 2007

$80

There are only a handful of wines in Australia where just the one word will do to convey the seriousness and romance of the contents of the bottle. The most obvious is Grange and in order to achieve this mythical status you often have to spend years, if not decades, making incredible wine. When Brian Croser planted the Tiers vineyard in the Piccadilly Valley in the Adelaide Hills he was not to know that the word "Tiers" would, in the future, carry so much weight. Or, perhaps he did, because when he sold Petaluma he made sure that he kept this vineyard for his new venture, Tapanappa – after all, it is his front garden. This prescient decision, along with the fact that he will also move back into his original winery soon, shows just how visionary this man is. Tapanappa Tiers 2007 is the finest wine from this vineyard to date, so don't miss out on drinking a slice of Australian wine history in the making.

$91 Leeuwin Estate Art Series Chardonnay 2006

2006 Art Series is one of the very greatest vintages of one of Australia's top Chardonnays ever made. On a world scale, this is as good as Chardonnay ever gets anywhere outside of Burgundy. It strikes the quintessential balance between control and concentration, power and finesse. Its length is so heroic that minutes later, nothing has changed the slightest bit in the mouth. As far as "art labels" go, we would prefer this to a bottle of Mouton-Rothschild.

Margaret River

Screw Cap

Best Price: $80

AU: 1st Aus Boc Chalk DMs DW Ed EEC GPO Nicks PWS Rand SMWM Sum VCs WLC

NZ: HWC SC WFW

$125 Giaconda Estate Vineyard Chardonnay 2006

Giaconda Chardonnay is a legendary wine. We have never before received a sample for this book but this year the planets realigned, something wonderful happened to the great Rick Kinzbrunner and his Chardonnay arrived on our tasting altar (we reserve this holy bench for legend wines only). And what a wine! It's massive, of Bâtard-Montrachet proportions. If you are familiar with this vineyard in Burgundy, you will have now dropped to your knees. Prepare yourself for the ritual of anointing your glass with this heavenly wine. Before you do, you need to put on your chain mail gauntlet and take up your Homer Simpson nuclear facility tongs just to manoeuvre the bottle around the room. This is another sensational Giaconda of revelatory proportions. There were little more than 5000 bottles made so speed is of the essence if you want to bring this legend home.

Beechworth

Screw Cap

Best Price: $90

AU: Aus Sel DMs Ed EEC PWS Rand SMWM VCs WLC

NZ: HWC WFW

rosé

South-Eastern Australia

Screw Cap

Best Price: $12

AU: 1st Boc DW VCs

See back page for key to stockists

De Bortoli Wines Windy Peak Cabernet Rosé 2008

$13

Windy Pants leads our rosé charge (again!) but don't pass it up as giggle juice and move on to the bigger boys further down our list before giving it a chance to work its magic. This wine is built in an intelligent style but it's so delicious that you shouldn't hesitate to pour it for your thicker mates. Its light, fragrant raspberry nuances freshen the palate and will do the same for your mood.

Maule Valley, Chile

Screw Cap

AU: 1st Boc Lland VCs

Casillero del Diablo Shiraz Rosé 2008

$14.50

The world needs more bargain-priced rosés like this. When it comes to clean, fresh wines that taste exactly as they should, Marcello Papa doesn't miss a thing. For a glass of strawberries and cream with a lively, balanced finish, stock up on this pretty little thing.

South-Eastern Australia

Screw Cap

www.cwines. com.au

Hardys Pruner's Cup Shiraz Cabernet Rosé 2008

$15

Our favourite blend of Shiraz and Cabernet appears in all styles from bubbly to monstrous, and here it looks just the part as a lively water-melon and raspberry jelly flavoured rosé.

Langhorne Creek

Screw Cap

Bremerton Racy Rosé 2008

$16

A wacy wosé made for a womantic evening in

with a wonderful wady. Webecca Wilson continues to craft wich, wipe wosés which will guawantee that you have a wipper of an evening with your bewoved. Fine and tight with a zesty acid backbone, great line and length, this is a fresh, well made rosé.

$16 Majella Melody Coonawarra Rosé 2008

Coonawarra

Screw Cap

www.majella wines.com.au

AU: Aus DW

Melody is the diametric opposite of Prof Lynn – delightful, clean, refreshing and light. This is an elegant, gentle rosé with pretty red fruits and it's as well made as anything from this great estate. Despite its delicate style it's the definitive wine for any pink crustacea and it will happily handle some chilli on the top.

$16 Trevor Jones Barossa Valley Cêbo Rosé 2008

Barossa Valley

Screw Cap

www.keller meister. com.au

AU: SMWM WLC

We booted a lot of rosés out of our list to make way for this one. This juicy, ripe cherry juice style with a smooth, slippery palate is just the thing for white wine drinkers. It's a medium weight rosé with plush cherry and strawberry fruit and a spice finish. A touch of sweetness on the end rounds it out nicely.

$18 Coriole Nebbiolo Rosé 2008

McLaren Vale

Screw Cap

www.coriole. com

AU: DW

We like this wine because it's off the wall and one of the least commercial styles in our book. They don't even make rosé like this in Piedmont (the home of Nebbiolo) because the grape has such assertive tannins. But the team at Coriole has

www.bremer ton.com.au

AU: Aus DW SMWM

> **Nebbiolo** (Neb-ee-olo) is a tough grape that often needs five years in the bottle to soften to drinkability. A great Nebbiolo can conjure up intense plummy flavours with leathery, spicy, gamey overtones and a firm, dry finish. Nebbiolo is a regal grape, at home in Italy but showing some promise in the Adelaide Hills and McLaren Vale.

cunningly side-stepped the tannins, preserving the trademark sour cherry fruit of this variety and adding a ton of McLaren Vale spice and liquorice. This means that when you sniff this wine, you'll likely do what we did – look quizzically at each other, count to ten, and then, like Caesar, do a thumbs up or thumbs down. You're reading about it because we both did a thumbs up. Which way is yours pointing?

Linda Domas Shotbull Rosé 2008 $18

Fleurieu

Screw Cap

www.ldwines.com.au

Shotbull Rosé is always a winner and the 2008 must be the best ever. With a colour that looks like it has an arc lamp behind it, a nose that is a spitter for Ocean Spray cranberry juice and a palate which tastes like crunchy, shiny red cherries, it is all ready to shock, amaze and refresh. The whip crack of acidity keeps it all in check and you crave another bottle – perfect.

Shelmerdine Yarra Valley Pinot Noir Rosé 2008 $19

Yarra Valley

Screw Cap

www.shelmerdine.com.au

AU: DW Sixty

Very fine, minerally and savoury with a great texture, there is no confected sweetness here, just stylish, fine, minerally strawberry juice fruit. Gorgeous and white-wine-like throughout, if you shut your eyes it drinks like a white wine, but if you open them it is a hauntingly pale Pinot Noir.

$19 Skillogalee Cabernet Malbec Rosé 2008

Clare Valley

Screw Cap

www.skilloga lee.com.au

AU: DW SMWM TWC

Next time you open a bottle of red and you suspect you're not likely to finish it, crack a bottle of this serious rosé instead. It smells honeyed and sweet and the palate is rich and ripe with blueberry and cherry fruit. This is a real step up in concentration from those before it in this list, but with a dry, long finish, making it your ideal drinking partner if you're eating Indian or Asian cuisine.

$20 Paxton Shiraz Rosé 2008

McLaren Vale

Screw Cap

www.paxton vineyards. com

AU: DW Sum VCs

This is a delicious rosé with pretty rose petal notes and juicy red cherry flavours, and there is some sweetness on the end which rounds it all out. A juicy but fresh style, serve it super-cold to ensure that the sweetness on the finish doesn't stick out. It's luscious, like a punnet of red berries in summer.

$21 De Bortoli Yarra Valley Pinot Noir Rosé 2008

Yarra Valley

Screw Cap

AU: 1st Boc DW VCs

Gorgeous and breath-taking by comparison with some of the more macho wines in this section, the quality of Pinot Noir fruit on show here is very plain to smell and taste. DBYVPNR is intellectual rosé for Pinot freaks, and that doesn't happen very often, so pick your moment well and only pour this wine for great mates. Its pretty, elegant bouquet and dry, finely textured palate make more of a statement about crafted shape than they do about overt fruit. Hooray for that!

the best wines of 2009

Turkey Flat Rosé 2008

$21

Barossa Valley

Screw Cap

Best Price: $18

AU: 1st Aus
Chalk DMs
DW Ed Nicks
Lland PWS
Rand Sum
VCs WLC

NZ: WFW

You may not have noticed it but this wine has become more and more grown up in recent years and the reason for this is that Turkey Flat Rosé has progressively decreased in sweetness by half over the last four years. This makes it a fresh, tight, clean style with lifted rose petal aromatics and a beautifully lively palate. It has great balance and it's much classier than it used to be.

Charles Melton Rose of Virginia 2008

$22

Barossa Valley

Screw Cap

AU: 1st Aus
DMs DW EEC
Ed GPO Nicks
Lland PWS
Rand SMWM
Sum VCs WLC

This is a big wine by any standards and please watch out that you don't let its great big feet stand all over your gorgeously elegant cuisine! You should only drink this wine with the sort of food that you would with a red wine made from the same grapes. Massive BBQ fare is the order of the day here, and its blackcurrant and blueberry fruit will chomp through any sizzling selection with consummate ease.

Burge Family Winemakers Shiraz Rosé 2008

$24

Barossa Valley

Screw Cap

www.burge
family.com.au

This is a bloody good rosé that happened by accident. When it caught my (Tyson's) attention at the Barossa Shiraz Alliance, I took my glass over to quiz Rick Burge on how a rosé ended up in a Shiraz tasting. As the story goes, he had to free up a fermenter in the middle of the heatwave so he decided to empty one early and make his first rosé. "I woke up in the middle of the night and thought, 'Bloody hell, what on earth have I done making premium Barossa Shiraz into rosé!?'" he said. The result is a grown up rosé made from serious fruit, with rippling spice and a swell of rich Shiraz fruit that's so fresh it tastes like it's still in that fermenter. This is one of the biggest rosés in our list, making it just the thing for a serious Indian or Thai banquet.

red wines

$6.50 McWilliams Inheritance Shiraz Merlot 2007

South-Eastern Australia

Screw Cap

Best Price: $5

AU: 1st Boc DMs Lland Sum VCs WLC

McWilliams Inheritance S&M (an unusual concept!) was up against its own Shiraz /Cab, which, as you know, would usually be our preferred combo. However, bearing in mind its 'nearly free' price point, we felt that this Shiraz Merlot would benefit from a listing because not only is it a more refreshing and happy-go-lucky style than the SC, it's better, too! With crunchy red berry notes and some pretty smart spiciness, this is a superb red wine that deserves to be glugged by the case load.

$8 Pepperton Estate Goodwyn Shiraz Cabernet 2007

South-Eastern Australia

Screw Cap

www.pepper tonestate. com.au

Two jokes in one wine – we are bursting at the seams, but Pepper Town is a Good Wine and true to its name there is a superb volley of pepper and red fruit on the nose and a darker, blueberry, cherry and summer pudding palate to back it all up. There is nothing complex going on here – after all, it's not called Cornucopiaville Awesomegear Shiraz Cabernet – but for eight bucks you get very good value for money and a wine that we would happily pour for any Vinoyawn Boreonandon.

South-Eastern Australia

Screw Cap

Best Price: $8

AU: 1st Boc DMs DW Lland SMWM VCs

Jacob's Creek Cabernet Merlot 2006 $10

Don't get label prejudiced about this wine because this is a very tight JC that deserves to be treated like a much grander wine. Be sure to give it a decent decant. You can even cellar it for a year or two with confidence to soften its dusty tannins and allow its superb blueberry fruit to loosen up.

South-Eastern Australia

Screw Cap

Best Price: $8

AU: 1st Boc DW Lland SMWM VCs WLC

NZ: Mill

Jacob's Creek Grenache Shiraz 2007 $10

In the 2007 vintage this Grenache Shiraz was a star performer for JC and if you haven't tried this combo before, then you will be amazed at the result. It's spicy and red-fruited with savoury herbs and fresh raspberries all jostling for attention. Hands in the air, who wants some more?

South-Eastern Australia

Screw Cap

AU: 1st DMs DW Lland VCs WLC

NZ: Mill

Lindemans Bin 40 Merlot 2007 $10

It is desperately difficult to make good Merlot at any price and this cheeky little entry level red from the mighty Lindemans operation is a bloody good effort. Plummy and immediately engaging, this is the sort of wine that shouts "Australia" from the rooftops and pleases experts and novices

red wines 97

alike. There needs to be a lot more wine like this flowing down the pipeline in order that you keep your enemies at bay and your fans close to your bosom.

$10 McWilliam's Hanwood Estate Cabernet Sauvignon 2007

South-Eastern Australia

Screw Cap

Best Price: $8

AU: 1st Boc DMs Lland Sum VCs

This wine is so readily available that you might be mistaken into thinking that it is from a massive multinational company, but in fact it isn't. The McWilliams squad is one of the most articulate and passionate we have met, with each of their divisions headed up by true experts in their fields. In a difficult vintage like 2007, this level of skill and determination really shines through, lifting this pure, accurate expression of Cabernet to one of the best under this label in years. If you're used to buying in sub-$10 land, we have good news for you because our spies tell us that the price on the street is a couple of dollars less than last year.

$11 McPherson Cabernet Sauvignon 2007

South-Eastern Australia

Screw Cap

www.mcphers onwines.com

The whole range of McPherson reds are surprisingly juicy and accurate. Each one nails the character of the grape while maintaining an enthusiastic style. This is a friendly Cabernet that comes up and says hello with its crunchy, fresh blackcurrant fruits. You'll be more than happy for it to stick around and chat for a while, too.

$11 McPherson Merlot 2007

South-Eastern Australia

This wine has no Merlot mates whatsoever at this

Screw Cap

www.mcphers
onwines.com

AU: DMs

price because we tasted more than 30 contestants under $25 and it was the only wine worthy of stepping into the spotlight. Make a Merlot happy today by giving this little darling some much needed mouth-to-mouth.

Adelaide Hills

Screw Cap

Best Price:
$8.50

www.topdrop
wines.com.au

AU: Aus WLC

Mike Press Adelaide Hills Cabernet Sauvignon 2007 $11

Since introducing Mike Press reds to my (Tyson's) friends last year he has single-handedly changed their wine buying habits. Not only have his Shiraz and Cabernet become their house reds of choice, but they now compare every other red wine prospect under $25 with these wines – and invariably conclude that his wines trump everything up to even twice their price. When it came time for the release of the challenging 2007 vintage there was a little apprehension that their favourite wine supplier might temporarily run dry, but they need not have doubted the talented Mr Press. When the samples arrived and we lined them up against last years' wines, the group vote went to the 2007s. The exuberant Cabernet is again built like a much more expensive wine. It demands a decent decant – and preferably a few years in the cellar. Thanks Mike, you will keep your adoring fans delighted for yet another year!

Adelaide Hills

Screw Cap

Best Price:
$8.50

www.topdrop
wines.com.au

AU: Aus WLC

Mike Press Wines Adelaide Hills Shiraz 2007 $11

We have always known that Mike Press has a touch of the dark side about him and it is all on show here in this epic, budget stunner. We tasted it, decanted it and then went back to this wine ten or more times, and on each occasion it grew and grew, stretching out and making the most of its release from its glass cell. This is an absolutely beautiful wine with five glorious years ahead of it and we are in awe of its swarthy deep black fruit and massively impressive stance. Stock your cellar and make this your house wine of choice. We do!

$11.50 Yalumba Y Series Shiraz Viognier 2007

South Australia

Screw Cap

Best Price: $9

AU: 1st Boc Chalk DW Ed Nicks Lland PWS SMWM Sum VCs WLC

NZ: Sel Glen HWC Mill SC

Made to be drunk young and with very few angles to grip onto, this cracking little wine is as slippery as an eel with its blueberry pie notes and jittery acidity. Y Series is a great little family of wines and, once again, our favourite turned out to be this fashionable blend – not surprising when you consider how much these gals and guys know about the two grapes concerned.

$12 Kemeny's Hidden Label KHL1028 Barossa Valley Reserve Grenache Shiraz Mourvèdre 2006

Barossa Valley

Screw Cap

www.kemenys
.com.au

Eagle-eyed Andrew Kemeny has smuggled this $25 wine into his emporium, whacked it into his own bottle and more than halved the price. It hails from a famous Barossa name that rhymes with "ball break" and begins with a "T" (you'll find it on the label, but only if you look for it before you drink this wine because you won't find it after!). This is a great value Barossa GSM with rich plum fruit and layers of spicy complexity.

presidential performance

Penfolds Rawson's Retreat Cabernet Sauvignon 2007

$12

South-Eastern Australia

Screw Cap

Best Price: $11

AU: 1st Chalk DMs DW Lland VCs WLC

NZ: Mill

Rawson's doesn't really behave like a classic Penfolds premium wine, in that it is forward, juicy, drinkable and up to racing speed the moment it lands on the shelves. For this reason it shouldn't be compared with its lofty Bin siblings, but rather with its like-priced peers on these pages. In this context, it's a precisely built wine with accurate Cabernet flavours of fresh redcurrant fruit.

Victorian Alps Winery Tobacco Road Cabernet Sauvignon 2006

$13

Victoria

Screw Cap

www.victorian alpswinery. com.au

AU: DMs

This aptly named wine actually does have hints of tobacco and herbs on the nose, and these fragrances cunningly overlay an impressive palate with a fresh black plum and cherry fruit core. This is a cool Cabernet style from a winery on the road to the snowfields. A beautiful wine from a beautiful place.

De Bortoli Windy Peak Shiraz Viognier 2007

$13.50

South-Eastern Australia

Screw Cap

Best Price: $12

AU: 1st Boc Chalk DW Lland SMWM Sum VCs

NZ: Sel Glen

With a stunning, baked blueberry muffin nose and a superb, stylish lick of iodine on the palate, this is a dead ringer for a super-smart Crozes-Hermitage, from the Northern Rhône in France, but it costs half the price of a dull one, let alone one of the more serious versions! Windy Pants pushes harder each year to ramp up its fan base and amaze its acolytes and this wine is a presidential performance! If you love crunchy, cool climate Shiraz then this is a must for your cellar. Try to give it until 2009 to polish off some of its youthful exuberance and you will be gobsmacked at the value here.

$14 BullAnt Langhorne Creek Shiraz 2006

Langhorne Creek

Screw Cap

www.lakebreeze.com.au

AU: WLC

NZ: SC

Apparently these hardnut ants can take on funnelwebs! We just saw a home movie of them carrying a big spider away with them for supper – there are some awesome takeaway joints in Langhorne Creek! We suppose that this wine echoes the menacing ants that march around these vineyards in that it is forceful, dense, powerful and a small amount of spend can go a pretty long way. Good wine, nice label, just don't fall asleep on a picnic in Langhorne Creek!

$14 Casillero del Diablo Cabernet Sauvignon 2007

Chile

Cork

AU: 1st Lland VCs

NZ: HWC

Australia and New Zealand have more than their fair share of genius winemakers but there is only one in Chile, his name is Marcello Papa, and he makes more than a million cases of this wine every year. When we caught up with him in London he told us that 2007 was the first year that he had the chance to blend a touch of Carmenère, Shiraz and Petit Verdot into this Cabernet. The result, he says, is the best Cabernet he's made in his ten years with Concha y Toro. He is absolutely correct, of course, as this complex and well-aligned capsicum and blackcurrant creation proves. It is mind-blowing that Marcello can make a wine of this quality in such massive volumes and it deservedly appears in every corner of the globe.

De Bortoli Windy Peak Pinot Noir 2008

$14

Victoria

Screw Cap

Best Price: $11

AU: 1st Boc DMs DW Ed Nicks Lland Sum VCs

NZ: Sel Glen

If you shop well, there is a chance that you could get two bottles of this wine for the same price as our cheapest Kiwi Pinot, which is all the more remarkable, because this wine is the best Windy Pants Pinot to date. It raises the bar further than we ever thought possible over last year's wine. Goodness gracious, this is lovely. A beautiful violet and spice nose, textured palate, classy, medium-weight finish that is already totally relaxed – this is incredible.

St Hallett Gamekeepers Reserve 2007

$14

Barossa Valley

Screw Cap

Best Price: $12

AU: 1st Aus Boc Chalk DMs DW Ed Nicks Lland Rand Sixty VCs WLC

NZ: Glen HWC WFW

Drunk cool, Gamekeepers must be the ultimate BBQ wine, but when savoured at normal temperatures it is able to take on a vast array of traditional dishes. This ranks it among the most multitalented red wines of the year (and it's a bargain to boot). The secret ingredient which puts it ahead of the pack is one of the most revered red grapes in Europe, responsible for Vintage Port's ageworthiness and silky texture – Touriga Nacional. A dribble of this variety transforms this covert huntsman into an Olympian marksman, hitting the target with unerring accuracy. You know what to do when the gun goes off.

red wines 103

$14.50 — Penfolds Koonunga Hill Shiraz Cabernet 2007

South Australia

Screw Cap

Best Price: $12

AU: 1st Boc Chalk DMs DW Nicks Lland SMWM VCs WLC

NZ: Mill WFW

You only have to flick to our incredible TGAR results (page 17) to see that Penfolds Bin 389 is our top dog of the year and it is clear to see (and taste) that this marvellous wine is its little brother. You can, if you are very eagle-eyed, pick this bottle up for a teeny price. What you will get in the glass is a beautifully balanced nose of freshly-picked blackberries, dusted with sweet and savoury spices and a long, smooth finish. What makes this wine sing so beautifully is the seamless mesh between these two awesome grapes. With Koonunga Hill it is the Cabernet that comes in like Batman, smashing through a skylight, and it totally brings the Shiraz fruit to order. There is a definition and freshness on the finish that only Cabernet tannins possess and this is what makes this wine gripping viewing. You really have a difficult decision to make with the exchange rate for this wine currently sitting at three bottles of KH to one bottle of 389.

$15 — 2Up Shiraz by Kangarilla Road 2007

Southern Fleurieu, McLaren Vale

Screw Cap

www.kanga rillaroad. com.au

AU: Aus SMWM

So three and a half bottles of this wine equate to one 7Up? If only that were true of the price, but by any standards this wine is still a bargain! With floral, rose petal and violet notes, reminiscent of the hills behind the winery, and a lively damson and plum palate, this is a really expressive wine. It echoes the grace and beauty of owner Helen O'Brien and leaves out all of the coarse notes of her ruffian husband Kevin! This is a very impressive quaffer and a wine that will appeal to all palates with its crowd-pleasing air.

Shiraz/Syrah *(Shiraz/Sirrah)* is Australia's most famous grape, invoking explosive blackberry and ground-pepper aromas with vanilla, smoke and charred-oak nuances. From warm regions, big, inky-black Shiraz often has high alcohol and a mouth-filling prune, chocolate, raisin and spice palate. In cooler places its pepper, herb and coffee bean characters come to the fore. Shiraz is called Syrah in Europe and elsewhere in the world. It's often blended with small amounts of the white grape Viognier and in Australia it makes a delightful partnership with Cabernet Sauvignon.

South-Eastern Australia

www.cwines.com.au

Hardys The Sage Shiraz Sangiovese 2007

$15

Australia is one of the best places in the world for cross-regional blending, and Hardys has been perfecting the art for nigh-on 150 years. The Sage makes clever use of Shiraz from the Adelaide Hills, Fleurieu Peninsula and Limestone coast to add sinew and definition to intense, black-fruited Shiraz from McLaren Vale. Adelaide Hills Sangiovese is the surprise element in the mix, contributing a dried herb spice and a lively freshness that makes this a very appealing quaffer.

Taltarni T Series Shiraz 2005

$15.50

Pyrenees and Heathcote

Screw Cap

AU: 1st Chalk DW Lland SMWM Sum VCs

T Series is a Taltarni for beginners. We say this because if the power and earthiness of the big Taltarni reds is a bit much for you, then throttle back a touch and let this wine be your guide to this famous estate. Having said this, you are still getting Taltarni class at bargain price, so dive into the depths of prune and cracked pepper, in the knowledge that a well-trained lifeguard is on standby in case of any difficulties. Remember to breathe, too – you and the wine!

$16 De Bortoli Gulf Station Yarra Valley Pinot Noir 2008

Yarra Valley

Screw Cap

Best Price: $15

AU: 1st Boc DMs DW Lland SMWM VCs

NZ: Sel Glen

More intense and with a tad more wood and more tannin than Windy Pants, what would we do without De Bortoli's Pinots? They both come in under the rest of the Pinots in our list and the black cherry, spice and grippy but supple tannins make this an impressive creation. Gulf Station is more closely related to De Bortoli Pinot than it is to Windy Pants, though. You can't buy a Bourgogne Rouge at this price so this is one of the best value and best tasting Pinot Noirs on the planet. Serious.

$16 Peter Lehmann The Seven Surveys Shiraz Grenache Mourvèdre 2007

Barossa

Screw Cap

AU: 1st Aus Chalk DMs DW VCs

This wine is not perhaps what you'd expect from a Lehmann red, with its Barossan roots and foreboding pedigree. It's actually a much cooler, more toned, fresher style of wine with a lighter, garnet colour and a frisky, perky flavour. Pretty red fruits bound around unfettered and pepper and spice call order every so often before it all becomes too hilarious. This is a clever 'session' red with a smooth finish so your pals will adore it.

Grenache/Garnacha (Gre-nash/Gar-natch-ah) is usually blended with Shiraz among others. It is a meaty, earthy, red- and black-fruit-drenched variety, often with highish alcohol and a garnet hue. It sometimes picks up a wild herbal scent not dissimilar to aromatic pipe smoke.

Fleurieu Peninsula and Adelaide Hills

Screw Cap

AU: 1st Chalk DMs DW Ed Lland SMWM VCs WLC

NZ: SC

Wirra Wirra Scrubby Rise Shiraz Cabernet Sauvignon Petit Verdot 2007

$16

Even though '07 Scrubby is still in its infancy, there is already an incredible amount of harmony on the go in this challenging blend. The nose is delish, but the flavour is even more expressive and despite its crunchy finish, there is a lot of slick fruit sloshing around the middle of the palate. While Shiraz is seemingly the master of the trio at this stage, Cabernet Sauvignon and Petit Verdot appear to stick their hands up at the back of the class to ask a question of the more exuberant grape and then quickly put them back down again to defer to its authority. This continual state of flux is what makes this wine such a fascinating red and the debate between these three grapes will rage on for many years.

Yarra Valley

Screw Cap

Best Price: $15

AU: 1st Boc Chalk DMs DW Lland SMWM VCs

NZ: Sel Glen

De Bortoli Gulf Station Shiraz Viognier 2007

$17

Remember to drink Windy Pants SV before you start screwing around (or rather 'off') with Gulf Station SV because it is a very different and far more grown up proposition indeed. This and the other Gulf Station wines are far more concentrated and engaging than they used to be, and they are edging ever closer to the top wines from this estate, which at this price is utterly incredible. With a ridiculously impressive dark chocolate nose and a monsoon of black fruit flavours, urged on by layers of spice on the palate, the only problem you'll have with this wine is trying to keep your hands off it! Good luck, we are having the same issues, too.

$18 Bremerton Tamblyn Cabernet Shiraz Malbec Merlot 2006

There are two ways to make a blend like this. One is to lob four parcels of disconnected fruit into a great big tank, stir it up and bottle it, which is how many makers around the world get rid of their leftovers at the end of vintage. The other way is to spend hours on end with hundreds of samples of these four grapes, assembling (the French word for blending is "assemblage") a wine that meshes together seamlessly. The resulting percentages are irrelevant because if you start with something in mind it will never turn out that way, anyway. The expert palates at Bremerton use their good taste to determine what goes into Tamblyn and the result is a polished blend of black cherry and plum fruit, spiced up with herbaceous complexity.

Langhorne Creek

Screw Cap

Best Price: $15

AU: 1st Aus Boc DMs DW Ed Lland SMWM VCs WLC

NZ: HWC WFW

$18 Pertaringa Understudy McLaren Vale Cabernet Petit Verdot 2006

This is the darkest Cabernet so far in our hall of greats, with a Petit Verdot element playing understudy to the Cabernet. We love the way that they work so well together, and this wine manages to retain the spice and fragrance of PV without attracting any of its unwanted brawn.

McLaren Vale

Screw Cap

AU: 1st Aus DMs DW VCs

Scotchmans Hill Swan Bay Victoria Shiraz 2006

$18

Victoria

Screw Cap

Best Price: $15

AU: 1st DMs
Lland VCs

This wine has a far nobler air about it than anything else at its price. In just one sniff we thought we were going to be diving into one of the peppery Shiraz icons from the Pyrenees, Canberra or Hawkes Bay. It doesn't have perhaps the amplitude of these big boys, but this only makes it all the more drinkable. At a quarter of the price of even the cheapest of them, this wine is your entry ticket to blackberry utopia.

Willunga 100 Cabernet Shiraz 2006

$18

McLaren Vale

Screw Cap

www.hasel
grovevigneron
s.com

Most of the epic Cab Shiraz or Shiraz Cab wines in this book are noble, structured, thoughtful wines, built with an 'architectural' degree in intellectual winemaking rather than a sports degree in vanity body-building. Sometimes, though, we relax our strict palates and allow in a fleshier, flashier red to frolic with the serious lads. Willunga 100 is a huggable red with sweet, open, vibrant, punter-friendly flavours and this is a wine to be enjoyed fully when you are having a night off and you want to kick back and not have to be troubled with the complexities of life (and wine). We love it, and for the cost of a takeaway pizza you can have the perfect match for one as well.

$19 Aramis Vineyards Shiraz Cabernet Sauvignon 2006

Aramis won a gold medal in TGAR this year and it narrowly missed out on a trophy. This is sodding good wine, with firm tannins, rich black fruits, lots of flavour and texture. Very smartly packaged, too, it's a serious McLaren Vale red at half the price that it should be. Don't muck around – buy it and let Aramis know that they've done good!

McLaren Vale

Screw Cap

www.aramis vineyards. com

AU: Rand

$19 Braided River Marlborough Pinot Noir 2007

Fresh and clean with red berries and pretty, lifted rose petal notes on the bouquet, there is a lightness of touch and delicacy which is compelling in this wine. It gently caresses the palate, as opposed to ram-raiding it at speed. This is the only NZ Pinot under $20 worth even looking at. We would love there to be more, and we ask everyone to play ball, but this is the one wine that we recommend to you this year.

Marlborough

Screw Cap

www.ager sectus.co.nz

AU: DMs DW

$19 Kangarilla Road Cabernet Sauvignon 2006

Kevin O'Brien manages to build a very deep bass drum footnote into his wines, which thumps away in the background. This gives his Cabernet drive and definition, allowing its fat black juicy jube fruit, plush liquorice and fine leaf flavours to dance along in time.

McLaren Vale

Screw Cap

AU: 1st Aus DMs Ed EEC SMWM VCs

Pinot Noir (Pee-no Nw-ar) ranks among our most beloved grapes on earth. When on form, the Pinot Noir bouquet is often reminiscent of wild strawberries, violets and redcurrants, with a black cherry flavour on the palate. There can be a degree of oakiness apparent in some styles. As these wines age, they may take on a slightly farmyard or forest undergrowth character and the colour fades to pale, brick red. Pinot has been dubbed "the heartbreak grape" because winemakers the world over are besotted with its charms, but it is the hardest grape to get right.

Clare Valley

Screw Cap

www.neagles rock.com

AU: Chalk WLC

Neagles Rock Misery Grenache Shiraz 2007

$19

Despite its name, The Misery vineyard is one of Neagles' best sites. A treat for the olfactory system, it's like a stroll through a Moroccan market with aromas of fragrant rose petals, potpourri and bundles of fresh spices. The palate continues this theme past a fine chocolate shop. You would be forgiven if you wanted to take out a texta and scribble out "Misery" on the label, replacing it with "Euphoria."

Victoria

Screw Cap

AU: 1st Chalk DMs Lland PWS Rand Sum VCs

Scotchmans Hill Swan Bay Pinot Noir 2007

$19

This wine is like fresh-picked, shiny cherries that you can't get into your mouth fast enough. With its really smart, black label, it looks as serious as it tastes. It's only going to get better over the next twelve months as well! This wine over-delivers, so much so that Scotchman's Estate wine, which is twice the price, simply isn't in the frame this year.

$19 Yalumba Barossa Shiraz Viognier 2006

Always the benchmark for entry-level SV blends and this year it's better than ever. Design teams are forever buggering up the labels of wines at this price but here they've done the opposite. It not only has brand new livery (and, boy, does it look smart!) but it's been livened up on the inside as well, with a purity of cherry and plum fruit that propels it faster and further than ever before.

Barossa

Screw Cap

AU: 1st DW Nicks Lland PWS Sum VCs WLC

NZ: Glen HWC Mill WFW

$20 Anvers Razorback Road 2005

We still haven't crossed the $20 barrier, and yet the variety of wines and talent on show in the Shiraz Cabernet class is nothing short of mind-expanding. Anvers Razorback tastes like it sounds, with savoury overtones, dark meaty flavours and great depth of spicy berry fruits. It's a big wine for a small spend, and we love that combination of traits.

Adelaide Hills

Cork

www.anvers. com.au

$20 Kangarilla Road Sangiovese 2007

There are only a couple of Sangioveses that really work in Australia and this is one of the best. The Chianti grape often loads the palate with moisture-eliminating acidity, but this version is quite the opposite. The aroma alone makes your mouth water with its sour cherry, violet and blackberry leaf notes, and the palate is perky, refreshing and not at all heavy. This makes it perfect for glugging at speed when you are on a mission, but classy enough to sip slowly with a

McLaren Vale

Screw Cap

AU: 1st Aus SMWM VCs

very smart Italian feast.

South
Australia

Screw Cap

AU: 1st Aus
Chalk DW
Sum VCs WLC

NZ: Glen

Kilikanoon Killerman's Run Cabernet Sauvignon 2006

$20

It seems rather amusing that the American market goes nuts for this wine because it sounds so tough and manly, a fact that we leant from the sensitive and educated Kilikanoon CEO Nathan Waks, prior to his performance of an incredible piece of classical music on his cello. Gangster rappers must be drinking this deliriously delicious wine without knowing just how many light years they are away from Nathan himself. Like the man, this is a highly polished wine with mint leaf notes accenting its fine red berry flavours.

Clare Valley

Screw Cap

AU: Aus DW
Sixty

NZ: WFW

Kirrihill Cabernet Sauvignon Clare Valley 2006

$20

With no discernable tannin, this wine is ripe and ready for drinking the moment you get home. You won't even need a decanter, such is its exuberance. But don't be tricked into thinking it is just a light-hearted, tomfoolery creation because this is a serious Cabernet with plush black fruits and a long, juicy aftertaste.

Langhorne
Creek

Screw Cap

AU: 1st Aus
DW Lland
SMWM VCs
WLC

Lake Breeze Langhorne Creek Grenache 2007

$20

The six rows of gnarled old Grenache vines in the Follet vineyard in Langhorne Creek look a lot older than they really are, because things grow

red wines   113

like crazy in this fertile flood plain. Impressive for seventy-five year old vines! Fruit from such old vines anywhere else would surely end up in ultra-premium-priced wines but Lake Breeze don't muck around and offer sensational value in every bottle they release. This wine is the definition of Grenache on a world stage. It's not far from the typical Aussie stewed strawberry style but much more like bright red Châteauneuf-du-Pape – scented, herbal and fragrant but without a caravan of alcohol that follows it and elbows you in the forehead like a fatty on bingo night. Thank goodness! We were both gobsmacked by this wine.

$20 Penley Estate Condor Shiraz Cabernet 2006

Coonawarra

Screw Cap

AU: 1st DMs DW Sum VCs

NZ: WFW

With fresh plum-dunked fruit and a really fit feel on the palate, this is a superb entry level wine from the great Kym Tolley at Penley. We have not included his more expensive wines this year because Condor and Phoenix Cabernet (read on) are doing so well (and the big boys need some time to mature anyway). With cracking (literally) pepper notes on the nose and stylish fruit concentration and length, this is a delicious wine that soars high! Not a blockbuster, more of a genial sort, just like Kym!

$20 Wyndham Estate George Wyndham Shiraz Cabernet 2005

South Australia

Screw Cap

AU: 1st DMs DW VCs WLC

NZ: HWC Mill WFW

We sometimes feel a little sorry for the historic names in Australia, because there are so many amazing new brands that pop up every day with super-flashy labels that try to steal their limelight. But when a wine named after the illustrious George Wyndham stands tall against the "Johnny come lately" opposition, you've got to think that the great man's legacy carries on in style. As you would expect flavour-wise, this wine is built to last, with fresh, spicy red berries and fine, well-structured tannins. Cheers George!

Yalumba "The Scribbler" Cabernet Shiraz 2006

Barossa Valley

Screw Cap

Best Price: $18

AU: 1st Aus Chalk Ed EEC Rand SMWM VCs WLC

$20

It's unprecedented in our **The Great Australian Red** competition for exactly the same wine to come back 12 months later and do the double, but The Scribbler, as it's now known (the company hadn't named it this time last year, but it's exactly the same wine) has proved its credentials. Two golds in two years, and two trophies as well. This is, by definition, Australia's finest value red wine. It has an air of freshness to its solid, dark berry and leaf flavours, which lift it and make it fly. No Scribbler really (perhaps they'll change the name again next year), we reckon it's The Comet.

Irvine Barossa Merlot 2005

Barossa

Screw Cap

Best Price: $16

AU: 1st Chalk SMWM Sum VCs WLC

NZ: HWC WFW

$21

There are five Merlots in this book. The first is $11 and the last is $120. Without knowing the price, we both thought that this Merlot would be priced closer to the latter than the former. Imagine our surprise when we discovered that this awesome creation, by Merlot guru Jim Irvine, was only $21. In terms of value for money this fruitcake and plum explosion is absolutely unmissable. Throw it through a decanter, bang it in front of your mates and pretend it has a three-digit price. They will nod sagely and ask for the merchant's number.

$21 Teusner The Riebke Ebenezer Road Shiraz 2007

Barossa and Eden Valleys

Cork

AU: Aus DW Nicks VCs

NZ: WFW

This wine is so pure and velvety that it's like wearing a black velour jumpsuit to the Antarctic, looking at everyone else in their Eskimo gear and saying, "What's wrong with you lot?" The reason for this incongruous and extraordinary image is that this wine wears no oak as an outer garment, preferring to let its fruit do the talking. And what absolutely extraordinary fruit it is, too. More wines should be made like this, and without Kym's brave Riebke, there would be no one blazing this white-hot trail.

$21 Yalumba Bush Vine Grenache 2007

Barossa

Screw Cap

Best Price: $18

AU: 1st DMs DW Nicks VCs WLC

NZ: HWC WFW

While Lake Breeze embodies world Grenache as we see it, this wine is a quintessential Aussie bush vine Grenache. It looks and tastes red and ripe, with juicy strawberries and spicy raspberries and it's great for matching with all those cuisines that don't go with anything else, like gorilla salad and Rogan Josh (not the band, the Indian lamb dish).

$22 Kangarilla Road McLaren Vale Shiraz 2006

McLaren Vale

Screw Cap

AU: 1st Aus Ed SMWM VCs WLC

McLaren Vale Shiraz is in a class of its own and

rather than heading straight to the end of this list and shuddering at the prices, why not kick off proceedings with this wine in the knowledge that it has all of the elements of the region tucked neatly into its twenty-two dollar frame. Tick these boxes – polished black fruit, velvety tannins, considerable length, fragrant oak, kangaroo breath and gorilla musk.

Clare Valley
McLaren Vale

Screw Cap

AU: 1st Aus
Chalk DMs
DW Ed Nicks
Rand Sum
VCs WLC

O'Leary Walker Clare Valley/McLaren Vale Shiraz 2006

$22

We test-drove this wine one evening after having tasted our way through a flight of more than 600 Shirazes during the day. It looked extraordinary and our friends all agreed. These two guys are operating out of a state-of-the-art facility and their wines, already brilliant, will no doubt continue to hit new levels of excellence in the coming years. Glossy black fruits and fragrant cinnamon signal a seamless join between the fruit of these two great regions. Impressive work, guys.

Coonawarra

Screw Cap

AU: 1st Aus
Chalk DW Ed
EEC GPO PWS
Sixty SMWM
Sum VCs WLC

Penley Estate Phoenix 2006

$22

More backward than the Penley's Condor, this is an impressive red for the money. It's built with the chassis of a far more expensive wine, with the same horsepower and accompanying tannin accessories. We suggest that you buy it as soon as you can, but hold off test-driving it for a year or so because it is still fairly dry. Given twelve months it will blossom beautifully into a spicy, black-fruited cruiser.

$22 Wirra Wirra Catapult McLaren Vale Shiraz Viognier 2006

The late great Greg Trott had a vision to build a medieval siege machine to bomb neighbouring wineries with bottles of fine wine in the hope that they would reciprocate the favour. We are not kidding! The Wirra team has named this wine in honour of his dream. If you bomb your friends with this classy wine then you will be certain to get something very serious in return, because it is one of the more refined SV blends in our list this year.

McLaren Vale

Screw Cap

Best Price: $19

AU: DMs DOr DW Ed SMWM

$22 Wirra Wirra Church Block 2006

Church Block is a lesson in blending and building flavour. This is a real skill and the main aim is to make the final wine seem effortlessly assembled and seamlessly in harmony. The 2006 vintage of this wine is honed, smooth, beautifully balanced and each of the varieties does exactly what is asked of it. Decant Church Block and allow the flavours to seep out of your glass. This is a $40 wine in every way apart from the price tag, so no prayer mat is needed when your credit card bill arrives, for once.

McLaren Vale

Screw Cap

Best Price: $19

AU: 1st Aus Chalk DMs DW Ed EEC Nicks Lland Rand SMWM Sum VCs WLC

NZ: WFW

$23 Lake Breeze Langhorne Creek Cabernet Sauvignon 2006

While Lake Breeze's "Bernoota" Shiraz Cabernet blend takes a rest from our list (my, we are tough markers this year!), three other wines have made the grade. In keeping with their mantra to please and convert as many people to Lake Breeze wines as possible, they are all stunningly good

Langhorne Creek

Screw Cap

AU: 1st Aus DW EEC Lland SMWM VCs WLC

value. The secret to the sheer class of this establishment is that the Follets sell more than two-thirds of their fruit to other companies. Guess where the best third ends up?! This means that even their $20 wines represent sensational value for money. In this Cabernet, hints of Langhorne Creek mint mingle with plush black fruits, creating a beautifully balanced, fruit-focused style.

Barossa Valley

Screw Cap

www.veritas
winery.com

AU: Aus DMs
EEC SumClare
Valley

Magpie Estate "The Fakir" Grenache 2006

$23

Spicy and savoury with red berry fruits and grippy, fine tannins, this is a Barossa Grenache with a modicum of control and complexity, unlike some of the rocket fuel versions out there. Pour yourself a glass and then run around the yard screaming the name of this wine and see if your neighbours complain. If they do, apologise politely and invite the Fakirs in.

Clare Valley

Screw Cap

AU: 1st Aus
Chalk DMs
DW Rand Sum
VCs WLC

O'Leary Walker Cabernet Sauvignon 2006

$23

Nick and David have a velvet thing going on with this Cabernet, which can either be made a part of the wine by picking the grapes later (this often results in clumsy red wines), or by very sensitive handling of the grapes. These guys never bully their wines into the bottle and the result is a line up of ethereally textured reds and whites at all price points. This is what makes O'Leary Walker such a reliable brand to follow. With baked mulberry pie flavours and rebounding black fruits, this wine has the appeal to stun any newcomer and the structure and balance to impress any wine snob.

$23 Off The Leash Max 2007

Max has finally been set free to maraud your palate. Welcome him with open mouth and open arms because this Shiraz Viognier blend was written up in our 2008 guide but was remanded in custody for bad behaviour and had to spend another year in detention in the darkness below The Lane winery. Drinking perfectly now, we should all raise a glass to this reformed character and wish him well.

$26 Paringa Estate Peninsula Shiraz 2006

This is the best Peninsula Shiraz from Paringa yet. With lifted florals and gamey complexity, it is a beautifully fragrant wine with a seamless finish. Packed with five spice and star anise and with a faint whiff of cigar smoke and Macallan 25 year old, the aromas are like a cross between an incredibly smart deli and a desperately exclusive gentleman's club. If you want to push this style even further, try **Paringa Estate Reserve Shiraz 2006** ($80) because this is also the best vintage yet, with a massive peppery finish and less overt alcohol and oak than usual.

$26 Wild Rock The Underarm Hawkes Bay Syrah 2006

You might think Craggy Range would have researched this name a little more thoroughly, because while we are sure they are referring to

Adelaide Hills

Screw Cap

www.thelane.com.au

AU: Chalk DMs WLC

Mornington Peninsula

Screw Cap

Best Price: $20

AU: 1st DW Ed PWS Sixty SMWM VCs WLC

Reserve

Mornington Peninsula

Screw Cap

AU: DW PWS Rand Sixty SMWM

Hawkes Bay

Screw Cap

AU: Chalk PWS Rand SMWM

NZ: Sel Glen HWC WFW

a sneaky bowling manoeuvre, the majority of the world's thirsty drinkers will assume it's something to look out for on the nose of this wine. We have a different theory because, knowing wine overlord Steve Smith as we do, and bearing in mind that he's one of the tallest blokes on the planet, the name on the label refers to the view that we get when we stand next to him. With a brilliantly lifted white pepper nose and a cool, long, refreshing black fruit coulis palate, this is a sensational Syrah with more than a nod to the French classics.

Adelaide Hills

Screw Cap

www.timknap pstein.com.au

AU: Aus Ed TWC

Riposte by Tim Knappstein The Sabre Pinot Noir 2007

$27

A decade ago there would have been a handful of Adelaide Hills Pinot Noirs queuing up to be in this book, but for some reason this region has changed its focus, favouring Shiraz and Chardonnay over the Sauvignon Blancs and Pinot Noirs of old. But you'll never find someone like Tim Knappstein ever dropping the ball. In fact, quite the reverse. He champions this style of wine and continues to push hard. The Sabre has juicy black plums and spicy baked plum cake flavours giving it the depth of fruit of a much more serious wine.

Hilltops and Young

Screw Cap

AU: 1st Aus Boc DW EEC Ed GPO PWS Rand SMWM VCs

Clonakilla Hilltops Shiraz 2007

$28

We've always felt that the magic of Tim Kirk's wines is derived from the vineyards at his own place. But for the first time the joy has spread to his Hilltops-sourced fruit and his own skills as conductor have set him apart as one of the nation's truly gifted vinous virtuosos. With layers of pepper and exotic spice rippling through its core, this is an everyday price for a special occasion wine.

$28 De Iuliis Show Reserve Hunter Valley Shiraz 2006

Hunter Valley

Screw Cap

www.dewine.com.au

AU: Sel DMs Sixty

With really attractive charcuterie notes on the nose, balanced by fresh, bright red fruits on the palate, this is a very impressive wine made in an old-fashioned Hunter Valley "Burgundy" shape. A touch of new RM Williams work on the nose gives it a fresh and lifted appeal and the overall impression is the very best of ancient and modern in one glass.

$28 Primo Estate Zamberlan Cabernet Sauvignon Sangiovese 2005

McLaren Vale

Screw Cap

www.primoestate.com.au

AU: Aus DW

Joe Grilli's Italian roots are legendary. And we can announce that Daniel from Scarpantoni has recently joined his brigade, so we expect to see yet more fireworks emanating from their stunning new McLaren Vale cellar door. To keep you titillated in the meantime, here is a cracking little number with layers of savoury complexity throughout its core of ripe black fruits.

$28 Skillogalee Basket Pressed Shiraz 2005

Clare Valley

Screw Cap

We normally describe wines from the nose via the palate to the finish, but let's turn this wine on its head and look at Skilly from the direction of its smashing rear end. The tannins on this wine are so devastatingly attractive and the texture of the aftertaste so silky smooth that we simply don't know how they've done it. Most wines from Clare at this age look meaty, raw and unshaven. Flipping Skilly around again, and with this in mind, take a look at how this wine builds into a crescendo of excellence and you will gaze at it open-mouthed, just like we do.

Teusner Barossa Valley Joshua Grenache Mataro Shiraz 2007

$28

Grenache is not supposed to be this polished. It hasn't usually had the pleasure of going to finishing school and it certainly doesn't have any social skills, but this one lives in Geneva, drives a vintage 911 and its bedposts have virtually fallen to pieces from "notch-abuse." Joshua has another remarkable trait: there are no barrels whatsoever used in its production, making this the most focused expression of GMS purity we have seen. This leaves the stage open for its spicy, sweet fruitcake characters to do their mesmerising act.

Paringa Estate Peninsula Pinot Noir 2007

$29

Quite a change of pace for Pinot Noir from our earlier examples around $20, and an enormous step up in intensity – Paringa has juicy red fruits and exotic spices with a beautiful palate and great length. It even manages to hold its 14.5% alcohol with real poise. The pretty mulberry fruit and silky structure enable you to crack on with this wine much earlier than you would normally – we suggest 5pm.

$30 Spy Valley Marlborough Pinot Noir 2007

With accurate black fruits and spice and a lifted violet bouquet, this is a delicious Kiwi Pinot Noir. Darker and more intense than the Braided River (above), with plum fruit and coffee/mocha oak, it seems ridiculous that in this $10 gap, 30 Pinots in our final taste-off did not make the grade. Your mission, if you choose to accept it, is to find and destroy this wine (*dans la bouche*).

Marlborough

Screw Cap

AU: DMs DW SMWM Sum

NZ: Sel Glen Mill

$31 Luke Lambert Yarra Valley Syrah 2007

We have very similar palates, almost unnervingly so, when we write notes and find similar words popping up here there and everywhere, but this is the only wine in the book where opinion is divided between us – not about the quality of the wine but the extent of its overall brilliance. In order to play this game, you'll have to buy a bottle, which in itself might be a challenge because there was bugger-all made. But when you do, send us your vote. The wine leads out with delightfully perfumed fruit but then closes in with stalky tannins that need time in the cellar to soften. The question is whether there is too much stalkiness. Were too many stalks used in the ferment with the grapes or is the freshness and aroma spot on for you? Either way, Luke Lambert is a precocious talent and we will be following him eagerly, glasses in hand.

Yarra Valley

Cork

www.luke lambertwines. com.au

AU: Rand

Majella Coonawarra Shiraz 2006 $33

Coonawarra

Screw Cap

Best Price: $28

AU: 1st Aus
Boc DW Ed
EEC Rand
Sixty SMWM
Sum VCs WLC

Under no circumstances should you drink this wine, and if you do, there is a GPS system embedded in the wine which will alert the Majella constabulary and they will pour in through your front door and caution you for crimes against drinkability. We place a priority of approachability on all of the wines that we include in our book but this is one which you must pop into your cellar because it is too good to miss – and it will all be sold out before our book is released next year.

St Hallett Blackwell Barossa Shiraz 2006 $33

Barossa

Screw Cap

Best Price: $28

AU: 1st Aus
Boc Chalk
DW Ed GPO
Nicks Lland
PWS Rand
Sixty SMWM
VCs WLC

NZ: Glen Mill
SC WFW

This is a red wine for the slightly larger man. With a massive punch of black fruit, plush liquorice, Barossa Kranskys and thick, seasoned oak, it very much has an Old Block feel, so save yourself $40 and buy this wine instead this year.

Majella Cabernet Sauvignon Coonawarra 2006 $34

Coonawarra

Screw Cap

Best Price: $28

AU: 1st Aus
Boc DMs DW
Ed EEC Rand
Sixty SMWM
Sum VCs WLC

Warning: Do not, under any circumstances, drink this wine. Do not buy it unless you have a very deep hole under your house where you can hide it until at least 2020. There is a magnum's worth of blackcurrant and capsicum intensity in every bottle and we would not advocate even opening one to see how tight it is because it would only be wasted. Just load your cellar with as much as you can afford (quite a lot at this bargain price, we would imagine) and you will be back to thank us in ten years' time. An invitation when you open the bottle will suffice.

$34 Ulithorne Paternus Cabernet Shiraz 2006

X marks the spot. Ulithorne is unmissable on a wine shop shelf so you'll be able to find it in seconds, thanks to its unique label. This is good news, because one glimpse of this wine and your search is over. A gold medal winner in **The Great Australian Red** this year, Paternus 06 very narrowly missed out on taking a trophy as well. This was an impressive feat, particularly when the wine that knocked it out was more than three times its price!

McLaren Vale

Screw Cap

www.ulithorne .com.au

AU: GPO SMWM

$35 The Yard Acacia Vineyard Frankland River Shiraz 2006

This is the only Frankland River Shiraz in this book, and it's no surprise that it comes from Larry Cherubino because he knows this region like no one else. With its gamey, charcuterie complexity and medium weight it has a genuine hand-crafted feel. It is cool, calm and controlled and will leave you feeling the same way.

Frankland River

Screw Cap

www.larrycher ubino.com.au

AU: Aus SMWM

$36 De Bortoli Yarra Valley Estate Grown Pinot Noir 2007

In a world of terribly skinny 2007 Victorian Pinot Noirs, this is the only one, after a long line in our tasting, which had balance. So many of its competitors have tragically fallen in this vintage of drought, frost and all of the plagues of Egypt.

Yarra Valley

Screw Cap

Best Price: $27

AU: 1st Aus Boc Chalk DW PWS VCs WLC

NZ: Sel Glen

You know, like we do, that competition is rife around the planet, and now is the time to strive for excellence, not mediocrity. Let the weak fall by the wayside. With lots of complexity and spice and great length and tannin texture, this wine is going to take until Christmas 2008 to even start to flatter, but it will run and run for five more years.

Scarpantoni Estate Reserve 2006 — $36

McLaren Vale

Screw Cap

http://scarpantoniwines.com

AU: DMs

If you have ever seen winemaker Daniel Zuzolo sprint around a touch footy pitch, you will realise that he is as nippy and agile as it gets. Many winemakers make wines in their own image, like the great Tim 'Bonecrusher' Adams (at his eponymous estate) and the elfin Geraldine McFaul (at Stonier), but Daniel's Estate Reserve 2006 is a colossus, ambling along the highway, picking up warm bitumen on its boots and scaring passers-by. Rich enough to be served with char-grilled marinades drowning in chipotli sauce, this is a big, black, gloopy, firmly oaky wine. Daniel must have a very big something... brain, heart... any ideas?

De Bortoli Estate Grown Yarra Valley Shiraz Viognier 2007 — $37

Yarra Valley

Screw Cap

Best Price: $24

AU: 1st Aus Boc Chalk DW PWS Sum VCs WLC

NZ: Sel Glen

This profound wine is made all the more seductive by the fact that on the label it states that it is made from Shiraz and Viognier but on the palate the texture is more Pinot-esque than any Shiraz we have ever seen. This is not surprising when you consider that De Bortoli is a Pinot Noir academy, but we have never before seen such levels of silkiness. There is no doubt that this wine

red wines 127

will mature beautifully over the next decade but, by golly, it tastes phenomenal right now.

$38 Dutschke St Jakobi Single Vineyard Barossa Valley Shiraz 2006

Barossa Valley

Screw Cap

AU: Aus DMs
DW Ed Nicks
SMWM VCs

Wayne has purple hands (Google his smart new kiddies book and you'll see why). St Jakobi is his other standout creation this year, with concentrated black plum and vibrant, spicy rhubarb flavours culminating in a flourish of black pepper. St Jak has secured its reputation among the best value single vineyard Shirazes in the Barossa, and with less obvious oak than usual, 2006 is one of the most stylish releases yet.

$39 Ravenswood Lane Adelaide Hills Single Vineyard Shiraz 2007

Adelaide Hills

Screw Cap

www.thelane.
com.au

AU: Aus PWS

The diversity of Shiraz in Australia is plain to see and taste in this book, from the inky monsters of the Barossa to the peppery, Rhone-like beauties of Victoria. There is a style somewhere between these two poles that flies under the radar and is about to hit everyone squarely over the back of the head. This style is perfectly displayed in RLS and, in order to describe it perfectly, you would have to go there to see what we mean. But, to give you an idea, this wine could not be made anywhere else, such is its minerality, fruit concentration and complexity. And with only a year under its belt it already has more drama than the opening of the Olympics and more length than the marathon.

Samuel's Gorge Shiraz 2006 $39

McLaren Vale

Cork

www.gorge.com.au

AU: Aus Ed EEC

Goodness gracious, Sideshow Bob's made a wine with alcohol under fifteen percent (it's 14.5%). He must have sprung a nose bleed making such "light" wine! Imagine, if you will, the fattest-duck-and-hoi-sin-roll-scented wine lining up to run the 100m. Only problem is that it wouldn't make the full distance at its first attempt, falling flat on its face at 85m, while every other contender sprinted past. Tortoise and hare initiatives come into play, though, and while the last 15m might take 15 months to complete, Samuel's Gorge Shiraz 2006, with duck and hoi sin coursing through its veins, will win the hearts and minds of the cheering crowd. It's not about being the fastest out of the blocks, it's about looking bloody good, tasting bloody good and occasionally not playing by the rules.

Clonakilla O'Riada Shiraz 2007 $40

Canberra District

Screw Cap

AU: DW PWS SMWM VCs

Prepare yourself for one of the best new wines of the year. It's pure transcendental meditation in a glass. We did a double-take on the nose of this wine, looked at each other and exclaimed "whoa!" simultaneously. Goose-bumps all round. We grinned, raised our arms in the air and shouted. And this was all before we even tasted it. If you are familiar with Clonakilla and its extraordinary wines you will understand. You must phone them immediately to secure your allocation of this miniscule production wine. We pointed this red with the same score that we have given any wine from this awesome estate – and it's half the price of the big boys.

Sangiovese (San-geeo-vay-zee) has red and black fruit flavours (mulberry, cherry, plum, blackcurrant and cranberry) on the nose with a whiff of fresh-cut herbs and leather for good measure. Famous for making Chianti, there is usually an oaky element tucked into the wine, and it always has an acidic kick on the finish.

$40 Jacob's Creek St Hugo Coonawarra Cabernet Sauvignon 2005

Coonawarra

Screw Cap

Best Price: $33

AU: 1st Aus Boc Chalk DMs DW Nicks Lland SMWM VCs WLC

NZ: HWC Mill WFW

We have been following St Hugo closely for decades, and its inaugural inclusion in our book is a massive statement on the standard of this vintage. It's inevitable that some of the Cabernets in our list will have quite dusty tannins, and this wine is one of them. It's a classically shaped Coonawarra Cabernet, because it is built for the long-haul but does not for a moment sacrifice any of its beautiful violet lift or precise blackcurrant fruit flavour.

$40 Kay Brothers Amery Vineyards Hillside Shiraz 2006

McLaren Vale

Screw Cap

AU: 1st Aus Boc Ed Nicks SMWM VCs WLC

NZ: SC

At 15.5% on the Richter scale, we advise that you drink this wine with a buddy at your side. You'll both be able to discover the extraordinary perfumes and amazing fruit density of one of McLaren Vale's oldest vineyards. It's got the full bouquet garni thing on the go, with wild thyme, liquorice, rosemary, chives and so on. Layers of rich black fruits and savoury spice build up to a massive concentration of flavours and phenomenal length. Attempting this wine on your own would put you in danger of waking up in the middle of the night, watching SBS and understanding every word.

Ocean Eight Pinot Noir 2007 $40

Mornington Peninsula

Diam cork

www.ocean eight.com

AU: PWS

We tasted all the Kooyongs, Giacondas, PHI, Farr and Bass Phillips and there was something nagging at the back of our brains, and that was to return to Yabby Lake and Ocean Eight because they offered twice the excitement for half the money. Brimming with a fruit compote of mixed berries and red cherries, Ocean Eight Pinot Noir delivers more action-packed excitement than Brad Pitt on the big screen.

Auntsfield Hawk Hill Pinot Noir 2007 $43

Marlborough

Screw Cap

Best Price: $37

NZ: Sel Glen HWC SC WFW

This wine embodies the perfectionism that Auntsfield seeks. It's an estate that prides itself in pushing everything to the limit. A relative newcomer to the international scene, Auntsfield is making waves in Europe as well as Australia, which proves that the restraint and complexity in this wine really appeals to all palates. Very pretty fruit characters with lots of raspberry and strawberry (typical of Marlborough) make this a more red-fruited wine than those from Central Otago.

Millsreef Elspeth Gimblett Gravels Elspeth Syrah 2006 $43

Hawkes Bay

Cork

AU: DMs DW SMWM

NZ: Sel Glen HWC

This is the best ever Elspeth (apart from Matthew's daughter, of course). Brilliantly pure and exceptionally refined, there is an entire mill

red wines 131

of white pepper in this wine but it never steps over the line. Despite its incredibly dark colour, it is a supple wine with liquorice and plum intensity. What it lacks in testosterone it more than makes up for in elegance and complexity.

$44 Bald Hills Single Vineyard Pinot Noir 2007

Central
Otago

Screw Cap

Best Price: $35

NZ: HWC Mill
WFW

2007 is tighter and prettier than the fine 2006, with ethereal red cherry and rose petal aromas. The palate is spicy and fresh with lovely length. It's quite grown up in style and made to last. When the calendar on the wall shows the same vintage as the one on the front of this book, then you have permission to unscrew. When you do, you ought to decant it to allow it to relax and lose some of the stage fright that it might have on its first appearance on your dining room table.

$44 Peregrine Pinot Noir 2007

Central
Otago

Screw Cap

Best Price: $33

AU: 1st PWS
VCs

NZ: Sel Glen
HWC Mill SC

Matthew opened the 2006 vintage PPN in a restaurant in London the other day with one of the most famous wine brokers in the UK, who rarely drinks anything other than classic French wines. He was so impressed that he ordered another bottle after having only just sniffed the first. You'll be delighted to know that the 2007 is every bit as epic with its swooping Volnay-like black plum fruit and pretty rose petal perfume.

$44 Ulithorne Frux Frugis Shiraz 2006

McLaren Vale

Screw Cap

This 2006 Frux Frugis is even better than the superstar 2005. Brilliantly balanced, with dense

AU: 1st Ed EEC
GPO Nicks
SMWM VCs

black fruit, acres of spice, plantations of coffee beans and kilos of dark chocolate, this cult wine has more length and concentration than ever. It's also under screw cap for the first time, which is great news for all of us. It goes well with stews, big game dishes, wild boar and Linkin Park.

Jim Barry The McRae Wood Shiraz 2005

$47

Clare Valley

Cork

Best Price: $35

AU: 1st Boc
Chalk DMs
DW Ed Nicks
Rand VCs
WLC

NZ: Sel Glen
HWC WFW

There is not a leaf or a misshapen berry that is allowed to make its way into this wine, such is the fastidious detail attached to making McRae Wood Shiraz. Polished to Aston Martin specifications and tuned up to Bugatti horsepower, this is a wine that is in perfect balance now but we know that it will last for a lifetime. It holds its 15.5% alcohol so well that the only afterburn you should experience is when you bury your foot on the accelerator of your glorious machine.

Fox Gordon King Louis Cabernet Sauvignon 2006

$48

Barossa Valley

Diam cork

AU: 1st Aus
DW VCs

What is amazing about King Louis is that, while he will be a king one day, at the moment he is gorgeous as a prince. Just don't drink all of your stock too soon, because when he ascends to the throne you will not want to miss the occasion. Look out for restrained blackcurrant fruit with structure, lovely leaf nuances and great balance. When we lined up our short-listed Cabernets we turfed out more than 100 between Majella and King Louis. Long live the king.

$50 Craggy Range Single Vineyard Block 14 Gimblett Gravels Syrah 2006

Hawkes Bay

Screw Cap

Best Price: $35

AU: Aus Chalk EEC Ed PWS Rand SMWM Sum

NZ: Sel Glen HWC SC WFW

If this wine ever comes on to your radar, then sound the alarm and find the biggest decanter around, because it needs air after having been submerged for so long. It has sensational purity of pepper, phenomenal intensity of fruit and ridiculously stealthy tannins. It's Red October in wine form.

$50 De Bortoli Yarra Valley Reserve Release Pinot Noir 2007

Yarra Valley

Screw Cap

AU: Boc DW PWS Rand VCs

Steve Webber manages to upholster his wines with so much plushness and texture without ever becoming gaudy. They are so classy and enviable that in order to complete the picture when you are drinking a glass of this wine, all you need is an Aston Martin DB9 to drink it in. Such is the complexity of this wine that it can only be compared with bresaola, wild heather honey, fresh picked mulberries and Provençal wild cherries – hoorah!

$50 Mitchelton Print Shiraz 2004

Central Victoria

Cork

AU: 1st DMs DW Rand Sixty SMWM VCs WLC

NZ: Sel Glen

This is the most detailed Print ever. How bizarre is it to taste a wine that is so ripe but yet so cool at the same time? With a uniquely captivating bouquet, highly polished fruit (which is more Burgundian than Shiraz-like) and restrained oak influence, Batman and Robin aka Toby Barlow and Ben Haines have combined forces to bring

Central Otago

Screw Cap

Best Price: $42

AU: 1st Chalk DMs DW Ed GPO PWS Rand Sixty SMWM Sum VCs WLC

NZ: Sel Glen HWC Mill WFW

power and sensitivity to this wine in equal measure. The result is unprecedented.

Mt Difficulty Pinot Noir 2007 $50

Normally we might expect to find this sort of complexity and palate gymnastics in Pipeclay Terrace or Long Gully but this year we are more than happy to save you a few dollars and champion the Estate Pinot from Mt Difficulty. And with a two-to-one exchange rate on the single vineyard wines, this means you can have twice as many people around to dinner! This is one of the three most impressive Pinot producers in New Zealand that continue to amaze us with their stellar wines. 2007 MDPN is ethereal and elegant, with a depth of sour cherry fruit.

South Australia

Screw Cap
.
Best Price: $33

AU: 1st Boc Chalk DMs DW GPO Nicks Lland Rand SMWM VCs WLC

NZ: Sel Glen HWC Mill SC WFW

Penfolds Bin 389 Cabernet Shiraz 2005 $50

With twelve top palates in the room, and a hundred wines to work through, the maths is very simple – there was a one percent chance of winning **The Great Australian Red** this year. But when you make a wine like 2005 Bin 389 the odds become seriously stacked in your favour. And when every judge marks this wine with a massive score, it begins to head toward the finish line with unerring velocity. Trophy judging is always nail-biting because, to a certain extent, and for the first time, personal tastes come into play, not just team consensus. When it came down to the line, this wine won over everyone's hearts with its perfect balance of power and poise. Winemaker Peter Gago's single-minded pursuit of excellence drives his beloved Penfolds to greater feats of winemaking brilliance every year, despite being part of a global beer company. This in itself is an awesome achievement. This wine is not considered by Penfolds to be one of its "super premium" offerings, preferring to group it in the Bin Series by virtue of its name. But we can assure you that at $50, this wine is a super-premium bargain. There will be a stampede when the results in this book are released and you would be well advised to grab as much of this wine as you can, because not only does it taste utterly outstanding right now, it will grow over the next two decades, and it might prove to be one of the best wine investments you have ever made. 389 has always been Australia's most consistent and celebrated Shiraz Cabernet blend, with forty-eight consecutive vintages under its belt, and we feel sure that this is one of the best ever made. Funnily enough, this wine won a silver medal in this very competition last year and clearly got the big gun this year. The 2006 vintage won a silver this year. Who knows what will happen next year?

$50 William Downie Yarra Valley 2007

Yarra Valley

Diam cork

Best Price: $44

AU: DMs EEC PWS Rand VCs

It's as much about texture with Bill's wines as it is about flavour. This is one of the most thoughtfully assembled wines in this book and it requires patience and some effort to coax the full array of flavours and aromas out of the glass this early in its lifetime, but this is a challenge well worth the effort. In an ideal world you would wait five years, but this wine sells out in seconds so grab a case, try one bottle, put your mind at ease about its enormous potential and extraordinary introvertedness and then save the rest of the bots for some very smart dinner parties. With very fine black cherry fruit and grippy, textured tannins, this is a serious wine with staggering length. Bear in mind all of these notes when you taste this wine and then think of one more mightily important point – this is a Pinot Noir! It doesn't say this on the bottle, because Bill wants you to enjoy it as a celestial red wine without any prejudice whatsoever. Adding this thought to the mix, go back to the glass and taste it again and then marvel at just how captivating this wine is.

De Bortoli Yarra Valley Reserve Release Syrah 2006

$52

Yarra Valley

Screw Cap

AU: Boc DW PWS Rand VCs WLC

This wine is a sniper and not an elephant gun. By this we mean that you cannot use the word "blockbuster" about it, even though some might group it with wines three times the weight and five times the width. If bigger means better to you then you are not going to understand just how superior this wine is by comparison to the clumsy blunderbusses of the wine world. Those of you who understand the finer things in life will absolutely adore this wine.

Wirra Wirra The Angelus Cabernet Sauvignon 2006

$52

McLaren Vale

Screw Cap

AU: Aus DMs DW Rand SMWM Sum VCs WLC

NZ: WFW

Wirra's stellar Cabernet enters our list at half the price of many of the top end reds on the shelves. It is typical of this company to make this wine and, for that matter, its entire portfolio more accessible to wine lovers, so more people can enjoy world-class Cabernet without having to go to Bordeaux. It's layered with gamey complexity, complex dark chocolate flavours and very fit tannins.

$53 Anaperenna by Ben Glaetzer 2006

Barossa Valley

Cork

Best Price: $45

AU: 1st Aus DMs EEC Ed Nicks Rand SMWM Sum VCs WLC

Ben Glaetzer continues to evolve and adapt his winemaking skills as the years pass by. Where once it seemed that the Incredible Hulk was his mentor, it now appears that Zorro is more his thing. The flashing blade of Anaperenna mesmerises the palate with small, sweet mulberries, plums, liquorice and black jubes. The velvety tannins are beautiful and it's all done with swash-buckling dexterity.

$54 Neagles Rock 'One Black Dog' Reserve Cabernet Shiraz 2005

Clare Valley

Cork

Best Price: $47

www.neagles rock.com

AU: DMs

Neagles top red wine did very well in **The Great Australian Red** and we noted its unique flavours, which emanate from its Clare origins, setting it apart from many of the other winning wines. The intense, sweet nose, scented with smooth, blue fruit and meaty, herbal notes made this a more pliable and expressive wine than some at this age. But there is ample tannin to ensure that this black dog will continue to run for years.

$55 S.C. Pannell McLaren Vale Shiraz Grenache 2006

McLaren Vale

Screw Cap

Steve Pannell is too young to be a legend, but

AU: Aus DW
EEC PWS
Rand SMWM
WLC

who said there were age requirements for this status? The latest vintage of his SG blend goes straight to the honours list. It's not hard to build a generous McLaren Vale red wine but the real talent here is displayed in its perfectly honed and controlled structure. Steve tames the wild elements of McLaren Vale like a veteran ringmaster, giving us yet another spectacular performance, making it look all too easy (which we can assure you, it certainly is not).

Thomas Kiss Hunter Valley Shiraz 2006 $55

Hunter Valley

Cork

www.thomas
wines.com.au

AU: DMs PWS
WLC

You might think that a bloke who names his icon Shiraz "Kiss" would either be a very romantic dude or enjoy eighties glamrock and over-the-top face painting. But if you ask Thommo, he'll simply tell you to say "Kiss Shiraz" very quickly and figure it out for yourself! Well, it seems that Thommo kissed his own Shiraz in 2006 because this is his best yet. It is very finely textured with exotic spices of all kinds ricocheting off the sides of the palate. This is classic, ageworthy Hunter Shiraz.

S.C. Pannell McLaren Vale Shiraz 2006 $59

McLaren Vale

Screw Cap

AU: Aus Sel
DMs DW EEC
PWS Rand
SMWM WLC

Rip the back seats out of your Evo 7, chuck the CD player in the bin, pull the shag pile from under your racing boots and fill this beauty with nitrous. Rather than bumbling along in your Mitsubishi Lancer, drive the bloody thing, which is exactly what Steve Pannell does with this Shiraz, taking full advantage of every inch of the road and all the aerodynamics money can buy.

$60 Domaine Georges Roumier Bourgogne Rouge 2006

Burgundy, France

Cork

AU: DOr PWS Rand SMWM VCs

Domaines Georges Roumier is the name on the label of some of the most ethereal Pinot Noirs in the world. From a vineyard of less than one hectare, this is a very complete Bourgogne Rouge which is ready to drink right from the start. The 2006 vintage has blessed it with a delicate, pretty, fresh shape and the invigorating aromas of walking through a dewey forest at sunrise.

$60 Domaine Jean Grivot Bourgogne Rouge 2006

Burgundy, France

Cork

AU: Ed PWS Rand SMWM

When I (TS) met Étienne Grivot, it became increasingly apparent that the unforced, serene, sensitive personality of the man was somehow translated into his wines. He described his different terroirs as a symphony, conducted and interpreted by the winemaker. Even his Bourgogne rouge accurately reflects its Vosne origins in its delicate red cherry fruit and savoury herb flavours, structured with firm, masculine tannins. This is a Bourgogne rouge for the cellar, and it demands at least five years before you dare to approach it.

$60 Petaluma Coonawarra 2005

Coonawarra

Screw Cap

Best Price: $40

We have had the great pleasure of drinking virtually every vintage of this wine, including the inaugural 1979 – which was and still is a staggering piece of crasftsmanship (see page 19). This glorious 2005 may be as delicious, too, after thirty years in a cellar. One thing is certain, though, and that is you can, without feeling too guilty, take a sneaky peak at this wine now to get a glimpse of the excitement that is to come. The blackcurrant fruit is stunningly lifted (Cabernet's trumpet call) and then the outriders of red berry notes flank this movement, thanks to the astute addition of top quality Merlot. On the palate the vanillin oak and woodsmoke notes call out, adding to the cacophony. While this wine will need a long time to soften and integrate, it makes for an extraordinary experience already. One of the incredible things about this wine was that we noticed that there was some left in the bottle three days after having tasted it and we couldn't resist dipping in again to see what changes had transpired (by the way, this is a top tip to determine how well a wine might mature). It was beautifully balanced and even more alluring with great length and savoury complexity. Initially, this wine was so compact that it felt like there was a barrel's worth of wine in this bottle and with time, albeit only three days, we could see how settled and magnificent this wine was and will be. Does the 2005 have the quality of the 1979? We are absolutely certain that it does.

Yabby Lake Vineyard Mornington Peninsula Pinot Noir 2006 — $60

This is a serious wine with valid delusions of grandeur. The robust fruit runs right up to where the firm tannins start. The bouquet promises a continued explosion of flavour which happens in style like a series of fireworks, setting the next ones off, over and over again. This is a big, crunchy wine with fairly chewy tannins that work extremely well with gamey dishes and serious, classic French cooking.

$62 Ghislaine Barthod Bourgogne Rouge 2006

Burgundy, France

Cork

AU: DOr Rand

Year in, year out, Ghislaine Barthod crafts a range of Chambolle-Musignys that represent the purest definition of Burgundy's most seductive commune. Her Bourgogne Rouge is always reliable and in 2006 it is one of the best from anywhere in Burgundy.

$64 Ashton Hills Vineyard Reserve Pinot Noir 2007

Adelaide Hills

Screw Cap

Best Price: $58

AU: Aus Boc DW EEC Ed GPO SMWM Sum

Stephen George continues to elevate his guru status ever further, and in the challenging 2007 vintage he has nailed it. What you must know is that a truly great winemaker manages to make stunning wine, year-in-year-out, and Ashton Hills is a label to rely on. Stephen is the Jedi Lord of the Hills. His is a Pinot Noir with silky texture, exotic fruit and wild hedge row spice – feel the force in this wine.

$65 Pyramid Valley Vineyards Growers Collection Calvert Vineyard Central Otago Pinot Noir 2007

Central Otago

Screw Cap

Best Price: $50

NZ: SC WFW

In the same way that the great wines of Burgundy are classified by their vineyard, the one Grand Cru vineyard in New Zealand is clearly

Angel Smoke and **Earth Flower**

Canterbury

Screw Cap

www.pyramid valley.co.nz

Calvert because it is the source of fruit for all three of the top New Zealand Pinots that have made it into our list this year. Each one of these wines perfectly demonstrates the character and the winemaking style of its owner. If you ever have the opportunity to taste all three side-by-side, as we did with twenty of our friends on the evening following our Pinot Noir tasting, you will be treated to one of the most complete and fascinating trios of wines that New Zealand has ever seen. Mike and Claudia Weersing at Pyramid Valley make wines with sensitivity, intricate detail and an other-worldliness that is both beguiling and hypnotic in equal measure. The supplest of these three Pinots is also the most aromatic and it is these perfumed aromas of Chinese five spice and cooled down plum skin that make it so alluring. For an even more intellectual experience of Pyramid Valley's Pinot Noirs, track down **Pyramid Valley Earth Smoke 2006** and **Angel Flower 2006** (both $80).

Skillogalee Trevarrick Single Contour Cabernet Sauvignon Clare Valley 2004

$65

Clare Valley

Screw Cap

www.skilloga lee.com.au

AU: Sel DMs DW EEC SMWM TWC

The way that Skillogalee handles the oak in this wine and in its Shiraz (see page 126) is reflective of its white wine expertise because the tannins are so fine-grained and controlled that they never take over the palate or dry out the tongue. This inevitably means that the wine is even more delicious than you could possibly imagine, in spite of its youth. Yet it will live for as long as the best of its competitors because there is such a mass of energy buried in its beautifully ripe core of cassis fruit.

$68 Craggy Range Pinot Noir Calvert Vineyard Central Otago 2007

Central Otago

Screw Cap

Best Price: $59

AU: Aus EEC PWS SMWM

NZ: HWC WFW

Winemaker Steve Smith is obsessed with Pinot and his dedication to this variety means that he travels the world eulogising on New Zealand's behalf about the wonders to be found within this variety. His own wine mirrors Steve's near seven-foot Spartan physique with a depth of fruit and a darkness of chocolate and spice that builds on the palate and pounds your taste buds relentlessly with sumptuous flavours of macerated red fruit compote, stewed rhubarb and violet perfume. It's a great wine to be drunk with great friends.

$68 Domaine Méo-Camuzet Bourgogne Rouge 2006

Burgundy, France

Cork

AU: DOr Ed EEC PWS Rand SMWM VCs

NZ: Sel Glen HWC RWM SC

The Domaine wines of Méo-Camuzet rank among the most sublime Pinot Noirs in the world and their top labels sell for ear-splitting prices. It is a joy that this brilliance filters down to the entry-level Bourgogne Rouge classification, and in the excellent 2006 vintage it is expressed in this lively, red-fruited wine with a long, finely structured finish.

$70 Kaesler W.O.M.S. 2006

Barossa

Cork

This Weapon of Mass Seduction has picked up gongs two years in a row in **The Great Australian Red**, and it's finally on the shelves for you to buy. So, if you're a fan of the classically-dimensioned, old-fashioned great Australian reds with dark fruits and a firm structure, grab a few of these and stick them away. You will be so chuffed in five year's time to put this seductress on your very own catwalk for your mates to fall in love with.

Kay Brothers Amery Vineyards Block 6 Shiraz 2006
$70

There is one cellar door in Australia that gets more mentions than any other when we are out and about. Every time we hear about the enthusiasm, integrity and willingness to spend time and pour wine with complete strangers, the name that crops up is Kay Brothers. The two Colins, one front of house, one back of house, do an exceptional job at explaining their wines and their phenomenal setting to us all. Block 6 is one of the legendary vineyards of Australia and the fact that this wine can be bought for a two figure sum is, frankly, baffling. Every year it kicks forty or fifty other so-called "cult" wines into touch with its brooding, bitumen, liquorice and black olive flavours. It is always an honour to taste this wine and it will remain an immense pleasure for us all to revisit this estate every time we are in the Vale.

Geoff Hardy K1 Tzimmukin Shiraz Cabernet 2005
$77

Geoff Hardy went back to the Bible to research this wine, but it would have been quicker to head to the Veneto in northern Italy, where this style is made by the truck load. "Amarone" is the technique here, and it involves partially drying the grapes to concentrate their flavours. In biblical times, wine made in this way was apparently called Tzimmukin. This savoury and spicy wine is loaded with charcuterie complexity and it is very full-bodied, too. One of the biggest wine in this year's competition, it managed to get through where others failed because it has balance and not just muscle. Geoff's next biblical event will be held at Russell's Pizza in Willunga, where he's turning water into wine on Friday night. See you there.

$78 Felton Road Calvert Pinot Noir 2007

It's not the delicacy, nor is it the power of this wine that attracts us, because this time Calvert expresses its fruit via the medium that is Felton Road, the most famous winery in the country. Nigel and Blair at Felton manage to enable this celestial variety to resonate in the glass so beautifully that the resulting wine has the whole gamut of Pinot flavours and sensations in one glass. It is absolutely mesmerising. You are lucky indeed if you get a chance to drink this wine.

Central Otago

Screw Cap

Best Price: $60

AU: Chalk Ed EEC GPO PWS Rand SMWM VCs

NZ: HWC WFW

$79 The Colonial Estate Alexander Laing Single Vineyard Old Vine Grenache 2006

A newcomer to our list of heroes, The Colonial Estate's vast portfolio has one true superstar wine in its throng. Alexander Laing is the lucky bloke on the label and whether he knows it or not his Grenache is one of the greatest examples of this grape we have tasted this year. Grab a morning

Barossa Valley

Cork

www.colonial wine.com.au

AU: Aus EEC

coat, pencil on a moustache and slide into some spats because only real gentlemen are allowed to partake of something this distinguished.

Penfolds St Henri 2004
$80

After the enigmatic nose has caught your attention and you momentarily suspend disbelief, you will sense a devastating power growing in the glass with dark chocolate, black pudding and more than a touch of freshly slaughtered pagan invader crackling away on a bonfire. Keep that thought and progress to the ultra-refined palate with its stupendous array of well-drilled flavours. Is this the very St Henri to overthrow the longstanding Penfolds monarch? We hear murmurings that suggest that support for this prodigy is growing like wildfire.

Tapanappa Whalebone Vineyard Merlot 2005
$80

Is this Australia's Merlot of the Year? Brian Croser's Whalebone vineyard is up to racing speed and it is always a joy to taste his new releases each year. Our vote this year went unanimously to this desperately distinguished Merlot. The detail and build quality of this wine require serious inspection. Tight, but expressive, this is a wine that should not be hurried. You wouldn't want to miss anything, would you? BTW, Brian's **Tapanappa Whalebone Wrattonbully Cabernet Sauvignon Shiraz Cabernet Franc 2005** ($80) is a beauty, too. If he hadn't chaired the judging teams in our The Great Australian Red Competition, he surely would have entered this wine. But being the

Barossa Valley, Langhorne Creek, Adelaide Hills

Cork

Best Price: $70

AU: 1st Aus Boc Chalk DMs DW Ed EEC GPO Nicks Lland PWS Rand SMWM Sum VCs WLC

NZ: Glen HWC Mill WFW

Wrattonbully

Screw Cap

AU: DW Rand SMWM

Cabernet Shiraz

Wrattonbully

Screw Cap

AU: 1st DW Ed Rand SMWM VCs

red wines 147

ultimate professional, we couldn't give it a swirl on the day. However, we both feel it would have been on the podium for sure.

Cabernet Franc (Cab-er-nay Fron) is often used in partnership with Cabernet Sauvignon and Merlot to give an aromatic dimension to the blend. On its own it has firm acidity, oodles of black fruit flavours and a wonderful violet element coupled with green, leafy notes on the nose.

$79 Castagna Genesis Syrah 2005

Genesis is an enigmatic puzzle of flavour. It has nuances of hand dried sausage, charcuterie, seaweed and fresh, rolled tobacco, in the most flattering proportions. With more than a nod to the Rhone Valley in France, this is a Cornas-style, Clape-shaped creation. It's a heroic wine for classicists only.

Beechworth

Diam cork

Best Price: $60

AU: Aus Boc
Ed PWS
SMWM WLC

NZ: SC

$82 Peter Lehmann Stonewell Shiraz 2004

Matt Cartwright, our over-qualified bottle monkey, who opens and closes every one of our samples each year with amazing dexterity, is a Stonewell groupie. So all three of us tasted this wine together – not just the usual dastardly duo. After the awesome 2001 and the ever-so-suave 2002, we knew that the next wine that Wigs and his team would release from this monumental vineyard would have to be up to the standard, or even eclipse, these two showstopping vintages. We knew we would have to be there with ringside seats and jeroboam-sized glasses in hand when this moment came. 2003 came and

Barossa Valley

Cork

Best Price: $75

AU: 1st Aus
DMs DW Ed
GPO Nicks
Lland PWS
Rand SMWM
Sum VCs WLC

NZ: HWC SC
WFW

went, as it did for the Rolling Stones (presumably their rig was being built for their next performance, too). So when the 2004 vintage arrived, our anticipation was at eruption point. It's hard with just a book of these diminutive dimensions (having said this, it is the biggest one yet), for us to list the reasons why we are completely and utterly spellbound by this wine. Stonewell 2004 is off the clock. This wine was the marker by which we compared every $100+ red wine, and you would be shocked at how many did not even make the retasting bench, let alone the final cut. With colossal, rampaging black fruit and incredibly fine tannins, this is undoubtedly a heavyweight wine but it has such perfect balance and composure that you cannot be anything other than awe-struck when it collides with your being. We had to double-decant it on the spot to wake this sleeping giant. Check this out – there is no choking stampede of new oak on the palate, nor is there a fiery blowtorch of alcohol on the finish, unlike almost every other wine at this price from this region. In short, is this wine the rightful successor to the brilliance of the 2001 and 2002? Drum roll, clouds part, thunder bolt moment – it is in a class of its own. Being blokes we love lists, and at the end of every tasting we always challenge each other to name the best wine of the day. Of the 600-odd Shirazes on that Monday in August, we both shouted in unison "Stonewell!"

Canberra District

Screw Cap

Best Price: $75

Clonakilla Shiraz Viognier 2007 $84

Tim Kirk has pushed the cool climate Shiraz thing so far in this country that he's lapped everyone else. This wine is very, very young and it needs a good deal of time to soften because the latent power and malevolent energy in its core are almost unnerving. While you are guarding this wine in your cellar we suggest that you drink the two other Clonakillas further up our list and wait for this big boy to give you the nod.

AU: Aus DW EEC Ed GPO PWS Rand SMWM VCs

$85 Castagna Un Segreto Sangiovese Shiraz 2005

Beechworth

Diam cork

AU: Aus PWS SMWM

We short-listed more than 200 alternative reds for our book – all the Italian varieties plus Zin, Durif, and anything else that didn't fit Pinot, Merlot, Grenache, Shiraz or Cabernet. The entire line up was an absolute disaster! We only found three wines, and this was the star by light years. In a world of Australian-made Italian varietals, where most winemakers are completely deluded about the quality of their wines, Julian Castagna is a beacon. In spite of its price, Un Segreto is utterly world class. Delightfully savoury and complex, with a bouquet of exotic spices and spankingly fresh leather, this unlikely blend forces you to revisit the glass more than any wine in this book because it compels you to attempt to unlock its secret. Good luck!

$95 Bilancia La Collina Syrah 2006

Hawkes Bay

Cork

Best Price: $88

AU: Rand

NZ: Sel Glen SC WFW

Three one hundred dollar New Zealand Syrahs from Hawkes Bay in our list? A few years ago we would never have imagined it, but these three wines are utterly sensational. While New Zealand doesn't remotely have the depth of talent with this variety that Australia does, they certainly have some extremely serious wines to consider. All three are different in style, with La Collina being of the chiselled Côte-Rôtie mould. This is an exceedingly fine, peppery wine with a heady, lifted perfume. It's fine, very tight and unbelievably long.

Clare Valley

Cork

AU: DMs DW Nicks WLC

Jim Barry Wines The Benbournie Cabernet Sauvignon 2004

$95

I (MJ) thought that the 2002 vintage of this wine was the best ever, but I spoke too soon. The Benbournie 2004 is a legendary wine with incredible intensity, but not an ounce of unwanted high tone oak or alcohol. This wine is in perfect harmony already and so decadent and attractive that you need all the self control you can muster to keep your hands off it.

Adelaide Hills

Screw Cap

www.thelane. com.au

The Lane JC John Crighton Shiraz Cabernet 2007

$100

Despite its youth (it was the only 2007 in the $50+ class of **The Great Australian Red** Competition) JC is already showing extraordinary class and elegance. While we don't differentiate **The Great Australian Red**s by style, it is clear that many of the wines are blockbusters, but a few of them are built with the texture, complexity and finesse of great red Burgundy. This wine accurately reflects its cool climate, single Domaine origins in the hills (not unlike Burgundy, then) and it's named after John Edwards' father – the man who worked so hard to give the Edwards family the opportunity to start their wine business. JC is a more than worthy homage to Pa Edwards, it being the finest

red wines 151

red ever made at The Lane.

$105 Moss Wood Margaret River Cabernet Sauvignon 2005

The density of Cabernet fruit in Moss Wood 2005 is truly staggering, but none of this power is misplaced, 'hot' or oaky – it is just introverted and brooding. With vigorous swirling you may encourage fragments of this wine to dislodge themselves from the mother ship and it is these tiny morsels that point to an epic future and some stunning evolution along the way. One of the greatest vintages of all time returns Moss Wood to its position as the Latour of Margaret River.

Margaret River

Screw Cap

Best Price: $95

AU: 1st Aus Chalk Sel DMs DW Ed EEC Nicks PWS Rand SMWM Sum VCs WLC

$112 Craggy Range Le Sol Gimblett Gravels Syrah 2006

If you are used to wandering around town with your underpants on the outside of your trousers, then hello brother – this is the wine for you. Only superheroes are allowed to drink Le Sol. Why? It is faster than a speeding bullet, more powerful than a locomotive, taller than the average bear and it also has a mullet that's ahead of it's time. Steve Smith creates this wine in his own image, and he is… the greatest superhero to come out of New Zealand.

Gimblett Gravels

Cork

Best Price: $85

AU: Aus Chalk DMs Ed PWS SMWM

NZ: Sel Glen HWC RWM SC WFW

$115 Brokenwood Graveyard Shiraz 2006

This is the best young Graveyard we have ever

Hunter Valley

Screw Cap

Best Price: $95

AU: Aus Chalk
Sel DMs DW
Ed GPO Rand
Sixty SMWM
Sum VCs

NZ: RWM

tasted and it must be among the finest wines ever created at this world-famous property. This is an exceedingly ageworthy Hunter Shiraz and it demands a very long time in the cellar, even though it appears to be delightfully integrated already. At only 13.5% it bucks the trend by being one of the lightest red wines in this book, not only of the Shiraz variety, but of all styles. We are delighted to see such precision, depth and composure, proving that alcohol is not everything when it comes to building quality and distinction into a wine.

Gimblett
Gravels

Diam cork

AU: DW

NZ: HWC Mill
WFW

Trinity Hill The Gimblett Merlot Cabernet Sauvignon 2006

$120

We tasted all of the top end Aussie Merlots and every one of them came out too green, too oaky, too bretty or just very bloody average. This is the only Merlot that really got it right at the top end. If you're one of the lucky people who snaffled a bonus this year, then splash out on this wine and you'll reap the rewards in about five years' time. It's peppery, spicy and grippy with dusty, firm tannins and a very tidy palate. There is only one condition to qualify for buying this wine – you must be able to carry the bottle out of the shop unassisted. Good luck!

Merlot (Mer-low) is a juicy red grape, with supple, smooth, silky, blackberry, plum, black jube and fruitcake flavours. It happily flies solo but loves the company of Cabernet Sauvignon in a blend. As Merlot is usually oak aged, the fruit flavours are often accompanied by a touch of sweet wood-smoke barrel nuances. It's time to get over Sideways and give Merlot another chance.

$129 Trinity Hill Homage Syrah 2006

Homage is a perfectly balanced wine because it's absolutely massive in every possible way, like the Kiwi rugby player Ma'a Nonu. Devastating on the palate, a little like the mind-blowing Northern Rhone wine Hermitage, this is the finest Trinity Hill wine ever made. Winemaker John Hancock should be extremely proud of what he has achieved, leading, as he always does, from the very front of the pack.

Hawkes Bay

Cork

Best Price: $110

AU: DW

NZ: Sel Glen HWC SC WFW

$131 Wolf Blass Black Label Cabernet Shiraz 2005

Continuing its run of excellence (2004 Black Label picked up last year's trophy for **The Great Australian Red**) this 2005 got a trophy as well, and we think that if you are into power-packed reds (black, not red, in this case) with unlimited rev counters and more horsepower than a stud farm, look no further than this iconic wine. It's brilliant in every way with really fit tannins, mind-blowing length and all manner of fruit flavours (all black, of course).

Langhorne Creek, McLaren Vale, Barossa Valley

Screw Cap

Best Price: $100

AU: 1st Chalk DMs DW Ed GPO Lland SMWM VCs WLC

NZ: Mill

$165 Penfolds Bin 707 Cabernet Sauvignon 2005

This is a very ancient style of wine, staying completely true to its original recipe of broad oak. It has a Viking ship hull of wide oak beams, laden with Ribena fruit. Built for long distance with the stamina to keep powering on for decades, this wine is no catamaran scudding

Barossa Valley, Coonawarra, Padthaway

Screw Cap

Best Price: $150

along at speed, it is a relentless vessel of doom which will crush unbelievers in its path. The only safe place is inside, and 2005 is the best vintage in more than a decade, so get on board.

Penfolds Cellar Reserve Cabernet Sauvignon 2006

$250

This is the best young Australian Cabernet that we have ever tasted. There you have it, one of the biggest statements in this book. And there's more. If you bring the rest of the world into play, the only region worth mentioning is Pauillac in Bordeaux, where Chateau Latour and the other big guns hang out. We are desperately serious about this statement and will watch this wine as closely as we can afford for the next fifty years (there's not much chance Jukesy will outlive this wine!). It has extraordinary persistence and concentration as well as masses of oak. Its sensational fruit needs decades to come out.

Penfolds Cellar Reserve Cabernet Sauvignon Shiraz 2006

$250

When we wrote up the 2005 last year with the biggest rave review we could muster, it was priced at $100 a bottle. Imagine our surprise when the sample of 2006 turned up this year and the sticker on the back said $250! We thought the inflation rate in Zimbabwe was insane, but clearly at Fosters it's even steeper. So, throughout our tasting exercise with this wine, we did something that we very rarely do, which was to attempt to justify the price of the wine in terms of its quality, rather than the other way around. We are happy, and somewhat shocked, to report that this wine ranks among the best in the world, and therefore, despite its stomach-churning cost, unlikely as it sounds, it still offers good value for money.

*Aristocratic, age-worthy **Cabernet Sauvignon** (Cab-er-nay Soe-veen-yon) forms the backbone of many sturdy, lusty reds. Its hallmarks are a deep colour, blackcurrant flavour, with occasional cigar-box or cedarwood notes and sometimes mint leaf. When it's on top form, a smooth, velvety, dark-chocolate texture and flavour emerge from the glass. It performs best when it is blended, usually with Merlot and Cabernet Franc. In Australia it also works brilliantly with Shiraz. Cabernet Sauvignon is the most celebrated red grape in the world, and the most age-worthy of them all.*

sweet & fortified wines

375ml

Victoria

$12 Brown Brothers Orange Muscat & Flora 2008

Screw Cap

Best Price: $10

AU: 1st Chalk DMs DW EEC Nicks Lland VCs'WLC

NZ: Mill

Another mainstay in our list this year, the consistency of this wine every vintage is remarkable. I (MJ) have enjoyed it every year since 1987 and it has not once dropped the ball. Nor has the price changed. Tyson was still in primary school in 1987 but he agrees that the 2008 is as heroic as always, with its fresh orange, honey and spice flavours.

Innocent Bystander Victoria Moscato 2008

375ml

Swan Hill

Crown seal

Fancy a lovely looking little firecracker of a

sweetie to serve with fresh fruit puddings and chocolate-stuffing-sofa-evenings-in? Bystander can do both with equal style and panache because it is a wine that is made to a very high spec, but it doesn't take itself too seriously. Grapey and thirst-quenching and with a delicious prickle of bubbles, you might find that the evening is not that innocent after you've squirreled one (or two) of these bottles away.

Brown Brothers Moscato 2008 $15

The brothers Brown have done it again, taken a style, nailed it and banged it on the shelves at a bargain price. Ross Brown pours every ounce of his forty years of experience with Moscato into this wine. He told me (TS) that it's more difficult to make sweet wines than most people realise, so he has to work harder than he does with dry wines to achieve finesse and delicacy. The result is as fresh and as professionally made as anything from this outfit, so even if you're a wine snob you'll get loads of pleasure out of its fresh ginger and lemon zest flavours.

La Gitana Manzanilla di San Lucar Hidalgo Sherry NV

This teeny little piccolo of the driest sherry you can imagine is an inspired way to kick off an awesome dinner party. Shove ten bottles of this nimble, sea salty thing in an ice bucket and hand them to your guests as they cross your threshold and we can guarantee that they will be uplifted to party mode in no time at all. Grab some salami, chorizo, olives, sundried tomatoes,

AU: 1st Aus DMs DW Rand SMWM VCs

See back page for key to stockists

750ml

South-Eastern Australia

Screw Cap

Best Price: $12

AU: 1st Chalk DMs DW Ed Nicks Lland PWS SMWM Sum VCs WLC

NZ: SC

500ml

Spain

Screw Cap

AU: DMs Nicks PWS

NZ: RWM

sweet & fortified wines 157

cashews, caperberries, salt and pepper squid, whitebait and any other nibbly bits you can think of and watch this Manzanilla (pronounced man-than-eeya) do what it is world famous for – waltz through the lot of them with a skip in its stride.

$18 Chalk Hill Moscato 2008

Jock Harvey's lighter style (yes, he has one, believe it or not) is on display in this elegantly beautiful, grapey sparkler. One bottle per head is the minimum entry fee, and you'll need more than that anyway because it disappears in milliseconds.

500ml

McLaren Vale

Crown seal

www.chalkhill.com.au

AU: Aus

$18 Wirra Wirra Mrs Wigley Moscato 2008

Mrs Wigley is the definitive breakfast wine to enjoy with fresh cut pink melon slices and the lightest of pancakes (or filthy great sausage sandwiches slathered in ketchup nestling in humungous buns – if you get our drift?). The colour alone of this impish sparkler might drive a strapping man to tears, such is its beauty, so take it steady. If all goes to plan you will be rewarded with the usual fairy-light Moscato flavours, this time punctuated with dribs of honey and drabs of fresh ginger – yum, yum, yum.

500ml

McLaren Vale, NSW, Riverland

Crown seal

AU: DMs DW SMWM VCs

$19 Dutschke Ivy Blondina Moscato 2008

Not as squeaky or Disney-like as Moscato tends to be, this is a more adult style with a complexity that Moscato rarely offers. It is not quite as sweet,

750ml

Barossa Valley

Screw Cap

nor as fizzy as the other soda-siphon styles in this book. This must be the only style of Moscato that James Bond drinks. "My name is Dutschke, Wayne Dutschke" is how we suspect the winemaker introduces himself when he is pouring this wine. It's one of the nicest revival tipples for breakfast-work that we could possibly think of, and we have road tested it on numerous occasions.

www.dutsch
kewines.com

AU: Ed

Kay Brothers Amery Vineyards McLaren Vale Moscato 2008 — $20

750ml

McLaren Vale

Crown seal

AU: 1st Aus
VCs WLC

NZ: SC

You can still drink a large glass of one of the finest wines in this book with the confidence that you shouldn't be troubling the RBTs because this wine is a mere 5% in alcohol, making it ideal for lunch parties or early evening drinks. It's refreshing and playful, just like it says on the label. It tastes like the chunky bits in home made apricot jam and it's extraordinary that the creators of one of the most revered Shirazes in Australia can also make a wine as serene and delicate as this jaw-dropping Moscato.

Lark Hill Auslese Riesling 2008 — $20

375ml

Canberra
District

Screw Cap

www.larkhill
wine.com.au

There are two types of wine drinker that will adore this wine. The first is the committed Riesling addict who, in search of even more polemic examples of this wine, feels compelled to buy it, drink it and adore it. The second is the sweet winophobe who trembles at the sight of a late-picked Muscat and orders a taxi when the Botrytis Semillons appear. Fear not, dear friend, you are not alone. Lark Hill is here to save you. Trust us, because this wine isn't heavy or cloying.

It is simply a gossamer smooth rivulet of heaven which runs across your taste buds, gently kissing them as it goes with lips of sweet pear, tarte au citron and the lightest of wild honeys. By the time you remember that you "don't like sweet wine" it's too late. You've been converted.

$23 Mount Langi Ghiran The Gap Passito Riesling 2006

375ml

Grampians

Screw Cap

www.langi.com.au

AU: DW SMWM

Sheesh! There should be so many more wines made like this in Australia, but so few makers put in the commitment to get it right, whether or not they have the talent. Shiraz wizard Dan Buckle has both. In the knowledge that this style of wine has been made at this estate since Dan's predecessor, Trevor Mast, was working with Viv Thompson at Best's, this is a heritage worth maintaining, and the proof is in the glass. We sneakily think that he has probably made this for selfish reasons, and we applaud his ingenuity because he is such a gourmand and we are sure that he desires this style in his entertaining repertoire. He has pushed it so far so quickly that it now ranks among the very best in the country. This is Langi's greatest Passito yet, not to be confused with purple-labelled kids' drinks of the same name (otherwise you'll find your kids grow up very quickly!).

$23 Peter Lehmann Botrytis Semillon 2007

375ml

Barossa Valley

Screw Cap

Best Price: $12

This straight-laced, youthful Semillon is already so attractive and refreshing that it had to go straight into this list. It will age well for a few years, but we rather like the fresh pineapple and mildly honeyed fruit that is already on display. There are plenty of other fat bot Sems for you to frolic with, so make a change and visit this nubile beauty as soon as you possibly can.

Baileys of Glenrowan Founder Liqueur Muscat NV

$25

750ml

Glenrowan

Cork

AU: 1st DMs
DW GPO VCs
WLC

The value here is staggering because this is a 750mL bottle, double the size of most Muscats in this list and half the price. It should win a design award, too, because it looks bloody serious and it tastes as good as it looks. It's got all the nice things about big fat plums, choccies and brûléed toffee in one bottle. Here's a thought for all you twenty-something budding trend-setters out there: Serve this in an old-fashioned low ball glass with a massive square ice cube instead of spirits as an aperitif and blow your mates away.

McWilliam's Hanwood Grand Tawny Port Special Reserve 12 Years Old NV

$26

750ml

South-Eastern
Australia

Screw Cap

AU: 1st DMs
Lland VCs

Here's another case of McWilliams nailing a wine style that everyone else should be getting right but so few do. They must be pouring some investment into this port because it looks the part with its dark colour and smart bottle. There is none of the spirity, rasping alcohol flavour that we hate – and saw in every other bottle of Aussie tawny that we tasted. By contrast, this wine showed super smooth, nutty fig and caramel notes with a beautiful, balanced finish begging you to go back for more. And we did.

$29 Turkey Flat Pedro Ximénez NV

375ml

Barossa Valley

Cork

www.turkey
flat.com.au

AU: DMs DW

Pedro's Cousin Pierro Ximénez made a fleeting appearance at **The Great Australian Red** dinner at Gianni's this year, thanks to a rather ill-informed but delightful waiter who introduced this new member of the Ximénez family to us in the form of a jus drizzled over a duck leg terrine! Whenever we talk about this variety, we remember that night with a smile and toast Pierro while we drizzle this sensational wine over legs and all sorts. Tasting like boozy raisins and dark powerful spirit, just make sure the leg you're aiming for is not a turkey leg, or you will certainly need a second bottle.

$30 D'Arenberg The Noble 2007

375ml

McLaren Vale

Screw Cap

Best Price: $24

AU: 1st Aus
Chalk Sel DMs
DW Ed Sum
TWC VCs

NZ: Sel Glen

The decadence and rumbustious nature of this mighty sweetie mirrors its owner and his fantastic theatrical outfits. Whenever we meet Chester Osborn we feel compelled to say, "You didn't let us know it was fancy dress!" and he winks back at us like we are naughty boys. If you are feeling dangerous and want to blow your guests away with a hedonistic and gallactically enthusiastic performance, then give centre stage to this peach crumble flavoured sweetie.

$30 De Bortoli Noble One Botrytis Semillon 2006

375ml

New South Wales

Screw Cap

This is Australia's most famous sweet wine, and justly so, because it is another iconic creation

Best Price: $25
AU: 1st Aus Boc Chalk DMs DW Ed GPO Nicks Lland Rand SMWM Sum VCs WLC
NZ: Sel Glen HWC WFW
500ml
Rutherglen
Screw Cap
AU: 1st Boc DW Ed Nicks PWS Rand SMWM Sum VCs WLC
375ml
Clare Valley
Screw Cap
AU: 1st Aus DW Ed Rand Sixty SMWM Sum VCs WLC

that never misses a vintage. We have tasted every wine since the inaugural 1982 (and we are looking forward to the anniversary release next year!). This 2006 continues an unbroken line of excellence with its crème brûlée toastiness and cinnamon and baked peach notes oozing out of every corner of the glass. Its core of lemon/grapefruit acidity and excellent length mark this as another vintage to adore.

Seppeltsfield Grand Muscat NV $30

To step into the Seppeltsfield winery in the Barossa Valley is to walk right into the middle of the heritage of the Australian wine industry. A glass of this wine will have the same effect. Very dark in colour, but in no way earthy, tannic or woody, this is a wine that parades its roasted coffee bean, Black Forest gâteau and port-soaked fig flavours. How such an estate can craft a Grand Muscat (aged for between ten and fifteen years) in a big bottle at this price is beyond us.

Mount Horrocks Cordon Cut Clare Valley Riesling 2008 $37

In light of the fact that 2008 is clearly a fantastic vintage for Clare Riesling (and we have a stunning selection in this line-up) it follows that Mount Horrocks' legendary Cordon Cut is an absolute stonker, too. And, like the dramatic dry Rieslings, it has a burst of freshness in its heart that, no doubt, will allow it to age for longer than ever. This theory is borne out by its grapefruit and wild honey flavours which are so determined and single-minded that we think this is one of the most entrancing MHCCRs in years.

$40 Skillogalee Liqueur Muscat NV

If you're looking for a present for a loved or lusted one then get your paws on this beautiful bottle of Muscat. It looks as good as it tastes and it tastes better than any South Australian Muscat we have seen this year. With a highly polished mahogany hue and Christmas spice flavours, this wine is red fruit scented, not black, which means you can conceivably drink a couple of glasses. It slips quickly over the palate, making it an ideal bottle to plonk in the middle of the table at a dinner party. Just don't expect there to be any left when your guests leave two days later.

750ml

Clare Valley

Cork

www.skilloga
lee.com.au

AU: DW
SMWM

$40 Taylor's LBV Port 2002

Without question the finest Late-Bottled Vintage Port of all, this is a masterful creation from the legendary house of Taylor's. As dark as Batman's cloak and every bit as powerful as the caped crusader himself, this mighty wine will amaze your guests with its complexity and impact. The great thing is that it will last for a month if you can't finish a bottle (you lightweight!).

750ml

Portugal

Cork

AU: 1st DW
PWS VCs

NZ: HWC Mill

$43 Pegasus Bay Aria Late Picked Riesling 2007

We know Matt and Lynette at Peg Bay well, and always expect greatness in the bottle, but with 2007 Aria they have completely exceeded even our wildest expectations. A full bottle will do eight

750ml

Waipara
Valley

Screw Cap

Best Price: $36

AU: DMs DW SMWM

NZ: Sel Glen HWC SC WFW

375ml

Marlborough

Screw Cap

www.forrest.co.nz

NZ: HWC

Botrytis

375ml

Marlborough

Screw Cap

AU: DW SMWM

NZ: Sel Glen HWC Mill SC

375ml

Rutherglen

Screw Cap

AU: DMs DW Ed PWS Rand VCs

large glasses for a dinner party, making this eminently affordable with its exotic, spiced honey and lemon nose and just-baked almond croissant nuances. Cheers guys – love your work.

John Forrest Collection Noble Riesling 2006

$52

Forrest's Noble is a proper, world-class sweet wine with ripe guava fruit and layers of complexity. This is a mighty price to pay for a half bot, but whoever gets the pleasure of drinking this wine with you will love you forever because it is New Zealand's finest sweet wine. If you are a tight-wad then you could always drop down a level to its younger brother, **Forrest Estate Botrytised Riesling 2006** ($37). We, however, cannot guarantee eternal love with this wine. Would a week suffice?

Campbells Merchant Prince Rare Rutherglen Muscat NV

$116

Merchant Prince? Bollocks. There's nothing prince-like about this offering – it is the King. This wine has a lifetime membership to our book and the only question we have for Colin Campbell is why he's not bottling it in magnums! Amazingly concentrated, with incredible fruit, balanced by savoury, powerful acidity, this is the ultimate Muscat experience. But why is it so bloody expensive? There is one simple reason. These grapes were picked at a time when dinosaurs roamed the earth – this wine predates civilisation as we know it. This tincture was the inspiration for the Pyramids of Giza, those cool statues on Easter

Island, the Hanging Gardens of Babylon (although it has to be said that they were a bit of a mess, but at least they caused a stir at the time) and Madonna's silver conical boobs. In short, this wine has made the earth and all of us in it the way it is today.

> **Muscat** *(Muss-cat) wines vary from the lightest, fizziest Soda-Stream of grapey juice, to the deepest, darkest, headiest liqueur that looks like a rugby player's liniment and tastes like knock-out drops. Muscat is the only grape variety that in its simplest form actually smells and tastes 'grapey'.*

FOOD AND WINE

COMBINATIONS

it's all about taste.

This chapter is about choosing the right wine for your next dinner party, casual lunch or restaurant experience. We'll lead you through the combinations that work and those that don't, guiding you toward the right style to impress the palates of your guests and your own along the way.

This is all a matter of taste – food and wine matching is a subjective topic if ever there was one. There are certainly principles that always apply, regardless of individual tastes, but we're not about to tell you exactly what to drink here. Instead, we'll provide plenty of general suggestions and gently guide you to a flavour or a collection of wines that would work well. It's up to you where to make your final decision, by lining up a bottle that you know you like. **The Best Wines of 2009** is the place to discover the very best bottles on the shelves this year.

You can therefore relax (and open a bottle – we would!). It no longer needs to be a nightmare trying to match wine to food when you're entertaining at home, or out and about. Forget the pressure to 'get it right,' simply follow our guidelines and get on with enjoying yourself!

Using this chapter is dead simple.

Once you've got an ingredient, dish or cuisine in mind, flick to its entry and check out the wines to suit. Then flick to **The Best Wines of 2009** to select your exact bottle. If you're up for making your own choice, use our **Who's Who** chapter to direct you to the best regions, vintages and producers to look for.

We wish you many exciting discoveries in your journey through **Taste**!

When in doubt, grab a few bottles of a multi-purpose, multi-talented style of wine. Some names pop up in this chapter more often than others – like **Sauvignon Blanc**, the crowd-pleasing, zesty, dry, white grape that is the perfect lunch partner and a winner with all things Asian. It also happens to be the wine fashion statement of the noughties, so get on board and stock up! **Aussie Riesling** is grossly underrated but absolutely brilliant, and shaping up to be the bargain of the decade. You'll find that it appears more than 100 times in this chapter! Equally versatile are the juicy, smooth, black-fruit-driven, **GSM (Grenache, Shiraz, Mourvèdre)** blends – try to keep a few bottles of this style of wine at hand in readiness for unexpected guests or impromptu cooking. They're also a safe bet when you're rushing off to a BYO and aren't quite sure what to expect.

appetisers

Champagne
Sparkling White
Sherry
Riesling
Sauv Blanc
Semillon

Pre-dinner nibbles like *dry roasted almonds, bruschetta, cashews, canapés, crostini, crudités* and *olives* are designed to give your palate a jump-start and get your juices flowing before a feast. It is important at this stage of the proceedings not to overload your taste buds with big, weighty, powerful wines. Save these bottles for later and zero in on refreshing, taste-bud-awakening styles that set the scene, rather than hog the limelight: Champagne is, not surprisingly, the perfect wine if you're feeling loaded but, if not, Australia and New Zealand take the prize for the best, authentic Champagne-taste-alikes. These are usually very good value, too (around half the price of Champs) – Tassie, and the cooler reaches of Vic, WA and SA are the places to go to find awesome quality, and you'll find plenty among **The Best Wines of 2009**. If you're feeling adventurous, go on the hunt for sparkling wines from the Loire Valley in France (Saumur), Crémant de Bourgogne (Burgundy) or California. Italy offers up superb, dry, palate-enlivening fizz in the form of Prosecco, from Veneto.

Fino and manzanilla-style sherries are wonderful palate cleansers, particularly with salty dishes, despite being thought of as perpetually 'out of fashion'. The least expensive option (and often the safest, particularly if you are eating out) is a zesty, uplifting, palate-sprucing dry white. Even a moderately expensive number is often half the price of a bottle of Champs and there are thousands of these around, so go for it. There are also loads of first-class examples in this book (page 47 is your starting point). Stay with unoaked styles like Riesling, Sauvignon Blanc and Semillon and keep the price under control. Then step up the pace with the next bottle when the food hits the table. If the choice is poor (a short restaurant wine list or a poorly stocked bottle shop) then grab a neutral, dry, inexpensive white wine (again, you have stacks to choose from) and pep it up with a dash or two of Crème de Cassis (blackcurrant liqueur). Spend up on the cassis (it will go a long way) and make a Kir. Use the same liqueur to turn a dry, sparkling wine or inexpensive Champagne into a glitzy Kir Royale. Flick on to our teeming 'Seafood' entry for canapés featuring *prawns, crab, smoked salmon* or any other delight from the depths.

starters and main courses

African see 'Moroccan'

Anchovies Strongly flavoured whether they are fresh or cured, these hairy little fish (whether you like 'em or not) require dry, unoaked, tangy, acidic whites or juicy, bone-dry rosés for maximum impact. Try a local Riesling or Sauvignon Blanc or head for Italy, Spain or France – but keep the budget low –

Riesling
Sauv Blanc
Rosé
Sherry

fifteen dollars will keep you in fine shape. There are a few worthy rosés up for grabs as well, but watch the sweetness and keep the alcohol under 14% – stay with **The Best Wines of 2009** (pages 33 to 170), to be safe. Dry sherry is also spot on, but consider what is in the rest of the dish, as it can be quite a strong flavour.

Antipasto

Semillon
Verdelho
Sem Sauv Blanc
Pinot Grigio
Valpolicella
Bardolino

The classic Italian mixed platter of *artichokes, prosciutto, bruschetta, olives, marinated capsicum and eggplant* enjoys being romanced with clean, vibrant, refreshing whites like young Hunter Semillon, dry Verdelho and Semillon Sauvignon Blanc blends or Italy's Pinot Grigio, Pinot Bianco, Verdicchio or Gavi. For reds, turn to chilled, light Italians like Valpolicella and Bardolino.

Artichokes

Sauv Blanc
Riesling

Dry, unoaked, refreshing whites are best here, especially if you are going to dip the artichokes in *vinaigrette* (see 'Vinaigrette'). Keep it angular and edgy with New Zealand Sauvignon Blanc or lighter Australian Riesling. If you want to head abroad, Alsatian Sylvaner, Pinot Blanc, Loire Sauvignon Blanc or Aligoté from Burgundy are perfect partners from France, as are South African or Argentinean Torrontés and the Italian whites listed above for 'Antipasto'.

Asian see 'Chinese', 'Thai'

Asparagus

Sauv Blanc
Pinot Grigio

Because of its inbuilt asparagusy characteristics (see our tasting note on page 66), Sauvignon Blanc is the perfect match here. New World styles of Sauvignon like New Zealand (Marlborough), Australian (Adelaide Hills) or Chilean (Casablanca) have tons of flavour and would be better suited to asparagus dishes that have *hollandaise, balsamic vinegar* or *olive oil* and *Parmesan*. Old World examples, like those from France's Loire Valley (Sancerre, Menetou-Salon and Pouilly-Fumé) are great if the dish is plainer. Northern Italian whites like Pinot Bianco or Pinot Grigio, as well as South African Sauvignon Blanc (somewhere between New Zealand and Loire geographically and in style) would also do the job brilliantly.

Australian

Australia can take the credit for inventing and mastering Asian fusion, juggling the freshest of land and sea ingredients, and weaving into them the best of Asian spice and presentation. This beguiling and thoroughly delicious style of cuisine is a real hit worldwide, as the cooking is virtually fat free and packed with zesty, palate-enlivening flavours. Back home, it is no surprise that trendy restaurants reward the palate with finely tuned Clare and Eden Valley Rieslings, fresh, grapey Verdelhos, zippy, perky Adelaide Hills and Western Australian Sauvignon Blancs and assorted Pinot Gris, Semillon/Sauvignon blends and keen, fresh, oak-balanced Chardonnays. Not all of our reds are huge and porty, with the vogue for more aromatic wines coming from McLaren Vale, Nagambie Lakes, Mornington, Great Western, Canberra or Frankland (Shiraz), Tasmania, Mornington, Geelong or Yarra (Pinot) and cooler Margaret River, Orange or Coonawarra (Cabernet and Merlot) really hitting form. You can't go wrong with any of these awesome wines if you stick with our recommended producers (see **Who's Who** on page 261) so be sure to keep a few all-purpose bottles in the fridge at all times ('In case of emergency, break seal!'). These are also just the thing for your local BYO – with a bottle of red in one hand and white in the other, you're set to settle in for an action-packed evening!

Riesling
Verdelho
Sauv Blanc
Pinot Gris
Sem Sauv Blanc
Chardonnay
Pinot Noir
Shiraz
Cabernet
Merlot

Avocado

If the avocado is *undressed*, you need light, unoaked whites, in particular New Zealand, Adelaide Hills or Loire (French) Sauvignon Blanc, Western Australian Semillon

Sauv Blanc
Sem Sauv Blanc
Pinot Gris
Verdelho
Riesling

Sauvignon Blanc, Muscadet or fresh, cheap, clean Italians. If *dressed* with *vinaigrette* or with *Marie Rose sauce* (in a prawn cocktail), richer Sauvignon Blanc (NZ and the Cape), Pinot Gris (New Zealand and smart Italians) or Australian Verdelho and Riesling are spot on, as are France's young, white Rhônes and Alsatian Pinot Blanc. *Guacamole*, depending on its chilli heat, needs cool, citrusy, dry whites to douse the palate and cut through the gloopy green mush.

Bacon This usually pops up as an ingredient in a dish and not

Grenache/Shiraz
Sparkling Shiraz
Pinot Noir

often as the main theme, unless you've had a heavy night on the sherbets and need the finest of all oily/crunchy miracle cures – *a bacon sandwich*! If you feel like a glass of wine to accompany this classic bread and hog delight, or your *full English breakfast* (I know I do – Matthew), then chilled, inexpensive Aussie Grenache/Shiraz blends or red Côtes-du-Rhône, Languedoc Rouge or Cru Beaujolais (all French) would be a joy. If you are brave (or foolish, or both) try it with one of Australia's very own sparkling Shirazes. If you are using fried or grilled *pancetta* or *lardons* in a salad, remember that the salty flavour and/or smoked taste could prompt a move away from a salady, light white wine to a juicy, fresh red. Red Burgundy (a smart Bourgogne Rouge is as far as you need go) is heavenly with *bacon and eggs*, if a little ostentatious. New Zealand or Australian Pinot Noir would happily keep our piggy smiling.

Barbecues The Great Aussie Barbie is an institution, always verging on the explosive, complete with platters groaning with red-blooded meat tending toward charcoal, spicy, lurid marinades and splatterings of bright red tomato sauce. Any wine risking its existence in this haphazard picture had better be up to the flavour challenge. Aim for good value gluggers, as long as they are assertive, juicy and fruit-driven. When *red*

Shiraz
Cab Sauv
Grenache
Zinfandel
Chardonnay
Chenin Blanc
Semillon

meats are the order of the day, reach for inexpensive Shiraz, Cabernet Sauvignon, Grenache, Zinfandel (or Merlot or Carmenère if you can find a worthy contender). If you don't want to spend up on your unworthy friends, this is the time to be creative in your choice from our **Best Wines of 2009.** You'll be amazed at the sub-$10 reds that we've hunted down for you again this year – this is where you should shop. Petit Verdot, Durif and funky, inexpensive blends can do their debut on the BBQ stage without any sideways glances. When it's time to turn up the heat and put on a display of *calamari, prawns, whole fish, chicken* or *white meat kebabs,* give white wines a chance to strut their stuff. The rules are the same: juicy, fruit-driven and inexpensive. Lightly oaked Chardonnay, Chenin Blanc and Semillon all work. Australia, New Zealand, Chile, Argentina and South Africa are the most likely candidates for your guest list.

Don't be afraid of **chilling** both whites and reds for maximum effect at a BBQ.

Beans If your *baked bean* diet extends beyond breakfast on

Grenache/Shiraz
Shiraz
Zinfandel
Chardonnay

toast, you simply need to find fruity, berry-driven reds because the tomato sauce flavour is so dominant and it takes over the palate. Youthful reds with refreshing acidity, such as those from anywhere in Australia, the Loire (France), Spain, South Africa, South America or Italy, will work well. Remember to keep the price down (you are eating baked beans, after all!). Not surprisingly, anything goes with *green beans*, as they are the least flavoursome of veggies. You'd have to mince along with a light, dry white to let a green bean truly express itself! *Bean salad* needs slightly chilled, light-bodied reds or fresh, zingy whites to cut through the earthy flavours. If you throw some beans into a stew, such as *cassoulet* (a French stew of beans and virtually any meat you have on hand) or any of a wide variety of Spanish dishes, then try to

track down a pure, fruit-charged Grenache or Grenache/Shiraz/Mourvèdre blend. Funky, edgy Shiraz from cool parts of Victoria, Western Australia and the Hunter Valley also does the trick. Grenache/Carignan-blends from the south of France, or Garnacha-based wines from Spain will easily deal with the beanie ballast. *Black bean sauce* requires a few moments' meditation and trepidation. The curious, oil-slick texture and intensity of dark sweetness must be countered by huge, juicy, mouth-filling, velvety smooth reds – Zinfandel is the only red grape brave enough to cope. *Refried beans*, either in *tacos* or other *Mexican* dishes, have a fair degree of earthy sludginess that needs either rich whites like a bright Chardonnay (Australian or New Zealand, of course, but Chile and South Africa make the best value if you have the inclination to stray beyond home soil) or any fresh, fruity reds. We list plenty of Aussies in our **Best Wines of 2009,** but keep the price and the temperature down. Break the bank and spend a fiver on a bottle of McWilliams Inheritance Shiraz Merlot blend (page 100) and stick it in the fridge when you get home. If your beans inspire your Latin streak, we would suggest you try Bonarda, Sangiovese or Tempranillo from Argentina as a starting point, then head over to Chile for some Carmenère or Merlot if you have no joy. Matthew's favourite bean is the noble *cannellini*, the base for all great bean-frenzy soups. What should you uncork? Sorry, but you'll have to wait with spoon and glass at the ready for the 'Soup' entry.

Beef There are so many different beef dishes, so it is lucky that the rules are not too tricky. Reds, predictably, are the order of the day, but it is the size and shape of them (the wines, not the cows) that determines just how accurate the match will be. *Roast beef* (or *en croûte/beef Wellington*) served up for Sunday lunch deserves a modicum of respect. When you gather around the dining room table do, by all means, push the boat out. Head to the top Cabernets from Margaret River (Western Australia) or Coonawarra (South Australia), top Aussie Cabernet

Cab Sauv
Cabernet Shiraz
Zinfandel
Malbec
Pinot Noir
Petit Verdot
Merlot
Rosé
Pinot Grigio

Shiraz blends (totally underrated) or Napa Valley in California. Try Margaret River for the more elegant, plainer cows and Coonawarra for the gamey, richer beasts.

It's times like these when old-fashioned gentlemen's red Bordeaux really comes into its own. Don't ask us why, but classy French wines such as red Bordeaux, Bandol, erudite Northern Rhônes – Hermitage, Crozes-Hermitage, Cornas, St-Joseph or Côte-Rôtie – or even Italy's answer to an Aston Martin V12 Vanquish, the Super-Tuscans, are simply magnificent with this king of beef dishes. As you'd expect, not one of these wines is remotely affordable (nor is the car, mind you). They are all special occasion wines, so if you are looking to shave a few bucks off your credit card bill, stick with the Aussies. You've guessed it, the best of these are again fairly dear, but at least these reds will give you the richness and complexity that you are craving. If you are on a strict budget, then don't change regions, just buy cleverly – not all wines from Margaret River or Bordeaux are exorbitantly priced. Cool climate Cabernet makes its debut in **The Best Wines of 2009** at just $11 (check it out on page 103). Try the less famous producers in our **Who's Who** or Bordeaux sub-regions like Côtes de Castillon, Bourg, Blaye and Francs, and go for a good vintage like 2004 or 2005. These wines can really hit the spot. Hearty Southern Rhône or Languedoc (both French) reds would also do very well. Most Aussie (try well-made and ripe vintage Clare Valley and cooler vintage Barossa and McLaren Vale in particular), South African, Chilean and Argentinean Cabernets or Cab/Shiraz blends around the $25 mark offer charm, complexity and competence, especially if you stick to our recommendations. It is at this price point that it really pays to buy Australian made. But even if you drop down to around $15, you can still have fun if you follow our picks, just remember to stay close to home, as European reds at this price are likely to give you a very unpleasant surprise.

Stews, casseroles and *meat pies* need richer, more structured reds, particularly if meaty, stock-rich gravy is involved. Cabernet Sauvignon, Shiraz, Pinotage, Piemontese (Northern Italian) reds, Zinfandel and Malbec are but a few of the superb, hunky, robust grapes to go for. Look for wines from Australia, South Africa, California and Argentina. Southern Rhônes will also be superb, as will Provençal or Languedoc reds made from a similar blend of swarthy red grapes. If you can track them down, Portuguese wines are worth considering with rich beef dishes – the red wines from Dão and the Douro Valley are still woefully under-priced and, from the best producers, mightily impressive (but hard to find in Australia – keep asking your independent, we'll do the same, and hopefully next year there will be more on the ground that we can point you toward). *Bollito misto*, the Italian stew made from beef and just about everything else you could find in your larder, demands the presence of medium-weight, high acid wines like Great Western Shiraz, inexpensive Yarra Shiraz and Shiraz/Cabernet blends. Northern Italy, smart Valpolicella, Barbera and Dolcetto would be quirky and yet inspirational local partners for your stew. *Boeuf bourguignon*, as the name suggests, usually pressgangs the help of red Burgundy ('Bourgogne,' to the French). Any of the entry-level Pinot Noirs from our recommended producers would do the trick.

> **How do you like your beef cooked?** If you are a keen carnivore and a fan of **rare** beef, you can safely drink younger, more tannic red wines, as the harder tannins balance perfectly with juicy, rare meat, slicing through the flesh and making your mouth water. If, however, you like your beef **well done**, then choose an older wine with smoother, more harmonious tannins.

Steak and kidney pie or any *meat pie* (swerve the beer and give the coke a very wide berth!) love manly, rustic reds with grippy, palate-crunching acidity and sturdy tannins. These wines slice through the gravy and often-chewy kidneys – Aussie Shiraz,

Malbec from Argentina and South African Pinotage and Syrah all enjoy this challenge. *Cottage pie*, with carrot, celery, onions and minced beef rarely requires anything more challenging than an inexpensive, fun lovin' red. You could try your hand with anything mass-produced from the Riverland (provided it's in our list – start from page 100) or Southern Italy or Sicily and then go crazy and buy two bottles. A heroic *Beef stroganoff* also demands rusticity in its dancing partner, so gather together some Grenache/Shiraz/Mourvèdre blends or southern Rhônes; even a straight Côtes-du-Rhône from one of the better domaines can be a joy. Otherwise, seek out The Barossa at its finest: sub-$25, sub 14% alcohol from a decent producer in our list. *Hungarian goulash* would be wonderfully authentic if a Hungarian red wine joined it. 'Nuff said! But if you want to play a straighter bat, reach for a cheapie Aussie Cabernet (there are some out there – we only found a few worthy of **The Best Wines of 2009**, but we love 'em) or head to Rioja, Navarra, La Mancha or Toro (Spain) or Chilean Cabernet Sauvignon.

Please **don't cook with anything expensive** – save your money for a 'drinking' wine and cook with a simple generic bottle (anything cheap and red works, even if it's from one of those ghastly cardboard boxes).

Straight *steak* has a more direct and controlled meaty flavour than a rich stew, so finer wines can be dragged out of the cellar (or local retailer). Bathe in cool climate Australian, New Zealand, South African or Argentinean Cabernet Sauvignon or Shiraz, Italian Chianti or Brunello di Montalcino, Spanish Ribera del Duero, Californian Merlot, Zin or Cab, top-end Cru Beaujolais, Crozes-Hermitage and St-Joseph (both Rhônes). Watch out that you don't OD on *Béarnaise sauce*, which, though great with a mouthful of steak, can clog up the taste buds (and the waist band) a little. With *steak au poivre*, the pungent, pulverised peppercorns make their presence known in each and every mouthful, so look for meaty (and pepper-flavoured) wines like Aussie Shiraz (look for spicy cool climate

Victorians, Western Australians or Hunters) or its cousins from further afield – northern Rhône reds (Syrah), or Shiraz from Chile or South Africa. *Burgers*, heaven in a bun (homemade of course, not mechanically reclaimed at the golden arches!), often served with ketchup, bacon, cheese or relish (or all of the above), crave fruity reds like Australian Petit Verdot (hard to find, but dead funky) or Shiraz blends, Italian Dolcetto or Barbera, Spanish Garnacha or young Rioja Crianza, juicy Californian Zinfandel, South African Pinotage or Chilean or South African Merlot. Once again, go for younger wines if you like your burger rare, and older, more mellow wines if you dwell at the well-done end of the spectrum. *Chilli con carne* is a difficult dish to match with wine. As with burgers it is necessary to search for fruitier styles like Aussie or New Zealand (Hawke's Bay) Merlot, or Negroamaro from southern Italy and Sicily – we quite like chilling them a touch, too. *Steak tartare* is a strange one, as we're still not sure whether we actually really like it (a side issue), but we must admit it works terrifically well with very light reds and rosés – Grenache-based rosés (stick with Aussies – we've found you some pearlers this year – or brave an offering from Spain or Tavel, southern Rhône) are perfect, as are snooty Pinot Noirs like France's Sancerre red or rosé. If you fancy splashing out, then rosé Champagne is the ultimate combo (although people are bound to think you're a show off).

Cold, rare roast beef salad and other cold beef dishes enjoy the company of fresh, light reds with low tannins. Chilled Pinot Noir is a treat with this style of dish (look to Martinborough, Marlborough or Central Otago in NZ, Tasmania, Yarra Valley and Mornington or, of course, Burgundy itself), as are darker-coloured Shiraz-based rosés – just make sure they are DRY (we

Whatever you do, make sure you go easy on the capers if they are served alongside – they are mini hand grenades on the palate, spoiling a seamless vinous performance.

are shouting through our megaphone!). You're safe if you buy from our list on pages 95-100. French Beaujolais, red Loires (either Cabernet Franc or Gamay) Italian Valpolicella, or Argentinean Tempranillo or Bonarda would also work. The only occasion when you are allowed to break the red-wine-with-beef rule (of course there has to be one) is with *carpaccio* (raw/rare) or *bresaola* (air-dried). These wafer-thin-sliced beef dishes can handle whites. Any dry, apéritif-style Italian white or light Montepulciano-style red would be fantastico. You'll find them if you look, but make sure they are dry.

Pinot Grigio, as opposed to Pinot Gris, is supposed to suggest a fresh, dry, tangy style, but Aussie and New Zealand producers are only just starting to grasp the importance of this.

Bread Plain, savoury bread tends to be uninspiring on its own. Base your wine choice on what you put in it or on it.

Bugs see 'Seafood'

Bruschetta see 'Appetisers'

Burgers see 'Beef', 'Junk food'

Burritos see 'Mexican'

Cajun see 'Mexican'

Calamari see 'Seafood'

Canapés see 'Appetisers'

Cannelloni see 'Pasta'

Capers Sauvignon Blanc, from Marlborough in New Zealand (or almost anywhere), or very dry Italian whites like Soave (Veneto) or Greco are very good matches,

Sauv Blanc

as they can cut through the peculiar, green, otherworldly, vinegary tanginess you experience when you crunch and burst open the exoskeleton of an unsuspecting caper. (For more options up to the challenge, see 'Appetisers')

Capsicum
Fresh, crunchy, raw capsicum crackles with zingy, juicy, healthy flavours. It should come as no surprise, then, that Sauvignon Blanc (from almost anywhere in the solar system) is the best grape for it – 'capsicum' is actually a recognised tasting note for this variety. It is a marriage made in heaven, but if you want to try something different, then dry Chenin Blanc from South Africa or Italian Pinot Grigio would also be splendid. *Piemontese peppers* (roasted half capsicums with a tomato stuffed inside) are a no-fuss favourite Saturday lunch dish of mine (Matthew), and with the olive oil, garlic, black pepper and tomato ingredients, dry whites are required, especially if the traditional anchovy fillets are criss-crossed on top of the shimmering tomato hemispheres. Assertive Sauvignon Blanc is the best option, although Italy's Verdicchio (or a less expensive, Cortese-based Piedmont white) would be appropriate. A *stuffed capsicum* depends more on its stuffing than the capsicum itself, so look to the filling for your inspiration. Generally speaking, meat or cheese stuffing goes well with light Italian reds. *Capsicum marinated in olive oil* loves any dry white wines. Good morning Western Australia, you can come right to the front of the queue! Capsicum is a word that is unavoidable when describing the cool green pepper aromas of any Sauvignon Blanc or Semillon from WA, on account of its cool climate. This makes it an ideal bedfellow for this cuisine. Otherwise, for consummate accuracy, Italian is best, so find a single varietal such as Pinot Grigio, Pinot Bianco, Traminer or Sauvignon Blanc. For *gazpacho* see 'Soup'.

Sauv Blanc
Chenin Blanc
Pinot Grigio
Semillon

Caviar
We know it is a sin, but we adore decent caviar. Sevruga or Oscietra (not Beluga – ridiculously decadent and a

Champagne
Sauv Blanc

little too 'fishy' for our taste) are our faves and Champagne is definitely the call of the day. Avoid rosé styles, though (they always tend to taste metallic with caviar in our experience), and there is no need to pop the cork of a prestige cuvée ($100 plus) unless you're desperately trying to impress (or are a tasteless lottery winner – congrats by the way). If you want to keep the budget down, and there is nothing wrong with that, then tighter, leaner New Zealand and South African Sauvignons or French Sancerre and Pouilly-Fumé (Loire) are all stunning combos. These styles also work if caviar is used in a sauce, but do look to the main ingredient as well as the caviar for guidance.

Charcuterie

Rosé
Pinot Noir
Riesling
Pinot Gris

A selection of charcuterie (*assiette de charcuterie* to be precise, including *saucisson, salami, ham* etc.) contains loads of diverse flavours along a similar textural theme. We love smart rosés (and we're not afraid to admit it – just look at the list in our **Best Wines of 2009**), particularly from McLaren Vale, Fleurieu Peninsula and the Barossa. Otherwise – if you can find it – this is the time for top quality, slightly chilled Beaujolais or Gamay from the Loire (France) to come out of the cupboard. Light to medium Aussie Pinots (just don't spend too much) and Italian reds, like Freisa (Piemonte) or Valpolicella (Veneto) would also be good matches (take a few degrees off these in the fridge, too). If you favour whites, then stick to firm, rich white grape varieties like Riesling or Pinot Gris (which usually manage to harness at least as much flavour intensity as the reds anyway). (For *chorizo* and *spicy salami*, see 'Pork'.)

Do watch out for **pickles, gherkins, cornichons** (wicked little French numbers) or **caperberries**, as excess vinegar will guarantee that you'll not be able to taste the next mouthful of wine! Our advice is to **shake your gherkin** first (hello boys!), endeavouring to knock off as much vinegar as possible before squirreling them away.

Cheese (cooked)

Chardonnay
Chenin Blanc
Semillon
Merlot
Pinot Gris
Riesling
Sauv Blanc
Pinot Noir
Gewürztraminer

There is a groaning cheeseboard section at the end of this hedonistic chapter, so flick on for non-cooked cheese joy! *Cauliflower cheese (leek Mornays, cheesy pasta* dishes etc.) and straight *cheese sauces*, depending on the strength of cheese used, need medium- to full-bodied whites such as Chardonnay, Chenin Blanc and Semillon. For reds, you must join the quest for fresh acidity coupled with pure berry fruit. This hunt should lead you to Merlot (Australian, New Zealand, Chilean or South African), the delicious wines from the Loire Valley in France (Saumur-Champigny, Chinon or Bourgueil), Italian Cabernet Franc or Dolcetto, or youthful Rioja or Navarra, reds from Spain. *Fondue* needs bone-dry whites (or pints of jolly good lager!) to cut through the waxy, stringy, molten cheese. However, if you are keen on rewarding your palate with pleasant-tasting, accurate wines, then Pinot Gris, Riesling, Chenin Blanc or Sauvignon Blanc from cooler regions of Australia or New Zealand would be ideal. If you're hankering for the French thing, look for well-balanced, fully ripe (as opposed to upsettingly lean and enamel-challengingly acidic) styles like Alsatian Pinot Blanc, Riesling and Sylvaner, and fresh Loire Sauvignon Blanc or Chenin Blanc. You could even try dry Portuguese whites and various north-eastern Italian single varietals like Pinot Gris or Pinot Blanc. *Raclette* (the Swiss dish of melted cheese over potato or bread) would love to be partnered with light Pinot Noirs (think northern Tasmania, Adelaide Hills, Victorian Central High Country, Geelong, Macedon, Yarra, Mornington, Gippsland, or New Zealand's Central Otago or Martinborough), red Burgundies or juicy Beaujolais-Villages.

With *cheese soufflé*, one of the true gems in the cooked cheese repertoire, you can really go out on a limb. Riesling (from SA's Clare or Eden Valleys, Victoria's Henty, WA's Frankland River or

Alsace in France), lighter Gewürztraminer (Tasmania or Alto Adige in Italy are worth a punt), Argentinean Torrontés, or any aromatic dry whites like Muscat (Alsace), would all be delicious. If the soufflé has any other hidden ingredients inside remember to consider them before plumping for a bottle – with *smoked haddock soufflé* you'd be wise to follow the fish – punchy, lemony whites, like Semillon or Riesling.

Mozzarella, with its unusual milky flavour and play-doh texture, is well suited to Italian Pinot Bianco, Pinot Grigio, good Arneis, Gavi and Verdicchio. Yes, these are all Italians! At home, Eden Valley Riesling, Adelaide Hills Pinot Gris and random Victorian High Country Italian whites all step up to the challenge. *Grilled goat's cheese* is equally at home in France with Sauvignon Blanc from Sancerre (the best goat's cheese hails from Chavignol, Sancerre's finest village) and Pouilly-Fumé (across the other side of the Loire river) and all other Sauvignon Blancs from around the world (Australia and New Zealand provide an arsenal of alternatives and South Africa would happily come to the party if your Loire fridge is empty). Lighter reds also work, particularly if you're tucking into a salad with some ham joining in the fun. Goat's cheese is pretty forgiving when it comes down to it, but avoid oaked whites and tannic or heavy reds.

Chicken

Chardonnay
Riesling
Pinot Noir
Gamay
Rosé
Viognier
Marsanne
Roussanne
Grenache
Sauv Blanc
Sauv Blanc Sem

Chicken is very accommodating – it loves both whites and reds. But be careful because it is a touch fussy when it comes to the precise grape varieties you want to set it up with. Chardonnay is chicken's favourite white grape by far, with Riesling coming in a close second. Pinot Noir is the bird's favourite red (it's every bird's favourite red, surely?), with Gamay perhaps surprisingly claiming the runner up spot. This means that a well-educated, classy chicken loves every village in our beloved Burgundy region, and who can blame it? At home, the bird is partial to

Pinot Noir on offer from northern Tasmania, SA's Adelaide Hills, VIC's Central High Country, Geelong, Macedon, Yarra, Mornington and Gippsland, and New Zealand's Central Otago and Martinborough.

Lighter dishes such as *cold chicken* or *turkey* are fairly versatile, so look to our al fresco-style wines in the 'Picnics' section. *Cold chicken and ham pie* works well with lighter, fragrant reds and deeper coloured, sturdy rosés from Australia and France's southern Rhône and Beaujolais. If you are feeling adventurous then try chilling down a bottle of rosé or Beaujolais-Villages to white temperature – it's a super, if unusual, match. *Poached chicken* can handle the same sort of wines but with a little more flesh – both Old and New World Pinot Noir work here. White wine companions include lighter Chardonnay or Viognier and Marsanne/Roussanne blends. Possibly my (Matthew's) favourite dish of all time, *roast chicken*, follows this theme once again, but takes it a stage further. Finer (by this we mean more expensive) cooler climate New Zealand or Australian or Californian Chardonnay and Pinot Noir, red and white Burgundy, elegant, and top flight rosé or Beaujolais (again) are all wonderful matches. *Coq au vin* also works well with Pinot Noir (red Burgundy is grand, but you can scale the wine down to a Chalonnaise version or an Aussie or NZ Pinot), Hautes-Côtes or Bourgogne rouge (from one of the better producers, of course). *Chicken casserole* or *pot pie* ups the ante even further and it enjoys a broader wine brief. South Australian Grenache or Grenache-based blends, medium-weight Rhône reds as well as mildly oaky Chardonnays, are all in with a shout. *Chicken and mushroom pie, fricassee* and other chicken dishes with *creamy sauces* call out to Chardonnay and beyond – dry Riesling from Clare Valley, Eden Valley, Henty, Frankland or Tasmania, Germany, Alsace (France), or, Alsatian Tokay-Pinot Gris and funky Rhône whites. New World Pinot Noir (from the Adelaide Hills, Tassie or Victoria, or an import from New Zealand or California) is the only red variety to feel truly at home here.

OK, so far things have been fairly straightforward, but we are now going to throw a few obstacles in front of our feathered friend, as *chicken Kiev* changes the rules completely. Full, rich and even part-oak-aged Sauvignon Blanc or Sauvignon/Semillon blends are needed to take on the buttery/garlic onslaught – Margaret River in Western Australia, white Graves (Bordeaux) and California do this well, but watch this space as this style is starting to be made all over the world. Not content with this hurdle, *coronation chicken*, depending on who is making it (we like a lot of spicy naughtiness in our sauce), can also have a bit of a kick, so dry Riesling from Clare Valley/Eden Valley or New Zealand would be worth unscrewing. Lastly, *barbecued chicken wings* can be nuclear-hot (Si Jukesy is a veritable Tardis when slotting these) and, in his experience, beer is usually the best bet. If, for some reason, you would like to try this dish with a bottle of wine (are you mad?), then a clean, inexpensive Aussie Chardy with a touch of oak won't do too much damage.

Chilli

Durif
Cab Sauv
Shiraz
Merlot
Grenache blends
Chardonnay
Semillon
Verdlho
Riesling

Enchiladas, chimichangas (nuclear waste in a wrap), *fajitas, chilli con carne, dragon's breath pizzas* (just ask Shrek) and any other fart-lightingly hot Mexican dishes all 'embrace the dark side' with a hefty dose of chillies. Thirst-quenching, chillable, juicy reds like Durif, Cab Sauv, Shiraz and Merlot or Italian red grape varieties like Primitivo, Nero d'Avola, Frappato or Negroamaro are needed to cool you down and rebuild your taste buds. South Australian GSM (Grenache/Shiraz/Mourvèdre) blends also work a treat, but look for juicy, fruity versions which don't register too high on the alcohol scale. If you need a bottle of white then Aussie Chardonnay, Semillon or Verdelho, thoroughly chilled, will have enough texture and body to handle the heat. We love Clare Valley Riesling with chilli-laden seafood or chicken dishes, but keep the price sub-$20. Good Luck – and May the Force be with You!

Chinese The perennial problem when matching wine to Chinese food is that the second you and your mates see the menu everyone wants something different and, of course, everyone is an expert! So, in the end, everyone's dishes end up orbiting the table on that giant Lazy Susan, and your palate is sent into a wild spin of different flavours. Sweet-and-sour dishes slam into spicy ones, stir-fried dishes envelop into crispy chilli ones, while poor old plain-boiled food struggles for a break in the non-stop, kick-boxing, palate action. Jackie Chan would be proud of the mayhem, but your taste buds are crying for a break, so this means Chinese-friendly wines must be multi-skilled, pure, fruit-driven offerings with lashings of all-important, crisp acidity. Tannic, youthful reds and oaky, full-bodied whites are completely out-of-bounds-thugs. White grape varieties to consider (in unoaked form) are big brand (but not posh) Sauvignon Blanc, Semillon, Pinot Gris, and the sweet and sour flavours of Riesling and Verdelho (totally underrated from Oz, and Queensland registers its first mention here). Greco (Southern Italy), and bone dry Gewürztraminer are also worth a look. Reds are a little more difficult, as there are only a few truly juicy varieties, but Australian Merlot and – if you can find them – cheaper Californian Zinfandels are good bets. It is no surprise that Antipodean wines work well with this style of cooking as Asia is right on our doorstep. If you're hot-tailing it to the local Chinese joint and don't have time to think, tuck a bottle of ice cold Brown Brothers Cienna under your arm (hee hee – give 'em some sales!). Hao chi, Ganbei.

Side panel:
Sauv Blanc,
Semillon
Pinot Gris
Riesling
Verdelho
Gewürztraminer
Merlot

Chutney see 'Pâté' and 'Pork'

Corn see 'Vegetables'

Crayfish see 'Seafood'

Curry see 'Fish' and 'Indian'

Duck *Roast* or *pan-fried* duck is often served with fruit or fruity sauces, so you need to be prepared to balance this with a fruity wine. Reds are the call of the day here – Australian and New Zealand Pinot Noir is hard to go past (loads to choose from in **The Best Wines of 2009**), good quality Beaujolais, Italian Barbera or Negroamaro, Australian Chambourcin (OK, this is rare, but what a challenge!), lighter Californian Zinfandel and any other super-juicy, berry-drenched wines would do the business. *À l'orange* swings the colour firmly to white, but full-flavoured, juicy wines are still the vogue. Top Aussie or Alsatian (French) Riesling, or Pinot Gris (Tokay-Pinot Gris in Alsace), or top Aussie, Southern French or Rhône Viognier all have enough richness and texture to crack this dish, as do top-end Northern Italian white blends (look for the best estates in Alto Adige and Friuli). With *cherries*, 'village-level' red Burgundy (utilising the beautifully cherry-scented red grape Pinot Noir), top-notch Barbera from Piedmont, smart, new wave Reserva-level Rioja (Spain) and medium-weight but classy Zins from California are all excellent. The more robust dish of *confit de canard* demands meatier reds with backbone, grippy acidity and tannin to cut through the sauce and fat that makes this dish sing, like posh Cabernet Shiraz blends (come on, step up to the mark!) or French offerings from Bandol in Provence, the Languedoc-Roussillon or the southwest of France. For an unlikely but first-class combo, give *crispy aromatic duck* a whirl with chilled Aussie Chambourcin or Durif, or juicy, fruit-driven Californian Zinfandel (if you can line up a cheap one) – they are a dead-cert.

Pinot Noir
Chambourcin
Zinfandel
Riesling
Pinot Gris
Viognier
Cab Shiraz
Durif

Eggplant If served grilled, with *pesto* or *olive oil*, *garlic* and

| Sauv Blanc |
| Durif |
| Grenache blends |
| Merlot |

basil, as always you must identify the most dominant flavours in the dish. In both of these recipes they are the same – garlic and basil – so tackle them with dry Sauvignon Blanc (Marlborough or Adelaide Hills) or keen, white Italians like Verdicchio, Inzolia, Fiano or Falanghina. Plain aubergine dishes are fairly thin on the ground as these glossy, sleek, black beauties are often used within vegetarian recipes (like *ratatouille* or *caponata*). If cheese or meat (*moussaka*) is involved, these more dominant flavours take over from the eggplant, so light, youthful reds are required. Aussie Durif or Grenache blends, Southern Italian or Sicilian Primitivo, southern French Grenache-based blends, Chilean Carmenère and Spanish Garnacha are all good matches (and great value, too). Just make sure they are not too ponderous or alcohol-heavy. If the dish is 'hotter' or spicier, or the eggplant is *stuffed*, you will need a more feisty, characterful red, but don't be tempted by anything too heady (avoid tannic red grapes like Cabernet, Nebbiolo, Zinfandel, Malbec and Pinotage). *Imam bayildi*, the classic eggplant, onion, olive oil and tomato dish, is a winner with green-tinged reds from Western Australia's Great Southern, with their inbuilt freshness and chillability. If you're feeling multicultural, call in juicy, slightly chilled Chilean Merlot, youthful, bright purple Valpolicella, spicy Sardinian Cannonau or black-fruit-imbued Italians like Barbera d'Alba.

Eggs For *quiches, soufflés* or *light, savoury tarts* consider the

| Chardonnay |
| Rosé |
| Riesling |

main flavours (ham, cheese, herbs etc.) and their impact on the dish. Also, think about what you're eating with it – these dishes are always served with something else. Once you have nailed these flavours, unoaked (just say no to oak) or lightly oaked Chardonnay is a fair starting point, and you'll find good examples from cooler areas in WA and SA. Chablis (France) is the classic Old World starting point, but north-eastern Italian Chardonnays would also be spot on. *Omelettes, frittata* and *savoury pancakes* follow the same rules. For *fried* and *poached* eggs, look at the other ingredients involved. If combined with a salad, utilising stronger-flavoured ingredients, try Aussie rosé or Beaujolais, but if you'd rather go white, then no oak Chardonnay, Alsatian Riesling or a top Pinot Blanc would be just fine. For *quails' eggs*, see the wine styles suggested for *Appetisers*. Finally, *eggs Benedict* has an awful lot going on, from the muffin base, via the bacon or ham and ending with the ridiculously wicked hollandaise sauce. Youthful Côtes-du-Rhône (France) is the classic combination – and you'll need a magnum.

Enchiladas see 'Mexican'

Fajitas see 'Mexican'

Figs
Riesling

The only entry to feature in both this section and the dessert category, if you are anything like us then these are the most decadently irresistible of all fruits, with exotic flavours lurking beneath their silky exterior. Served with serious ham (Italian) or in a salad, they manage to hold their own carnal flavours despite coming up against ingredients as combative as Gorgonzola and balsamic vinegar. Clearly these are the dominant flavours, not the figs, but if you really want to know what a fig wants to be drunk with there is only one answer (and the same variety appears later on in the second entry) – Riesling, made with passion, knowing and all encompassing sensitivity. Figs are, after all, the most erotic of ingredients and they must be rewarded with the most exotic and sensual of grape varieties.

Fish see also 'Anchovies' and 'Seafood'. The flavour intensity of fish depends not only on the sort of fish you are cooking but also, crucially, on how it is cooked. The general rule is the milder the flavour, the lighter the white wine, and the richer the flavour, the heavier the white wine – we know this is obvious, but it is worth stating. Fish cooked in red wine is one of the few

Pinot Gris
Marsanne
Semillon
Chardonnay
Riesling
Viognier
Sauv Blanc
Albariño
Rosé
Sem Sauv Blanc
Roussanne
Gamay
Gewürztraminer
Champagne
Sparkling White

exceptions to this white-dominated section, as a light, fresh red would simply meld better with the sauce. From heady Australian or New Zealand Pinot Gris, plump Marsanne or whip-cracking Hunter Valley Semillon, Bianco de Custoza and Soave (Italy), Austrian Grüner Veltliner, Sauvignon de Touraine (Loire, France), white Burgundy (Mâcon, Rully, Pouilly-Fuissé, Meursault and so on), fine Californian Chardonnay, zesty Jurançon Sec, to any aromatic Riesling or Viognier – the opportunities are literally endless. This is why there are more wines listed in this category than any other in this book. Just remember that poaching and steaming are gentler, non-taste-altering ways of cooking fish, while grilling, searing, frying and roasting all impart distinctive charred or caramelised nuances to the flesh. Also consider what you are cooking the fish with; check through your recipe for strongly flavoured ingredients, such as lemon, capers, balsamic vinegar, flavoured olive oil and pungent herbs. Often, the finer the piece of fish, the more money you should chuck at the wine. If you are spending up on the finest fish, you should endeavour to complete the picture by splashing out on a worthy bottle of top-shelf Aussie or New Zealand Chardonnay or white Burgundy. Failing that, for under $30 you could pick up a top Australian Semillon, Eden Valley or Clare Valley Riesling, Adelaide Hills Chardonnay, South African Chardonnay, Riesling from Alsace, posh Lugana or Gavi from Italy, dry white Graves (Bordeaux), white Rhône wines or trendy Spanish Albariño to go with these fish.

John Dory, Sea Bream, Mullet and *Skate* all enjoy these styles of wine, while *Swordfish* and *Hake* can take on slightly weightier whites (or even a fresh, light red, such as Beaujolais). *Salmon* (poached or grilled) also likes Chardonnay, whether it is from the Old or New World, but give oaky styles a wide berth. The

starters and main courses 191

delicate sweetness of *Whiting* is perfectly partnered to young, fresh Clare Valley Riesling. *Barramundi* and the *Dories* deserve nothing less than a posh Chardonnay – look for low oak, cool climate styles. Not to be outclassed, the *Emperors* are suited to Semillon (reach for top shelf Hunter Valley), but *Garfish* does not care much for what you drink with it, provided it is wet and cold. *Coral Trout* loves Riesling and the all-time classic Chablis. But, for an especially wicked combo, try to track down the unusually scented, dry French wine, Jurançon Sec. Margaret River Chardonnay is the perfect thing with *Jewfish* (*Dhufish*), assuming you're living it up on the pier at Fremantle (cheers!) – and still your best bet if you're not. *Flathead* demands a change of pace to young Viognier or Chardonnay Viognier blends. For *Spanish Mackerel*, set yourself a mission to track down Matt Gant's *First Drop* Albariño (and if you find it in retail, tell us immediately!). *Fish cakes*, especially proper ones with a high salmon content, go wonderfully with dry Riesling, richer Sauvignon Blancs or fresh Semillons, particularly if you are keen on a generous spoonful of tartare sauce (the grapes can handle it). The same rules apply for Thai fish cakes with sweet chilli and coriander. *Red Mullet* (get a haircut) has more than enough character to cope with rosé wines, making a beautiful pink partnership between plate and glass.

Sauvignon is the grape to enjoy with *fish 'n' chips* because it can handle the batter (sometimes made with beer), and it shines with *fish pie* – poshest partnership being the Loire all-stars Pouilly-Fumé or Sancerre. If you fancy a trip across the ditch then Marlborough in New Zealand has to be the starting point for fans of this zesty grape, with South Africa being next, and our very own Margaret River pulling out the best Sem/Sauv blends outside of Bordeaux.

Fish soups and *stews* need more weight in the glass, and one of the finest matches is white Rhône (France), made from Marsanne and Roussanne, or Viognier. Aussie Marsanne or Pinot Gris would also be great options. *Sardines* require masses of perky acidity to cut through their oily flesh, and once again Sauvignon Blanc is the winner. Having said this, don't forget poor old Muscadet or Italian Pinot Grigio, Arneis, Verdicchio or Gavi. Spanish Albariño, French Aligoté and even light reds, like Gamay, would also be smashing. *Canned Tuna* just needs unoaked, dry white wine – boring. However, *Albacore*, the finer, paler version, is more delicately flavoured so take care not to swamp it. *Fresh Tuna*, seared and served rare, desperately craves juicy, fresh, baby-light reds and chilled rosés (you could sneak a Sauvignon in, if you wish). *Brandade de morue* (salt cod), with its garlic and oil components, can stand up to whites with a little more soul. Albariño, from Galicia in Spain, is a perfect choice. However, Penedès whites and even light rosés are all within its grasp. *Herrings, Kippers* and *Rollmops* all have a more robust texture and aroma thanks to the curing process. Once again, dry whites and rosés work well, but steer clear of oaked whites, as the pungent barrel nuances will overshadow the subtleties of the dish.

Smoked eel is often served with crème fraîche, and cream is always a little problematic for wine, but look to Australia's own bone-dry, world-class Rieslings, Austrian Riesling or Grüner Veltliner, top end Italian Pinot Grigio or almost any dry white wine from Alsace. These will all relish the challenge. *Smoked Salmon* is perfect with Gewürztraminer, whether it is home grown, or from New Zealand, Alsace or Chile. Just make sure you buy a 'bone-dry', not 'off-dry' version. The scent and tropical nature of Gewürz works amazingly well, but so does Viognier and even Canadian Pinot Blanc. Don't forget Champagne, top-end Tasmanian or Californian sparkling wine, particularly if serving blinis topped with smoked salmon and caviar. *Smoked Trout* or *Smoked Mackerel pâté* is a challenge – fishy, smoky and creamy flavours all in one dish. Cool climate Victorian Riesling, Hunter Valley Semillon, Adelaide Hills Sauvignon Blanc or Pinot Gris, southern French Viognier, lighter Alsatian Riesling and Pinot Blanc are all perfect matches. Lastly, *curries* or *Asian* fish dishes often sport spices, such as turmeric, ginger and chilli, so turn to two of our favourite saviour white grapes for a solution – New World Sauvignon Blanc's supreme confidence and Australia's own world class, mind-blowing array of Rieslings – these are all stunning value – yum.

Foie gras see 'Pâté'

Fondue see 'Cheese (cooked)'

French Visits to France rank among our favourite past-times after eating and drinking, perhaps because of all of the eating and drinking that invariably goes on while we're there! At home, French cuisine covers a myriad of dishes and styles, so you'll have to look up the specifics in this section to find that perfect wine match. You'll note that having an English co-author, we have not left any stone unturned in the French kitchen. If you're en route to a French BYO, take a rapide swerve past the best bottle shop you can find. You're looking for a bottle each of Yarra Valley Chardonnay and 2002 Cabernet (this is a cool vintage and the wines are more elegant). Between them they'll navigate their way through most options on the French menu. Trade up to Margaret River on both fronts if you're feeling loaded, or flick through our **Best Wines of 2009** for a bargain duo if you're not. If your detour has landed you at the local drive-through with exactly seven wines to choose from, pick the best Aussie or New Zealand Chardonnay and Cabernet that you can afford. Bon Appetit!

Chardonnay
Cab Sauv

Game All flighted game, including *pheasant, quail, guinea fowl, woodcock, teal, grouse, snipe, wild duck* and *partridge* adore the majestic red grape Pinot Noir. This means red Burgundy is our first choice, with New Zealand, Tasmania, Victoria, California and Oregon somewhere in the pack behind the leader. The longer the bird is hung, the more mature the wine required (this can mean ten- or even twenty-year-

Pinot Noir
Shiraz
Nebbiolo
Zinfandel
Cab Sauv

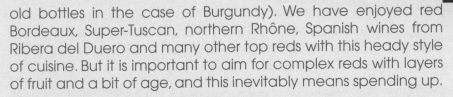

old bottles in the case of Burgundy). We have enjoyed red Bordeaux, Super-Tuscan, northern Rhône, Spanish wines from Ribera del Duero and many other top reds with this heady style of cuisine. But it is important to aim for complex reds with layers of fruit and a bit of age, and this inevitably means spending up.

Jugged hare, the favourite food match of Aussie wine writers, it seems, often uses port and/or redcurrant jelly in the recipe, so a pretty serious red wine is needed. More structured Australian Shiraz (Clare, McLaren Vale, Heathcote or Barossa Valley) and new-style Italian Piemontese reds made from Nebbiolo or Nebbiolo/Barbera blends would have the stuffing, as would Zinfandel from California or South African Shiraz and Pinotage. If you can track it down, one slightly cheaper and worthy source of full-bodied red is the Douro Valley in Portugal – not only would you have a meaty wine, but it would also be in perfect synergy if you've used port in the recipe (the Douro Valley is the home of port). *Rabbit*, as well as being a less athletic version of hare, is also less pungent and has lighter-coloured flesh so, although big reds are essential, they don't need to be quite as powerful as those suggested for hare. The classic combo of *rabbit with mustard and bacon* packs a pungent flavour punch, so aim for swarthy bottles of red with feisty tannins and a youthful, purple hue – turn up the volume, pull out a big old Bavarian work from the Barossa, scribble out the alcohol on the label so no one knows, book a taxi in advance and go for it! If you're not in the mood for such antics, opt for Chianti, Carmignano, Vino Nobile di Montepulciano (all from Tuscany), Bandol (from Provence), Lirac, Vacqueyras and Gigondas (from the southern Rhône), Argentinean Malbec, South African Cabernet and Shiraz, or smarter Chilean Cabernet blends.

Wild boar favours rich, brooding red wines and, depending on the dish, you could choose any of the aforementioned reds but, this time, add a few more of the finest of all Italian wines – Brunello di Montalcino, Barbaresco and Barolo. The only problem is you might need a lottery win to buy a bottle. *Venison* loves reds, and any bottle in this section would do, including top Australian Cabernet Sauvignon and some of the better New Zealand Hawke's Bay reds.

Finally, *game pie,* served cold, behaves like cold chicken and ham pie (see 'Chicken'). If served hot, open any wine suggested for steak and kidney pie (see 'Beef').

Garlic *Roast* garlic tends to emasculate fine wines so, if you are partial to lobbing a few bulbs in the oven, keep the wine spend down and follow the main dish's theme. Garlic *prawns, mushrooms* and *snails* all need aromatic, bone-dry, rapier-sharp Sauvignon Blanc. Watch out for *Aïoli (garlic mayonnaise)* because you'll get a shock if your wine isn't up to it. Once again, Sauvignon Blanc can provide you with a shoulder to cry on, but you will have to find a bottle with a lot of character and vivacity – Marlborough in New Zealand or SA's Adelaide Hills are probably the best answers. (For *chicken Kiev* see 'Chicken'.)

German Frau Stelzer has kept us honest by making sure that

Riesling
Sauv Blanc
Grenache blends

Deutschland is well-represented throughout this chapter, so hoist up your lederhosen, grab your wurst and flick to the entry you're looking for. If you're headed to Hahndorf to indulge yourself, grab a bottle of Adelaide Hills Sauvignon or Eden Valley Riesling and a Barossa Grenache blend on the way – sehr gut! Who says you need Bavarian lager for a good time?

Goose The best wines for roast goose lie somewhere between

Pinot Noir
Chardonnay
Riesling

those suited to game and those for chicken. In short, this means smooth cherry-scented Aussie or NZ Pinot Noir and lighter red Burgundies in the red camp, and big, rich, sultry Chards and Rieslings in the white. If you can afford it, step up to Alsatian Grand Cru Riesling – heaven.

busty Viognier and lusty Chardonnay

Goulash see 'Beef'

Greek This would be the chance for dry Greek whites to shine,

Sauv Blanc if only they made it to our shores. Instead, look for New Zealand Sauvignon Blanc, green, tangy WA Sauvignon, any Tassie whites, dry Aussie, Spanish or Portuguese Muscat, Pinot Blanc or Sylvaner from Alsace or Argentinean Torrontés. Albariño from north-western Spain also works well. If you must go for reds, keep the budget and the temperature down.

Guacamole see 'Avocado'

Ham Pinot and rosé are the order of the day for our porky

Pinot Noir friend. We should be drinking a lot more rosé
Rosé in Australia and New Zealand, but the rules
Merlot are the same as always: keep it dry, and keep
Viognier it cheap. If your trotters lead you abroad,
Chardonnay smart Cru Beaujolais, Chilean Merlot or
Riesling Carmenère, youthful Spanish Tempranillos,
Verdelho Italian Nero d'Avola, Montepulciano or
Cabernet Franc Negroamaro and youthful, inexpensive South
Pinot Gris African Merlot also have the essential
Semillon juiciness to complement a glorious ham. The golden rule is to avoid any tannic or heavily acidic reds – stick to more mellow styles. There is a splinter group for whom heady whites also work – busty Viognier and lusty Chardonnay would do the task well. *Parma ham and melon, prosciutto, jamón Serrano* and *pata negra* all like dry Australian or German Riesling (Mosel, Rheingau or Pfalz), many of the aromatic whites from Trentino, Alto Adige and Friuli (northern Italy), and Verdejo or lightly oaked Viura from Rueda (Spain). *Honey-roast ham* needs mouth-filling, textural, bone-dry whites like 'dry' Muscat, Viognier, Verdelho and Riesling. You'll find plenty of home-grown options, as well as French alternatives from Alsace, the Rhône Valley and from the vast array of terrific

starters and main courses 197

French Country wines (and grab some ripe figs to eat alongside – so exotic and erotic!).

Ham hock with lentils or boiled Jersey potatoes and beetroot (or garden peas) is a treat with posh, dry rosé, and there are a fair few out there. Seek out Grenache rosés from McLaren Vale or the Barossa or head to the southern Rhône, richer examples of Sancerre rosé or Garnachas from Spain. *Smoked ham* has a fairly strong aroma and lingering flavour, so older Aussie Rieslings would be exact, as would Tokay-Pinot Gris and young Vendange Tardive level Rieslings from Alsace . If you favour red wine then choose a Merlot, a Cabernet Franc (from Australia or the Loire in France) or a Beaujolais, and chill it a degree or two to perk up its acidity. *Ham steak* (sling the grim addition of pineapple or peaches) makes a neat partnership with oily, unoaked whites. The world-class Rieslings from Australia's Clare Valley, Eden Valley, Tasmania and Frankland would be delicious, as would all Alsatian wines and most dry German Rieslings. New Zealand Pinot Gris would also be fantastic. Semillon rarely gets the call up for a specific dish, but versions from the Hunter Valley and dry white Bordeaux (both with a smattering of oak) are simply stunning with it, too.

Hare see 'Game', 'Rabbit', 'Terrines'

Indian My (Matthew's) Indian food and wine matching career is taking off. In fact it is now nothing short of a fully-fledged passion. When I designed and wrote the wine list for the re-launch of top London Indian restaurants Chutney Mary, Amaya and Veeraswamy it was clear to me that unoaked or mildly oaked whites were to be the driving force in my selection. Smooth, juicy rosés were also essential, as were overtly fruit-driven reds, avoiding any that were noticeably tannic. The surprise came when I made the final selection and found that Italy, Australia, South Africa and New Zealand had claimed the lion's share of the list. There were a few wines from other countries but virtually no classics like red Bordeaux, Burgundy or

Rosé
Pinot Grigio
Sauv Blanc
Riesling
Viognier
Verdelho
Gewürztraminer
Pinot Noir
Merlot
Grenache
Zinfandel
Sparkling White
Champagne

Rhône. Shock horror! This just proves that, depending on the style of cuisine, a wine list can be balanced, eclectic and hopefully thoroughly exciting, without relying on France. The grape varieties or styles of wine that go particularly well with *curries* and all variety of Indian food are: whites – Pinot Grigio/Gris, Sauvignon Blanc, Riesling, Viognier, Verdelho, light Gewürztraminers, Verdicchio, Pinot Bianco, Fiano, Torrontés, and Albariño; reds – Pinot Noir, Merlot, Grenache (and Spanish Garnacha), Beaujolais (Gamay), Zinfandel, Barbera, Valpolicella and Negroamaro. Other styles that work well include rich rosé, Aussie sparklers, Prosecco, Asti (with desserts), rosé Champagne and good-quality ruby port. Your all-purpose, last-minute options for an Indian restaurant should be a bottle of Eden Valley Riesling and a posh Barossa Valley Rosé.

Italian There's not much to report here that you won't find under 'Pizza,' 'Pasta' or any other dish you're

Semillon
Sauv Blanc
Cab Shiraz
Rosé

looking for. If you're half way to Giuseppe's for a feast of the first order, take a detour (pronto!) via your nearest bottle shop, because he won't be happy unless you rock up with at least a couple of bottles. Your first target is a lean, mean, young, flavoursome (but not floral) white. One-year-old Hunter Semillon or Adelaide Hills Sauv Blanc would be perfecto. Then you're looking for a solid quality Cabernet Shiraz blend (our **Best Wines of 2009** is burgeoning with epic examples at every price). And, while you're at it, pick up a dry rosé as a backup – always just the thing for inter-course (grin).

Japanese *sushi* is a strange, but utterly delicious dish to match wine to. Surely green tea or sake (yuk) would be more appropriate? Well, we beg to differ – sparkling wines and

Sparkling White
Champagne
Sauv Blanc
Pinot Gris
Riesling
Semillon
Rosé
Shiraz
Merlot
Zinfandel
Pinot Noir
Sparkling Rosé

Champagne are a treat with the best sushi, especially bone dry cuvées – 'Ultra Brut', 'non dosage' or Zero Dosage (see page 41 of **The Best Wines of 2009**). Not surprisingly, the ever-ready Sauvignon Blanc grape is there, waiting in the wings to save you and the bill, too. Perky Pinot Gris and Riesling from Australia and New Zealand are also a great idea. You could always look to zesty, unoaked Italian whites for joy – Vernaccia, Arneis and Gavi are all ideal. Similar rules apply to *Tempura*, with light, fresh, dry whites the order of the day. A super-cool 2006 or 2007 Hunter Semillon would be a treat.

Teriyaki dishes are a nightmare to match wine to, though, as the sweetness and fruitiness in the glossy soy and saké glaze is incredibly flavour dominant on the palate. This year we have again lined up for you the perfect *Teriyaki* wine to handle this challenge with consummate ease – Charlie Melton's Rose of Virginia (page 99). If you're not man enough for ROV, you'll have to settle on lighter, modern Shiraz or Merlot from South Australia, Zinfandel or rich Pinot Noir from California, super-ripe Chambourcin, and Nero d'Avola or Negroamaro from Sicily – but chill for effect. Our picks for multi-talented wines for Japanese cuisine are Tasmanian sparkling whites, sparkling rosés and sparkling reds (only joking on the last one!).

You will always be offered a blob of nuclear green matter called **wasabi** with your sushi. We're afraid wasabi is a stealthy, committed, highly trained and silent wine assassin – thank God it's green so at least you can see it coming!

Kangaroo Skippy bounds in close to Bambi and Babe in the taste game (unless it's overcooked when, like anything, it tastes like chicken). Kangaroo can be a bit chewy, as it's not like true

blanched brontosaurus

Junk food *What on earth* should you drink with a *hamburger, cheeseburger, chicken nuggets,* bargain bucket of *fried off-cuts,* blanched brontosaurus or any of the other palate-knackering, mass-produced, fast-food delicacies? A high-sugar, monstrously carbonated, brain-banging **soft drink**, of course, for that all-encompassing explosive gut/nauseous cold-sweat feeling that you look forward to enjoying ten minutes after racing this *demonic* cuisine down your cakehole. If you are seriously considering opening a bottle of wine (*hello?*), you'll have to wrestle this **toxic waste** back into its day-glo polystyrene container and haul it back to your cave. Now you've got to warm it up again – do you bother? Course not, you're either starving or distinctly worse for wear, or both. But what should you uncork? Entry level Aussie Shiraz/Cabernet (albeit a sacrilege of our most noble blend), or, better still, Grenache/Shiraz (nothing too righteous here), Chardonnay or white blend (just keep the price down, for goodness' sake, you don't want to regret opening it in the morning). If you're well organised you'll always keep an 'emergency' white in the fridge and a red in the cupboard for times like these. That way you can't muck up and open a serious bottle by mistake. Either way, while you are guzzling, Dante is hastily reworking his epic, inventing yet another circle of hell for your internal organs to slumber in overnight.

Coke
Shiraz Cab
Grenache Shiraz
Chardonnay

game (more like an oversized rat with a tail that overtook its body on the evolutionary ladder). Perhaps it wouldn't be so tough if it were hung like venison? But we wouldn't know – never got close enough to see. On the wine front, scale it down a bit and look for crunchy, fresh, GSMs, youthful Victorian Shiraz or Yarra Valley Cabernet. Consider carefully the spices that you are likely to be up against, as the intense flavours of the meat are often married with the likes of tamarind

Grenache Blends
Shiraz
Cab Sauv

starters and main courses 201

Wine emergency!

You have exactly **29 seconds** to *nail* the perfect bottle. — **What do you do?** —

You pull out **Taste 2009**, flick straight to the centre-fold thrust it at the bottle shop attendant and tell them you'll take a bottle of *everything* on the list, please.

This crucial **emergency** guide is your **easy ticket** to

The Best Wines of 2009 under $20

sparkling wines

Pepperton Goodwyn Brut Cuvée NV $8
Jacob's Creek Sparkling Rosé NV $13
Jacob's Creek Sparkling Shiraz NV $14
Wolf Blass Red Label Chardonnay Pinot Noir NV $14
Orlando Trilogy Cuvée Brut Pinot Noir Chardonnay Pinot Meunier NV $15
Orlando Trilogy Sparkling Rosé NV $16
Taltarni Brut 2006 $20

white wines

Lark Hill Auslese Riesling 2008 $20
Oxford Landing Sauvignon Blanc 2008 $8
Hardys Nottage Hill Chardonnay 2007 $10
Jacob's Creek Classic Sauvignon Blanc 2008 $10
Lindemans Bin 65 Chardonnay 2007 $10
McWilliam's Hanwood Estate Chardonnay 2008 $10
Mike Press Wines Adelaide Hills Sauvignon Blanc 2008 $11
De Bortoli Windy Peak Sauvignon Blanc Semillon 2008 $13
De Bortoli Windy Peak Chardonnay 2007 $13.50
Peter Lehmann Barossa Riesling 2008 $13.50
Possums The Springs Unwooded Chardonnay 2008 $13.50
Bleasdale Langhorne Creek Chardonnay 2008 $14
Leasingham Magnus Riesling 2008 $14
St Hallett Poacher's Blend Semillon Sauvignon Blanc 2008 $14

Tahbilk Marsanne 2008 $14.50
Jacob's Creek Reserve Sauvignon Blanc 2008 $15
Tyrrell's Wines Verdelho 2008 $15
Willow Bridge Estate Sauvignon Blanc Semillon 2008 $15.50
Alkoomi Wines Unwooded Chardonnay 2008 $16
Jim Barry Watervale Riesling 2008 $16
Wirra Wirra Scrubby Rise Sauvignon Blanc Semillon Viognier 2008 $16
Chapel Hill Verdelho 2008 $17
De Bortoli Yarra Valley Gulf Station Chardonnay 2007 $17
McWilliams Mount Pleasant Elizabeth Hunter Valley Semillon 2008 $17
Ad Hoc "Hen and Chicken" Chardonnay 2007 $18
Ad Hoc Wall Flower Riesling 2008 $18
De Iuliis Show Reserve Hunter Valley Verdelho 2008 $18
Devil's Corner Tasmania Sauvignon Blanc 2008 $18
Peter Lehmann Eden Valley Riesling '08 $18
Bremerton Verdelho 2008 $19
Leo Buring Eden Valley Riesling 2008 $19
Nepenthe Sauvignon Blanc 2008 $19
Penfolds Thomas Hyland Chardonnay 2007 $19
Pewsey Vale Eden Valley Riesling 2008 $19
Audrey Wilkinson Semillon 2008 $20
Fox Gordon Princess Fiano 2008 $20
Linda Domas Vis à Vis Viognier 2008 $20
St Hallett Eden Valley Riesling 2008 $20
Tempus Two Zenith Hunter Valley Semillon 2008 $20

rosé wines

Casillero del Diablo Shiraz Rosé 2008 $14.50
De Bortoli Wines Windy Peak Cabernet Rosé 2008 $15
Hardys Pruner's Cup Shiraz Cabernet Rosé 2008 $15
Bremerton Racy Rosé 2008 $16

See dust jacket for complete quick-reference pocket guide

Melody Majella Coonawarra Rosé 2008 $16

Trevor Jones Barossa Valley Cébo Rosé 2008 $16

Coriole Nebbiolo Rosé 2008 $18

Linda Domas Shotbull Rosé 2008 $18

Shelmerdine Yarra Valley Pinot Noir Rosé 2008 $19

Skillogalee Cabernet Malbec Rosé 2008 $19

Paxton Shiraz Rosé 2008 $20

red wines

McWilliams Inheritance Shiraz Merlot 2007 $6.50

Pepperton Estate Goodwyn Shiraz Cabernet 2007 $8

Jacob's Creek Cabernet Merlot 2006 $10

Jacob's Creek Grenache Shiraz 2007 $10

Lindemans Bin 40 Merlot 2007 $10

McWilliam's Hanwood Estate Cabernet Sauvignon 2007 $10

McPherson Cabernet Sauvignon 2007 $11

McPherson Merlot 2007 $11

Mike Press Adelaide Hills Cabernet Sauvignon 2007 $11

Mike Press Adelaide Hills Shiraz 2007 $11

Yalumba Y Series Shiraz Viognier 2007 $11.50

Kemeny's Hidden Label KHL1028 Barossa Valley Reserve Grenache Shiraz

Mourvèdre 2006 $12

Penfolds Rawson's Retreat Cabernet Sauvignon 2007 $12

Victorian Alps Winery Tobacco Road Cabernet Sauvignon 2006 $13

De Bortoli Windy Peak Shiraz Viognier 2007 $13.50

BullAnt Langhorne Creek Shiraz 2006 $14

Casillero del Diablo Cabernet Sauvignon 2007 $14

De Bortoli Windy Peak Pinot Noir 2008 $14

St Hallett Gamekeepers Reserve 2007 $14

Penfolds Koonunga Hill Shiraz Cabernet 2007 $14.50

2Up Shiraz by Kangarilla Road 2007 $15

Hardys The Sage Shiraz Sangiovese 2007 $15

Taltarni T Series Shiraz 2005 $15.50

De Bortoli Gulf Station Yarra Valley Pinot Noir 2008 $16

Peter Lehmann The Seven Surveys Shiraz Grenache Mourvèdre 2007 $16

Wirra Wirra Scrubby Rise Shiraz Cabernet Sauvignon Petit Verdot 2007 $16

De Bortoli Gulf Station Shiraz Viognier 2007 $17

Bremerton Tamblyn Cabernet Shiraz Malbec Merlot 2006 $18

Pertaringa Understudy McLaren Vale Cabernet Petit Verdot 2006 $18

Scotchmans Hill Swan Bay Victoria Shiraz 2006 $18

Willunga 100 Cabernet Shiraz 2006 $18

Aramis Vineyards Shiraz Cabernet Sauvignon 2006 $19

Braided River Marlborough Pinot Noir 2007 $19

Kangarilla Road Cabernet Sauvignon 2006 $19

Neagles Rock Misery Grenache Shiraz 2007 $19

Scotchmans Hill Swan Bay Pinot Noir 2007 $19

Yalumba Barossa Shiraz Viognier 2006 $19

Anvers Razorback Road 2005 $20

Kangarilla Road Sangiovese 2007 $20

Kilikanoon Killerman's Run Cabernet Sauvignon 2006 $20

Kirrihill Cabernet Sauvignon Clare Valley 2006 $20

Lake Breeze Langhorne Creek Grenache 2007 $20

Penley Condor Shiraz Cabernet 2006 $20

Wyndham Estate George Wyndham Shiraz Cabernet 2005 $20

Yalumba "The Scribbler" Cabernet Shiraz 2006 $20

sweet and fortified wines

Brown Brothers Orange Muscat & Flora 2008 $12

Innocent Bystander Victoria Moscato 2008 $12

Brown Brothers Moscato 2008 $15

La Gitana Manzanilla di San Lucar Hidalgo Sherry NV $15

Chalk Hill Moscato 2008 $18

Wirra Wirra Mrs Wigley Moscato 2008 $18

Dutschke Ivy Blondina Moscato 2008 $19

Kay Brothers Amery Vineyards McLaren Vale Moscato 2008 $20

and chilli, cardamom, cumin seed or coriander seed.

Kebabs see 'Lamb'

Kidneys

Shiraz

Lambs' kidneys tend to absorb a fair amount of the flavour from the ingredients in which they are cooked, so follow these themes. Mustard is often used, so keep the reds firm, chunky and with a lick of perky, palate-refreshing acidity – Mornington Peninsula, Yarra Valley or Geelong Shiraz, Chianti, Barbera (both Italian), Rioja, Toro, Navarra (all Spanish), Languedoc and the Rhône Valley (both French) would all be worth a punt. (For *steak and kidney pie* see 'Beef'.)

Lamb

Cab Sauv
Pinot Noir
Shiraz Cabernet
Shiraz
Merlot
Rosé
Chardonnay

Red Bordeaux is, strictly speaking, the classic combination with *roast lamb* or *lamb chops*. However, reds from nearby Bergerac or Madiran and, further afield, Australia's Shiraz and Cabernet blends, Burgundy, South Africa's smarter Pinotage and Shiraz, California's Merlot, Spain's Rioja, and Argentina and Chile's Cabernets and Merlots are all in with a very solid shout. Keep the wine firmly in the middleweight division and you will do well. You could, of course, go bonkers on the price or stick within a tight budget, as lamb is less particular than beef or game. The way it is cooked, though, should definitely influence your final choice. If cooked *pink*, the range of suitable wines is enormous (any of the above). If *well done*, then a fruitier style of red should be served, as lamb tends to dry out and it needs resuscitation, and this is where Australia's reds really come into their own. Cabernet from McLaren Vale (from a cool vintage like 2002), Clare (from a good producer – see page 268) or Coonawarra (stick close to our picks because you don't want it to get too eucalypty here – like chewing on a gum leaf). Watch out for gravy and mint sauce, as an abundance of either could test the wine if it is not forewarned.

enlightening incarnations

Lamb pot roast and *casserole* tend to be a little richer in flavour than a chop or roast lamb because of the gravy. Again, don't spend too much on the wine, as entry-level Aussies or authentic Languedoc or southern Rhône (both French) reds will do fine. *Shepherd's pie* is incredibly easy to match to red wine. In fact, just open whatever you feel like – if it's red and wet, it will be spot on – a no brainer. Plain *lamb shank* is another relatively easy dish to match to red wine, with young, fresh (read: not room temperature) Clare Shiraz and Langhorne Creek Shiraz topping the list. Decant them if you have time, but a slight chill is more important than air at this point. Inexpensive European examples from Portugal, Spain, Italy and France also offer enough acidity and structure to cut through the juicy, mouth-watering meat. *Moussaka*, with cheese, onion, oregano and eggplant, is altogether different. Lighter, fruit-driven reds such as Aussie or New Zealand Pinot Noir, inexpensive workhorses from Toro in Spain, or cheaper South American reds will work well. *Stews* like *navarin* (with vegetables), *Irish stew, cassoulet* or *hot pot* all have broader shoulders when it comes to reds. Medium-weight, scented Aussie Shiraz (McLaren Vale, Pemberton or Yarra Valley) would suit these dishes. From further afield, beefier southern French examples would be perfect, as well as Malbec from Argentina or Carmenère from Chile. *Cold roast lamb* follows the same rules as cold slices of beef and, to a certain extent, ham in that fruity, light reds and juicy medium- to full-bodied whites work pretty well. Rosé or Beaujolais, served cool, but not cold, is a great partner, while Chardonnay in any of the following guises would augment the dish – try medium-priced white Burgundy, Chardonnay from Margaret River, Adelaide Hills or Yarra Valley or Nelson or Marlborough (New Zealand), or lighter South African and Chilean styles. Also, don't forget proper manly rosés – they are such an underrated drink, especially with cold cuts.

Lastly, *kebabs*, one of lamb's most exciting and gastronomically enlightening incarnations whether you've lovingly marinated and skewered the meat yourself or just adoringly watched it being shaved off that elephantine mass of meat in a kebab shop. We suspect you'd struggle to balance a kebab and a goblet of wine while stumbling down the street after a late-night gig. But on the off chance that you make it home before tucking into this taste sensation, then a glass of big brand, ten-buck Aussie Chardonnay would be a welcome break between mouthfuls, and not something you'd be too upset about having opened in the cold, stark light of a new day.

Lasagne see 'Pasta'

Liver *Calves' liver with sage* (an old-fashioned but ever-so-tasty

Pinot Noir
Shiraz
Cabernet Franc
Cab Sauv

retro dish) needs medium-weight reds with prominent acidity. The texture of medium rare liver is relatively delicate, but the flavour is rich and pure, and the wine's acidity cuts through this intensity with style. It's time to call on high acid, fruit-driven wines like Tassie Pinots (although they're probably a bit wasted here), Central Victorian Shiraz or any pretentiously labelled, heavy bottled, big brand red that you can land for under $20 (but give it a light chill to bring it back to earth). Loire reds from France made from Cabernet Franc are a perfect match; Saumur-Champigny, Chinon, St Nicolas de Bourgueil and Bourgueil would be a snap. Personally we wouldn't look any further, but if you need a larger choice then head to Northern Italy to some well known and less so names – Valpolicella, Teroldego from Trentino, Lagrein, Marzemino and Cabernet (Franc or Sauvignon – sometimes Italians don't specify which you're getting). These all have the required fruit richness with the balancing acidity, freshness and grip needed for this task. *Liver and bacon* needs a touch more spice in a red wine, but not much more weight, so spend a little more on your Central Victorian Shiraz or move to a warmer part of France or Italy (head further south or look for a hot vintage). Red Bordeaux and Chianti would be ideal, but this is likely to push the price up a few dollars.

Lobster see 'Seafood'

Marron see 'Seafood'

Meat Balls (see 'Pasta'), *pies* (see 'Beef') and *loaf* (see 'Terrines')

Mexican *Fajitas, enchiladas, tortillas, quesadillas, tacos, burritos* – loaded with chilli and salsa – lead to the consumption of copious quantities of lime-stuffed (leave it out) beer, which has excellent thirst-quenching properties but bugger all flavour, or tequila, which has bugger all thirst-quenching properties and enough flavour to take out any amigo (one tequila, two tequila, three tequila, floor!). A glass of wine is a much safer call, but you must go in search of ripe, fruity, chillable red grapes like cheapie Aussie Cabernet or Merlot, Nero d'Avola, Negroamaro and Primitivo (from southern Italy), Carmenère and Merlot from Chile, inexpensive Zinfandel from California to cool you down and smooth out your battle-scarred palate. As for whites – they are likely to get bashed up no matter what you choose, so this is a great excuse to pull out that bottle of boring white that you were given last Christmas and haven't been game to face, or find an inexpensive, mildly oaked Chardonnay or Semillon, and chill it down to sub zero. Watch out for refried bean reflux – good luck.

Cab Sauv
Merlot
Zinfandel
Chardonnay
Semillon

Interestingly, *Cajun* cooking follows a similar pattern to Mexican food when it comes to wine styles, as cayenne, paprika, oregano, garlic and thyme all cook up a storm and need to be tempered with similarly juicy whites and reds. Your all-purpose companions for your next voyage to Jose's or Pepe's are Pinot Noir (only joking), ripe, juicy, inexpensive Cabernet (the sort of wine you think you'll never enjoy, but secretly love) and anything white (the cheaper the better).

Minestrone see 'Soups'

Mixed grill

Grenache Blends

A vital part of every real man's cooking repertoire, mixed grill is the dish of choice for superheroes the world over. You need a rich, robust red and there is nothing more macho than a feisty southern Rhône (from a top performing producer) or its Aussie counterpart, a South Aussie 'GSM' blend (Grenache, Shiraz and Mourvèdre in any combo – we are still waiting to see the first maker brave enough to market an MSG!).

Moroccan/North African

**Sauv Blanc
Grenache
Albariño
Viognier
Pinot Grigio
Tempranillo
Rosé**

The most important factor to remember when matching this intriguing style of food with wine, is the level of spice involved in the dish. Once you have gauged this, you can do one of two things – either choose fresh, clean, neutral whites which sit in the background and let the food do most of the talking, or go head-to-head with the flavours and drink a stunning aromatic white. Sauvignon Blanc from Australia, New Zealand, Chile or South Africa has the herbal, lime-juice intensity to face the challenge. In the red department, Barossa Valley Bush Vine Grenache, with its pure red-berry fruit and herbal, smoky nose is a good bet. Heading for the Mediterranean, Spain, Italy and France are the most obvious and geographically closest ports of call, and within these three great wine nations, our favourite aromatic white styles would be Albariño (from Galicia in north-western Spain), Viognier (south of France) and Traminer and richer Pinot Grigio (northeast and northwest Italy). Other Italian whites that would be a little more intriguing and competitive with the food are Grillo from Sicily and Greco from Southern Italy. Reds that work well are Rioja or similar-style Tempranillo/Garnacha blends (Spain), chilled and ripe Côtes-du-Rhône (France), and Primitivo (southern Italy and Sicily). If you want to go down the neutral route, choose any inexpensive rosé as a red, or Alsace Pinot Blanc or Loire

Sauvignon Blanc as a white.

Mushrooms Although mushrooms traditionally form an integral part of a vegetarian diet, we are delighted to forego our rampant carnivorous tendencies if mushrooms form the backbone of an evening's cooking. The inbuilt 'meatiness' in field mushrooms or the intensity, flavour and texture of wild mushrooms really work for us. Clearly the mushroom family is a diverse one and you can cook them in every way imaginable, so this is a pretty long entry. When matching wine to mushrooms, ignore the fact that they are fungi and look at the task they are employed to do in the dish. *Baked* or *grilled* mushrooms usually retain their essence, moisture and flavour, and cellar temperature reds (i.e. chilled a touch) should allow them to express themselves. Make sure that you choose relaxed, fruit-driven reds with low tannins – simple Grenache blends, Pinot Noir or Gamay, for example. *Creamy sauces* are always difficult; if you overdo the cream, a robust, oaked Chardonnay or Semillon is needed, but if the cream features only in a supporting, 'whisked in' role, then refreshing red grapes such as Merlot, Barbera and Bonarda would be superb. *Mushroom omelettes* and *mushroom tarts* are both classic examples of how a mushroom can hold its own in the competitive egg world – here, again, light, fruit-driven reds must be mobilised. *Wild mushrooms* can be intensely scented, gamey and foresty, so look to our 'Game' entry and trade down in terms of muscle (and expenditure). *Mushrooms on toast* are ever so fashionable again (hooray) – good news, as there is nothing better for setting up your palate for a Viking-sized main course. This is one of the easiest dishes to make at home and, even if you splash out on fancy bread and top 'shrooms, it is still a dead cheap dish. Wine-wise, look to the main course you are preparing and downsize the wine a touch for your starters. If you are having a double serving as a stand-alone main dish,

Grenache blends
Pinot Noir
Gamay
Chardonnay
Semillon
Merlot
Riesling

then try Pinot Noir but don't spend too much (look to Tassie) or Barbera or Dolcetto from Northern Italy for their truffley, black cherry aromas and flavours. Wines to accompany *Stuffed mushrooms* depend on what they are stuffed with. We know this sounds obvious but cheesy or veggie ones work well with lighter reds. If you lose the cheese, rich whites are in with a shout – medium-sized Chardonnays and Rieslings are ideal. For *mushroom risotto* see 'Risotto'.

Mussels see 'Seafood'

Mustard Make sure you turn up the volume on any red or white wine if you are contemplating a mustard sauce/dressing or an accompanying dish with a strong mustardy theme. You do not need to go too far in terms of size or style, but a notch up in quality and flavour is needed to accommodate the flavour intensity – this will probably mean you'll have to spend a bit more on your bottle.

Noodles see 'Pasta'

Nuts see 'Appetisers'

Octopus see 'Seafood'

Olives see 'Appetisers' if you are restricting your intake to pre-dinner olives. If you're cooking with olives the trick, as usual, is to look to the main ingredient in the recipe and make sure that your chosen wine can be enjoyed alongside a sliver of olive (munch on one and taste the wine –

Sauv Blanc

Cooking with olives? Take care not to pour in the liquor (water, brine or oil) from the jar or can, as it is very pungent (and often not of the highest quality) and can cast too strong an influence over the final taste of the dish. This, of course, would affect your wine's – and your own – chances of happiness.

a road test). *Tapenade* is a funny old thing – totally unfriendly when it comes to wine (unless you find refuge in dry sherry), so it is best to go for very dry whites from cooler-climate regions, like cheap but dry WA Sauvignon Blanc, or a cheap but reliable Sauvignon from a big brand (you know where to find them). For European matches, look to Gavi and Soave (both Italian), Sauvignon de Touraine or Muscadet (both French).

Omelette see 'Eggs'

Onion
As a stand-alone dish, onion is at its best in a classic French onion tart, and Alsatian Riesling is the only true wine to drink with this noble offering. If you must stray from this advice (verbal warning from the wine police!) Clare or Eden Valley Rieslings would work beautifully. For *French onion soup* see 'Soup'.

Riesling

> Occasionally you see **caramelised onions** offered as a side dish – watch out! They are often delicious, intensely sweet (of the same order as a caramel tart) and, although you can moderate this by combining mouthfuls with the other elements of your meal, they are a real danger to a glass of dry wine so don't eat them with anything remotely serious in the wine department. Our advice is to eat enthusiastically and sip cautiously.

Oysters see 'Seafood'

Paella
Not worthy of its own listing really, except for the fact that it is such a desperately cacophonous mix of ingredients. Drink anything you want – it's cooked in a dustbin lid, after all. But just because you've opened this book specifically to look up paella (hello? anyone out there?) we will tell you that chilled, ripe Cabernet Franc (red Loire), Albariño or Godello (Spanish white grapes) or French Grenache-/Spanish Garnacha-based light reds and rosés all do well in a crowd-pleasing way. Substitute

Cabernet Franc Rosé

any of the above with the cheapest Aussie versions you can find in our **Best Wines of 2009.** You'll be drinking them from a plastic cup and eating off a paper plate, anyway!

Pasta

Shiraz
Sauv Blanc
Tempranillo
Grenache
Pinot Grigio
Riesling
Sem Sauv Blanc
Cab Merlot

Naked pasta tastes pretty neutral, which is why it is never served on its own. The trick with pasta and wine matching is to consider what you are serving over, under, around or in it. Stuffed styles such as *cannelloni, agnolotti, cappelletti, tortellini* or *ravioli* can contain veg, cheese, meat and all sorts, so think inside out and select accordingly. *Spinach and ricotta tortellini* soaks up juicy Italian reds like Freisa, Dolcetto and Barbera from Piedmont, and young, simple Chianti, Franciacorta, Bardolino and Valpolicella. There are a few Italian varieties grown in Oz, but very few have grabbed us by the short and curlies, so we suggest that you instead opt for funky, entry-level Shiraz from cooler climates (see our **Who's Who** for recommended producers). *Seafood* pasta dishes, including the all-time favourite *spaghetti vongole* (clams), love serious, crisp Sauvignon Blanc (from anywhere), decent Frascati (spend up, if you can find it!), Soave and Verdicchio.

Meatballs, spaghetti Bolognese, lasagne and *meaty sauces* all respond well to juicy reds. Keep the budget down and head for expressive, fruit-driven examples that work in harmony with the dish, as opposed to trying to dominate it. Consider all of Italy, most of Australia and many other New World regions, but steer clear of overly alcoholic wines (read the label and stay under 13.5%) and, although heretical, anything bright and juicy made from Tempranillo or Garnacha from Spain would also be delicious. These dishes are fun places to go out on a limb and try a different red from outside your standard wine diet, so go for it and have some fun with **The Best Wines of 2009**! *Roasted vegetables* often pop up in pasta dishes, allowing you to choose between richer whites and lighter reds. *Pesto* may be a classic pasta combo but it is remarkably argumentative on the wine front. Oil, pine nuts, Parmesan and basil seem innocent enough, but combine them and you are forced into lean, dry whites for safety. Go to the famous Italian regions of Friuli, Alto Adige or Veneto as your guide. Sauvignon Blanc is made here, so at least you can rely on that stalwart grape but, otherwise, Pinot Grigio, Riesling, Picolit, Tocai Friulano, posh Soave and Pinot Bianco are all good bets. *Red pesto* is a funny old fish (not literally). This time go for light red wines and keep their temperature down (15 minutes in the fridge – 30 in Queensland!) to focus the fruity flavours.

Cheesy and *creamy sauces* tend to be more dominant than the ingredients bound therein, so Bardolino and Valpolicella (both from Veneto), Dolcetto, Freisa and Barbera (all from Piedmont), Montepulciano (from Marche) and medium-weight Chianti (from Tuscany) are all accurate. If you need to stray from Italy's idyllic shores then there are plenty more to be found; medium-weight reds and dry whites are everywhere. Cheap high acid whites like SSB, SBS, BSS(?) and fresh, youthful Cabernet Merlot Blends should be out in force at this time. Just remember not to overshadow the dish, particularly with higher-alcohol wines. For *tomato sauce*, see 'Tomato'. For *mushroom sauce*, see 'Mushrooms'.

Pâté Regardless of its main ingredients, pâté is, perhaps surprisingly, keen on white wines. The only reds that really work are featherweights such as rosé, Beaujolais and Bardolino. In the white world, you need to hunt down fruity, aromatic wines from any decent estate in our **Who's Who**. The crucial taste character that you are searching for in these wines is a degree of sweetness (not much, just a hint – we won't let you forget that rosé should be dry!). All styles from technically dry (but still ripe and fruity – Riesling, Gewürztraminer, Muscat, Chenin Blanc and so on) up

Rosé
Riesling
Gewürztraminer
Chenin Blanc
Late Harvest Riesling
Botrytis Semillon
Riesling

to genuine rich/sweet wines can be considered. Pâté is usually served as a starter, so pouring a sweet wine at the beginning of the meal might seem a little about face. But if you are serving dessert or cheese later on in the proceedings (make sure you plan this carefully beforehand), you can happily open a bottle of sweet wine, serve a few small glasses for starters and finish it off later. Many sweet wines are sold in half (375ml) or 500ml bottles, so if it's a small gathering, anything up to six, you won't waste a drop. Clever drinking!

Chicken liver pâté favours older Aussie Rieslings (Eden and Clare Valleys), dry to medium-dry German Riesling, Alsace Riesling, Pinot Blanc and mildly sweet white Bordeaux styles (Loupiac or Saussignac). *Country pâté*, a clumsy catch-all term that often hints at a coarser texture pâté of indeterminate origin, again likes light white wines with a degree of sweetness (or a pint or two of real ale). If you are pushed into choosing from a short wine list or are confronted with an undernourished bottle-o, then play safe, buy a dry white and hope for the best. But if you have the luxury of choice, then Australia has an abundance of Riesling. Heading abroad, Alsace is a great region to start hunting, with Riesling and Tokay-Pinot Gris the plum picks here, while Chilean Gewürztraminer is an unusual but rewarding style.

With *duck pâté* and *foie gras (goose liver)*, we are firmly in sweet wine territory – Aussie botrytised, cane cut or late harvest Semillon and Riesling, Sauternes, Loire and Alsace sweeties (France), or, on a tighter budget, Monbazillac, Ste-Croix du Mont, Loupiac, Cadillac and Saussignac, Sauternes' taste-alike neighbours. If you have never tasted this heady food and wine combo, you are in for a very pleasant surprise indeed. *Parfait*, the smoother, creamier, Mr Whippy version of pâté, tends to reveal its covert brandy ingredient more than a coarse pâté, so make sure your wine is rich enough to cope with this. If you don't want to sip a very sweet wine, then less sweet whites from Alsace also work. Vendange Tardive (late-picked) wines offer richness without cloying, sugary sweetness and will appease those who don't go for turbo-sweet wines. Grapes to consider are Tokay-Pinot Gris, Muscat, Gewürztraminer and Riesling. Look to the Adelaide Hills, Tasmania, Marlborough in New Zealand and Western Australia's Great Southern to keep you out of trouble here. *Smoked salmon* pâté and other *fish* pâté incarnations are well served by dry aromatic whites (see 'Fish'). One thing to remember with pâté dishes is that occasionally *chutney* (or *onion confit/ marmalade*) is served on the side, giving an intense, sweet fruit or veg explosion of flavour, which may confuse the wine. Alsatian Vendange Tardive wines, mentioned above, have tons of spice and richness of fruit and they will simply cruise through these added flavours – dry wines will choke. We have already talked about *gherkins* and *capers* in the 'Charcuterie' section, so keep them well patrolled.

Pesto see 'Eggplant', 'Pasta'

Picnics You simply must find screw cap-sealed bottles for

Rosé
Sauv Blanc

picnics (or any occasion, for that matter!). And, thank goodness, there are even more around this year than there were last year. Quite apart from retaining the quality of the wine, the benefits are numerous – there is no need for a corkscrew, you can reseal the bottle with ease and you also don't have to worry about anyone knocking it over. Your first port of call for all-round picnic-matching skills has to be rosé. It is multitalented when it comes to all manner of cold food dishes, and it will get you through all of your courses, from crudités and dips, via smoked salmon, to rare roast beef and finally some good cheese. Other varieties that enjoy *al fresco* food are Sauvignon Blanc for whites and Beaujolais for reds. Once again, chill all of your wines right down prior to

Chill a bottle of rosé down ice cold before departure and it will drink like a fresh white early on, and as the day hots up, it will behave more like a red.

departure and, to enjoy them at their best, drink them in order from white, via rosé to red, and bring some ice if you can.

Pies For meat pie, see 'Beef,' for fruit pie, see 'Desserts'

Pigeon see 'Game' but spend less!

Pizza We adore pizza and, if prepared well, there is nothing to touch it for taste bud satisfaction and that warm, pudgy tummy thing afterwards (or is that just us?). Heroic pizzas rarely allow white wines enough space to be heard. However, we suppose a simple *vegetable* or *seafood* pizza might need a weedy, dry white wine. Assuming you have a tomato (or red capsicum – much tangier) base and some mozzarella cheese on top, the real point of a pizza is the unlimited number of toppings that you sling on – mushroom, onion, anchovy, caper, olive, beef, ham, egg, pepperoni and, crucially, chillies. A real man's pizza has these and more, so you will have to find a feisty red and cool it down. Our all-Italian pizza wine line-up includes: whites – Arneis, Soave, Bianco di Custoza, Verdicchio, Pinot Bianco, Pinot Grigio and Orvieto; chillable reds – Sardinian Cannonau, Freisa, Barbera and Dolcetto from Piedmont, Marzemino and Teroldego from Trentino, Bardolino and Valpolicella from Veneto and Chianti, Montepulciano d'Abruzzo, Morellino di Scansano, Sangiovese di Romagna, Primitivo di Puglia, Nero d'Avola di Sicilia, Negroamaro and Aglianico all from further south. Time to tune in again if the last sentence means as much to you as the credits at the end of an SBS film! For Aussie and New Zealand wines, keep the price under $20, and from there it doesn't really matter too much. This isn't a copout – these countries makes such a variety of great wines at this price and all you need to do is flick a few pages back to the ultimate list. If you insist on drinking non-Italian wines with pizza, you might just find you are the victim of far more than your normal share of cork-spoilt wines in the coming twelve months (you have been warned).

Pinot Grigio
Sangiovese

the big daddy

Pork The noble hog has so many different gastronomic guises that we've given the gallant sausage its own section. And, no doubt, *pâté* and *terrine* lovers are delighted that these two dishes warrant their own headings, too. We've also dealt with *charcuterie, cassoulet, bacon, full English breakfast* and *ham* in other sections – it just gets better! Here we endeavour to cover the porcine dishes not otherwise mentioned. First in this section, is the princely *pork pie*. A good pork pie is a real treat and, while we're sure that a pint of ale is the ideal partner, a glass of rosé or Cru Beaujolais is also a perfect fit.

Rosé
Sherry
Cab Shiraz
Zinfandel
Riesling
Pinot Noir
Chardonnay

Chorizo and *salami* fall into the aforementioned 'Charcuterie' section, but remember that the spicier the salami, the greater the need for cool red wine. A plate of chorizo is excellent with dry sherry – manzanilla and fino are the two best styles. Next on the menu, *spare ribs* – whether drenched in barbecue sauce or not, these are prehistoric fare, so Neolithic reds are needed to slake your thirst. Juice and texture are the essential ingredients, so head for Australian Cabernet/Shiraz blends, Argentinean Sangiovese, Malbec, Bonarda or Tempranillo or Chilean Carmenère. Californian Zinfandel would also work well, although it might be disproportionately expensive for the dish. *Rillettes* (smooth paste which can also be made from duck or rabbit) expose one of pork's lighter sides. This mild, oddly fondanty, savoury dish is often served as part of a plate of cold meats. White wine is called for and Aussie Riesling will find this a doddle; otherwise Pinot Blanc, Sylvaner and Riesling from Alsace all work well.

We have left the big daddy to last – *roast pork*. There are a number of ways to serve this, so, when it comes to matching it to wine, the brief is fairly open. One thing is certain – if you are going to serve a red, make it light (Pinot Noir is best). Pork is far more excited by white wine, particularly if there is apple sauce sidling up to your plate. Classy, unoaked Chardonnay from

Chablis or Burgundy would be exact, although New World Chardonnays can hack it as long as they are not too overtly oaky. (Our little piggy is grunting in approval of the trend toward less oaky Chardonnay in Aus!) Riesling (dry and luxurious), Condrieu (the super-dear northern Rhône Viognier), Vouvray (make sure it says 'sec' – dry – on the label) and southern Rhône whites (thin on the ground but a lot of bang for your buck) are all worth a substantial sniff.

Potatoes If you're hoeing into a potato on its own, you're not in any mood to crack a bottle of wine. In all other situations, consider whatever is served under, over, in or beside it. Sweet potato may be painfully trendy, but it does not warrant special treatment on the wine front.

Prawns see 'Seafood'

Prosciutto see 'Antipasto', 'Ham'

Quail see 'Game'

Quiche see 'Eggs'

Rabbit Rabbit *rillettes* love a little more musk and exoticism in their wines than plain pork rillettes, so Marsanne, Roussanne and Viognier from anywhere in the world (try Eden Valley, Victoria or Hawke's Bay, or if you're in an international mood, Rhône is your starting point, then California) or Pinot Blanc and Riesling (go for an older Aussie Riesling or the richer styles from Alsace) would be mouth-wateringly spot on. All other bunnies should hop along to 'Game'.

Marsanne
Roussanne
Viognier
Riesling

Ravioli see 'Pasta'

Rice see 'Chinese,' 'Thai,' etc

Risotto

Generally, the richness and texture of a risotto needs to be 'cut' with the acidity of a clean, dry, white wine, but what else have you folded into your risotto? It is these magic ingredients that matter the most when finding the perfect wine to counter the creamy, cheesy rice, particularly if you've whacked a spot of grated Parmesan and butter in with the stock. Light reds can work with *wild mushroom* risotto but, even with this, we prefer scented, cool, classy whites. *À la Milanese*, with saffron, can force a light, dry white into submission unless it has enough fruit and 'oomph' – Riesling from a good Australian or Alsatian producer is worth a go, as is Arneis or Gavi from Piedmont in Italy. *Chicken and mushroom* risotto likes Chardonnay and light Pinot Noirs, just as a non-risotto-style dish might. *Primavera* favours fresh, zingy, green whites – Sauvignon Blanc anyone? For *seafood* risotto see 'Seafood'.

Riesling
Chardonnay
Pinot Noir
Sauv Blanc

Roast

see whatever it is that you are roasting!

Salads

A huge subject that just needs a moment's common sense. Basic *green* or *mixed* salad without dressing is virtually tasteless, as far as wine is concerned, but be careful if it's dressed – particularly if vinegar is involved because this changes all the rules. *Seafood* salad enjoys the white wines that go well with seafood (obvious, we know, see 'Seafood'); *Niçoise* likes tangy Sauvignon Blanc, Sauv/Sem blends and neon green Margaret River or Hunter Valley Semillons; *chicken* salad works well with middle-weight Chardonnays and Rhône whites; *feta* salad, not surprisingly, is perfect with dry Greek whites and New Zealand or Aussie Sauvignon Blanc; *French bean and shallot* salad likes lighter, inexpensive Australian or New Zealand Pinot Gris (try Central Otago), Alsace Tokay-Pinot Gris and Pinot Blanc; *tomato and basil* salad is best matched with rosé, Sauvignon Blanc,

Sauv Blanc
Sauv Blanc Sem
Semillon
Chardonnay
Pinot Gris
Rosé
Chenin Blanc

inexpensive, unoaked Semillons, or anything fresh, dry, keenly acidic, white and Italian; *Caesar* salad, if made properly, is great with Sauvignon Blanc, Grüner Veltliner (Austria) or Gavi; *Waldorf* salad needs softer, calmer white grapes like Pinot Blanc and Sylvaner (Alsace), or South African Chenin Blanc; *pasta* salad can get a little stodgy, so uplifting, acidity-rich, dry whites are essential. Every country in the wine world makes salad-friendly wines, so don't be afraid to experiment.

Salami see 'Charcuterie', 'Pork'

Salmon see 'Fish', 'Pâté', 'Picnics'

Sausages (Meaty ones, please, not fish or veggie!) Any

Shiraz
Cab Sauv
Shiraz Cab
Zinfandel
Merlot

sausage dish, including *toad-in-the-hole* and *bangers and mash*, needs manly, robust, no messin' reds. Shiraz or Cabernet from Western Australian, Victoria or McLaren Vale (or, even better, blends of the two), Cahors (southwest France), Spanish Garnacha blends from Tarragona, Malbec from Argentina, any Languedoc or southern Rhône reds, Barbera from northern Italy, Primitivo from southern Italy, and Chinon or other red Loires are all suitable. Zinfandel, Merlot and Cabernet from California would also be awesome, as would a bottle of plain old red Bordeaux. Hurrah for sausages and their global compatibility with red wine! They're not fussy and nor should you be.

Scallops see 'Seafood'

Seafood See also 'Fish' and 'Anchovies'. Any buttock-clenchingly dry, unoaked Australian or New Zealand white is perfect with seafood. If you're going further abroad, you can't go wrong with Muscadet, Cheverny, Sauvignon de Touraine, Quincy, Pouilly-Fumé or Sancerre (all white Loire wines), Chenin Blanc (South Africa), Albariño (Spain), Verdicchio, Soave or Pinot Grigio (Italy). *Squid* and *octopus* both need very dry

finish the job properly

Chenin Blanc
Pinot Grigio
Sauv Blanc
Riesling
Sem Sauv Blanc
Chardonnay
Viognier
Semillon
Rosé

whites with aromatic fruit, so hook your calamari on Sauvignon Blanc, northern Italian or Penedès (Spain) whites, and resinous Greek whites if the dish is served in its ink. The curious, bouncy texture of both squid and octopus does not embrace wine in the same way fish does, so concentrate on the method of cooking and the other ingredients to help you make your final choice. Aussie Riesling is a must if you have a spicy dipping sauce.

Tiny shrimp, eaten whole as a pre-dinner nibble, are stunning with Muscadet or Sauvignon Blanc from Australia, New Zealand, or the Loire. *Crayfish* and *prawns* are a step up in terms of flavour and simple, dry Riesling, Sauvignon or Semillon/Sauvignon Blanc blends are all lovely. If you are a *prawn cocktail* fiend (a stunning dish if ever there was one), then decent Sauvignon Blanc (no need to spend over $20) is dry and sharp enough to wade through the livid pink Marie Rose sauce.

Lobster, the noblest of all crustaceans, served cold or in a salad, should tempt you to delve into the deepest, darkest corners of your cellar and uncork the finest whites. Burgundy (no upper limit), Australian and New Zealand (ditto) and Californian Chardonnay (only the best – not too oaky) and Viognier (from its spiritual birthplace in Condrieu, in the northern Rhône) will all set you back a fortune but, hey, you've already bought lobster, so go the extra nine yards and finish the job properly. *Marron* slots in close to lobster, but make sure it's WA Chardonnay this time, and steer clear of overtly oaky styles. *Lobster thermidor* is not our favourite dish, as we feel that lobster loses its magical texture and elegant flavour when served hot, but you can easily uncork richer (but less expensive) whites like Aussie Semillons or South American Chardonnays. If you feel like a slice of lobster class, but for a slightly reduced price, then *langoustines* or *bugs/yabbies* are the answer. Lobster-wines are perfect here, but just adjust the price downwards a little. If you're feasting on *Moreton Bay Bugs* (spooky-looking prehistoric things) then look for a fuller-bodied wine like Pinot Gris to counter the meatier flavours. *Dressed crab* is a fabulous dish and, once again, dry whites are the go, and Sauvignon Blanc is probably the pick of the grapes (it always is). Don't only look to Australia and New Zealand, though, as the white wines from France's Bordeaux and Bergerac often have a fair slug of Sauvignon in them and, of course, Sauvignon is grown all over the world. Loire whites like inexpensive Muscadet are also spot on, as is 'village' Chablis.

Mussels probably do best in *gratin* or *marinière* form, where dry Riesling, Hunter or Barossa Valley Semillon, New Zealand Pinot Gris or any New World Sauvignon Blanc are all worthy contenders. *Scallops* require a little more weight in a white wine (mildly oaked Sauvignon Blanc, for example – you'll find some exciting options appearing from Marlborough in New Zealand, and Australia's Adelaide Hills, Margaret River and Southern Victoria, not to mention Fumé Blanc from California). They can even handle a spot of light red or rosé (chilled). *Scallops sauté Provençal* (with tomatoes and garlic) and *scallops wrapped in bacon* are wicked with smarter rosé. *Scallops Bercy* (with shallots, butter, thyme, white wine, parsley and lemon juice) are superb with top French Sauvignon blanc from Sancerre or Pouilly-Fumé – spend up, it will be worth it. *Oysters* are traditionally matched with Champagne – but not by us. We prefer a simple dry white like Muscadet, with its salty tang, or a 'village' Chablis or Sauvignon de St-Bris. On the local front, slide your oysters down with Sauvignon Blanc or unoaked, cool climate Chardonnay – head to the Adelaide Hills for both. Finally, *seafood risotto* – here dry wines like New Zealand or Chilean Sauvignon Blanc, West Australian or South African Chenin Blanc or Italian wines including decent Arneis and Verdicchio Classico make a rather delicious combination. For *clams*, see 'Pasta'.

Side dishes see 'Vegetables'

Snails see 'Garlic'

Soufflé see 'Cheese (cooked)', 'Eggs'

Soups Dry sherry is often quoted as soup's ideal soul mate. But

Shiraz
Sauv Blanc
Riesling
Sem Sauv Blanc
Viognier
Sherry
Chardonnay
Verdelho
Grenache Blends
Chenin Blanc
Gamay

it seems a little ludicrous to crack open a bottle of fino every time you fancy a bowl of broth. And, what's more, it isn't always the best wine for the job, as the soup dynasty is a diverse collection of individuals – no one wine can expect to cover all of the flavours. *Minestrone*, with its wonderful cannellini bean base, and *ribollita* (the stunning, next-day minestrone incarnation, re-boiled with cabbage and bread thrown in for extra body) like to keep things Italian, with chilled Valpolicella being a superb candidate. If you want to hop over the mountains to France, then simpler southern Rhônes (a well-made Côtes-du-Rhône would do) make a refreshing and accurate alternative. At home, settle in with a young Shiraz, but keep the price under control. *Spinach and chickpea* soup goes well with bone-dry whites like Sauvignon Blanc from New Zealand, South Africa or Chile or whites from Verdicchio (Italy), Penedès or Rueda (Spain). *Vichyssoise* (chilled leek and potato soup) needs creamy, floral whites, such as straightforward Alsatian Riesling, Aussie Semillon Sauvignon Blanc, South American or French Viognier, or light, white Rhônes.

Lobster or crayfish bisque has a creamy texture coupled with a deceptive richness, so dry sherry could conceivably make an appearance here. If you don't fancy that, then youthful Australian or New Zealand Chardonnay or white Burgundy is best. *Bouillabaisse with rouille*, the serious fish, garlic, tomatoes, onion and herb broth with floating toasty crostinis topped with garlic, chilli and mayo, is a mighty dish and yet it only needs very simple whites like Sauvignon Blanc (keep it cheap – Jacob's Creek Reserve would do the trick brilliantly – see page 48) or our old favourites Muscadet and Sauvignon de Touraine.

Consommé is a definite Fino sherry dish (at last). *Gazpacho* (chilled *tomato, cucumber, onion, pepper* and *garlic* soup) likes nothing more than Spanish new-wave (unoaked) Viura or cheeky Verdejo from Rueda, but if you can't find one, grab an Aussie Verdelho and chill it to death. *Mushroom* soup is another dry sherry candidate (you might use some in the recipe), while *French onion* soup goes well with dry Riesling from South Australia or Alsace. *Oxtail* demands hearty reds – rustic, earthy inexpensive GSM blends or southern French bruisers like St.-Chinian or Minervois. When you're on a budget Lake Breeze Grenache (page 117) will do the trick. *Lentil and chestnut* and *lentil and bacon* soups both crave dry sherry (this time trade up from a fino to a richer amontillado, for complexity and intensity), while *clam chowder* is basically a fishy soup with cream (and sometimes potato), so Sauvignon Blanc, Chenin Blanc and all seafood-friendly whites (see above) are perfect.

Vegetable soup can be dull but it can also be excellent; either way, rustic reds at the bottom of the price ladder are needed. *Tomato* soup is a strange one. Always avoid oak. We favour light reds or dry whites – Gamay (Beaujolais or Loire) or Sauvignon Blanc (Australia, New Zealand, Loire, South Africa or Chile) all do the job admirably.

Spaghetti see 'Pasta'

Steak see 'Beef'

Stew see 'Beans', 'Beef', 'Fish', 'Lamb' or 'Veal'

Stroganoff see 'Beef'

consummate ease

Sushi see 'Japanese'

Sweetbreads With *butter and sorrel, sauce ravigote*
| Riesling | (mustard, red wine vinegar, capers and tarragon) or *sauce gribiche* (like ravigote but with chopped hard-boiled eggs and parsley as well), sweetbreads (euphemism for the edible glands of an animal) demand aromatic, decadently textured, luxurious, self-confident whites. South Australian (Clare or Eden Valley) or Alsatian Riesling with a bit of age would be our first choice. For a variation, try creamy, oily, nutmeg- and peach-scented Rhône whites. These can be a little dear, but there's no way around this quandary, as this is a demanding sector of the food repertoire. *Ris de veau aux morilles* (veal sweetbreads with a very rich, creamy wild mushroom sauce) needs the most intense Rhône whites or Alsatian Rieslings. A well-cellared Australian Riesling will also handle the challenge with consummate ease.

Sweet potato see 'Potato'

Tacos see 'Mexican'

Tapas Sherry and dry white wines, preferably Spanish and
| Sherry | avoiding oak, are perfect partners for these
| Sem Sauv Blanc | addictive Spanish snacks. This is also another occasion to pull Aussie Semillon Sauvignon Blanc blends out of the cupboard.

Tempura see 'Japanese'

Terrines A terrine is a more robust, often hearty, pâté, generally
| Chardonnay | served in slices, so what's good enough for a
| Gewürztraminer | pâté is often perfect with terrine. One of the
| Riesling | classics is *ham and chicken*, which loves white
| Sauv Blanc | Burgundy or elegant, non-French, mildly oaked Chardonnays. Another white Burgundy

lover is *jambon persillé*, the sublime parsley, jelly and ham dish. This is not surprising, as it is a Burgundian recipe in the first place. We would dive in with a youthful, inexpensive Bourgogne Blanc from a reputable Domaine, or head south to Rully, Mercurey, Montagny, Pouilly-Fuissé or a crisp Mâconnais wine for a match. Beaujolais, Alsatian Gewürztraminer, Riesling and Tokay-Pinot Gris love *rabbit, hare* and *game* terrines, particularly if there are prunes lurking within. If you're not in the mood for globetrotting, reach for an Australian or New Zealand Riesling or Pinot Gris at the fatter end of the spectrum with a touch of sweetness. This is also an opportunity for aged Riesling to make its way out of the cellar. Leasingham Classic Clare comes ready-aged for you (page 81). *Fish* terrines follow the lead of fish pâtés and mousses with Sauvignon Blanc, Riesling, clean, fresh Chardonnays like Chablis, Fiano di Avellino from Campania in Southern Italy and finally the enigmatic Spanish stunner, Albariño.

Thai

Riesling
Viognier
Semillon
Verdelho
Pinot Gris
Sauv Blanc
Sparkling White

Along the same lines as Vietnamese and other 'Asian but not overtly so' styles of cuisine, it's best to look to the main ingredient and then concentrate on appropriate southern hemisphere, fruit-driven wines. Likely candidates are: Australian or New Zealand Riesling, Viognier, Semillon, Verdelho, Pinot Gris and Sauvignon Blanc. New World sparkling wines in general work well, as do dry Muscats from Portugal and Pinot Gris, Torrontés or Viognier from Argentina. Thai faces the same 'Lazy Susan flavour spinout' challenge as Chinese, so you're better off arming yourself with a few all-purpose styles than trying to be tricky matching a bottle to every dish. We eat a lot of Thai, and have trouble going past Aussie and New Zealand Riesling and Sauvignon Blanc.

Toasted sandwiches

Shiraz

Whether you make toasties for late night nibbling or wolfing down on the run, you deserve a meaty, rustic red swimming alongside. A chunky, inexpensive Shiraz will do the trick nicely, but if you're up for some action, anything from the south of France, southern Italy or Spain would be a delicious match. Just make sure it's not too dear.

Tomatoes Strangely, tomatoes are pretty fussy when it comes to wine matching (see 'Soup'). Pinot Noir works well but, generally, New World versions perform better than their Old World counterparts, as they often have more fruit expression and lower acidity. Other reds, like Sicilian Nero d'Avola, Aglianico, Primitivo (all southern Italy) and any juicy, warm-climate Merlot or Zinfandel are accommodating. When *raw*, as in a salad, rosé or Sauvignon Blanc is a good choice. A *tomato sauce* demands dry, light whites and Italy is the best place to look for these, as they are often ripe and cheap.

Pinot Noir
Merlot
Zinfandel
Rosé
Sauv Blanc

Beware of Tomato sauce and Ketchup! While delicious, they're so sweet and vinegary that they give wine a hard time, so use sparingly on your burger if you like drinking fine wine. Drench it if you're gunning down a cheap glugging red!

Tortellini see 'Pasta'

Tortillas see 'Mexican'

Truffles Foresty, feral and musky – hooray! Choose similarly scented wines to match this unusual life form – Burgundian Pinot Noir, Piedmont's magnificent Nebbiolo and Barbera, and Syrah (French and serious, please). If you want to cook chicken or fish with truffles, then vintage Champagne (or go crazy and find some vintage rosé Champs) or

Pinot Noir
Nebbiolo
Barbera
Shiraz
Champagne
Rosé Champagne
Riesling

you'll be belly dancing

top Alsatian or Australian Riesling would be spectacular.

Turkey The thing to watch out for with *roast turkey* is the

**Pinot Noir
Grenache
Sparkling Shiraz**

cranberry sauce factor. Often a juicy New World Pinot Noir or fresh, young Crianza Rioja (Spain) complements this outlandish red-fruit flavour. At Christmas, Aussie Grenache or Rioja is again a winner as mountains of cocktail sausages, bacon, sprouts and the rest take the flavour spotlight away from the turkey. If you are feeling very brave, totally ahead of your time, or just a little barking, our very own sparkling Shiraz would be fantastic, celebratory and the perfect December red. You'll find three superb examples in our **Best Wines of 2009** this year – without spending much more than $20 (see pages 35-37 and order your Christmas dozen now!). Otherwise, see 'Chicken'.

Turkish We have already covered lamb kebabs (with lashings

**Sauv Blanc
Riesling
Shiraz**

of chilli sauce) in the 'Lamb' section but, essentially, Turkish food is best with Greek wines (endeavouring to be non-political) if you can find them, as the cuisine styles are linked and the resinous, aromatic whites and purple, earth-and violet-scented reds are spot on. On the Aussie and NZ front, look for more fragrant, herbal wines tinged with green flavours, like WA Sauvignon, Tassie Riesling or go for young, unoaked Shiraz, no older than last year. Pour yourself a big glass, and you'll be belly-dancing before you know what happened!

Veal There are some mightly good dishes in this section, but sadly there is no hard and fast rule as to what to follow on the wine front, so read carefully. In general, veal prefers to keep the company of grown-up white wines and classy, lighter reds. *Saltimbocca*, the terrific veal, sage and prosciutto dish, needs a wine to 'jump in the mouth'. Mornington Peninsula Pinot Noir knows how to pull all the tricks, and you can comfortably stick to estate (not reserve) level wines from our best producers (see

**Pinot Noir
Sauv Blanc
Chardonnay
Viognier
Roussanne
Marsanne**

page 115). Pinot Nero (Italian Pinot Noir) would be fine as well, but is hard to find and often a little dear. If your search is unsuccessful, try another unusual wine – Trincadeira from Portugal would be an inexpensive and inspirational substitute. *Vitello tonnato*, a phenomenal dish of contrasting flavours, using thinly sliced, braised veal and served cold, drizzled in a sauce made from marinated tuna, lemon juice, olive oil and capers, is one of the world's most sumptuous starters. Taking the tuna and anchovy (used in the braising stage) as your lead – fresh, sunny, seaside whites like Verdicchio, Greco and Vernaccia work especially well. If you are snookered for decent Italian whites, then just go for a Kiwi Sauvignon for safety. *Wiener schnitzel*, fried veal in egg and breadcrumbs, can often taste a little on the dry side, so what else is on the plate? If there is nothing of enormous character to deflect your mission, give it the kiss of life with a juicy, mildly oaked Chardonnay. *Blanquette de veau*, the French classic with a creamy sauce, is definitely a white wine dish. Again Chardonnay will do, but for perfection go for Viognier, Roussanne or Marsanne blends from Victoria, South Australia or the Rhône. *Osso bucco*, veal shin with wine, tomatoes, parsley, garlic and zesty gremolata, is a lighter, yet more heady stew than most, and Tasmanian, Yarra Valley, Adelaide Hills, New Zealand or Oregon Pinot Noir would be great, as would huge, full-on Chardonnays from anywhere.

Vegetables

**Pinot Grigio
Malbec
Shiraz
Sauv Blanc**

Vegetables (served on their own, or as an accompaniment) taste, on the whole, relatively neutral. But, depending on how they are cooked, they can require a moment or two of thought on the wine front. Any *gratin* (baked with cheese) or *dauphinoise* (thinly sliced potato baked with cream and garlic) dish needs light reds or firm, self-confident whites.

Beetroot is a tad tricky, but Alsatian whites generally have the texture and flavour to make it through (hang on, are you really ordering a wine to match your beetroot?). *Cabbage, leeks, spinach, parsnips, cauliflower, sprouts, courgettes, carrots, peas* and *potatoes* are usually innocent so don't worry about them, but *gnocchi* (plain or flavoured with spinach) needs juicy, fruit-driven wines with perky acidity to cut through their weird texture and lubricate the palate.

Marinated vegetables and *polenta* both love clean, green, unoaked Aussie wines and Italian whites – Pinot Grigio, Soave, Verdicchio etc. *Lentils* often dry the palate out and rustic, earthy reds are essential. Look to French Country wines for an endless supply of candidates or to Chile and Argentina for Malbec or Syrah/Shiraz. *Corn on the cob* is a dead ringer for New World Sauvignon Blanc. Open a bottle and you may sometimes detect a canned sweetcorn aroma! *Celeriac* is a stunning accompaniment to a dish and it has a pretty strong aroma and flavour, so make sure your wine is up to it.

Vegetarian
If you are a strict vegetarian or vegan, look at the label (usually the back) on the wine bottle, as most organic and vegan associations have stickers or a logo to let you know the contents and production techniques of the wine. If you are still unsure, ask at your local wine shop.

Venison see 'Game'

Vinaigrette
A passion killer for wine, vinegar is strongly flavoured and makes any wine taste flat for a few seconds. This can give your palate an annoying stop-start sensation, which is a little like someone switching the light on and off every so often. Dressing made with lemon juice and oil is more wine-friendly and healthier.

Vinegar
See above! Balsamic vinegar seems to be more accommodating than most, perhaps because you tend to use less, and it is more winey in depth and flavour.

Yabbies see 'seafood'

desserts

It's pretty obvious that port, muscat and tokay drinking have taken something of a hit of late in the after-dinner drinking stakes. Fashion is a cruel thing. Many of our friends now prefer to end a feast on a sweet wine, as it enlivens the palate and wakes you and your taste buds up. For our part, there is nothing better than finishing off dinner with a sweetie, particularly if it accompanies a tasty dessert. Read on for a comprehensive list of our favourite desserts and their dream dates. Thankfully there is only one rule to remember when matching wine to sweet dishes – **you must make sure the wine is at least as sweet as the dessert, otherwise it will taste dry.** Most wine shops have a few sweet wines lurking on the racks, but sadly not as many as one would like. You may have to find a decent independent retailer to get a good selection of sweeties, so check out our **Directory** on page 287 for a merchant near you. But also run through our **Best Wines of 2009** for a serious list of sweet wines. Between them they cover every dish in this decadent section.

Almond tart Despite its heavenly flavour and fantastic texture, this dish needs careful handling

Late Harvest Muscat
Botrytis Semillon

on the wine front, as an overbearing sweet wine would crush the delicate almondy nuances. Lighter, youthful sweeties like Brown Brothers Late Harvest Muscat or fresh young Botrytis Semillon would do the trick. Look for a lighter-coloured wine as darker wines are older and richer. If you're feeling multicultural, Muscat de Beaumes-de-Venise, Muscat de Rivesaltes, Moelleux (sweet) Loire whites and Jurançon Moelleux would all be spot on. Stick to these styles if your almond tart has fresh fruit on top.

Apple *Strudels, pies, fritters* and *crumbles* all enjoy varying degrees of nutty, cinnamony, buttery pastry and burnt, brown sugar flavours. These overlay the intrinsic fruitiness of the filling

Late Harvest Muscat
Late Harvest Riesling
Botrytis Semillon

and, therefore, demand a richer, heavier style of dessert wine than you might expect. Having said that, we are still in the foothills of sweetness! Late-picked Muscat or Riesling or botrytised Semillon from Australia, late-picked New Zealand Riesling, German Riesling (of at least Auslese status), classic French Sauternes (don't blow too much dosh) or lighter, youthful Hungarian Tokaji (less sweet, as indicated by a lower number of Puttonyos, say 4) are all runners. *Baked apples* (assuming they are served warm/hot) ought to have ice-cold, light, fresh German or Austrian Riesling (Spätlese or Auslese level) and clean, light Muscats. This will give your palate a marvellous and invigorating sauna then plunge pool sensation every time you take a sip! If they are served cold, don't bother with wine. See below for *tarte tatin*.

Apricot A sensationally accurate apricot match is Vendange

Late Harvest Viognier

Tardive (late-picked) Condrieu (from the northern Rhône) for *apricot crumble*. Unfortunately, this wine is extremely rare and exceedingly expensive (best to buy it on hols in the Rhône), so where else should you look? Australia makes some copies of this wine and they look great (Yalumba Late Harvest Viognier is a good one). Another answer is sweet Jurançon (Moelleux), bursting with tropical quince and peach flavours, or Monbazillac or Saussignac – a friendlier-priced Sauternes-style offering from southwest France.

Bananas *Raw* – you are joking! *Banoffee pie*, the hideous

Liqueur Muscat

love sprog of sticky toffee pudding and banana 'pennies', can only be tamed by the most outrageous of sweet wines – Hungarian Tokaji (although we wouldn't waste it), Australian liqueur Muscat (this will slow you down, hee hee) and Malmsey Madeira (we might even turn up if this was served). With *banana splits*, the candied sprinkles, shaky shaky things and ice cream flavours are more dominant than the neutered banana, so watch out on the wine front. We personally wouldn't serve wine at a kiddie's birthday party, unless the adults are really desperate – in which case we'd head straight for the Aussie liqueur Muscat.

Berries *Black, goose, blue, rasp, berri-berri* (bad joke), *logan,*

Late Harvest Muscat
Botrytis Semillon

straw, Halle (good joke), *mul, cran, bil* and his amoureuse *damson* bounce around in many different recipes. Whether they are served au naturel (naked!), in a juicy *compote*, or cooked in a *summer pudding*, they all love the talented sweet wine superhero Semillon and his trusty sidekick Muscat. Track down these grapes from France – Sauternes, Saussignac, Monbazillac, Loupiac and Cadillac all fall neatly into the Semillon camp; while Muscat de Rivesaltes, de Beaumes-de-Venise, de Frontignan and de Lunel all advertise Muscat on the label, so are easier to spot on the shelves. Aussie late-picked Muscats are all great and inexpensive, but watch out for liqueur Muscats, as they are wildly different and will destroy a delicate *fruit purée*. Having said that, you won't care, as you'll be a giggling wreck in the corner.

Biscuits/Biscotti (and proper shortbread) Vin Santo is

Botrytis Semillon
Late Harvest Chenin Blanc

the top choice for the extended biscuit family. Sweeter Madeira styles and good old cream sherry also work very well, counter-pointing the crumbly texture, butter and fruit or nut ingredients well. None of these wines need be served in large quantities (unless you are feeling particularly gung-ho!), as they are all sipping styles. Sauternes (heady, sweet white Bordeaux) or New World botrytised Semillon (exactly the same style but better value) come in a worthy second. Other lighter biscuits enjoy the company of simple sweet wines – we would still stick to Semillon or Chenin Blanc-based French or Aussie versions.

desserts 233

Brandy snaps

Liqueur Muscat

God, I love brandy snaps (Matthew – I thank my lucky stars for Ma Jukesy, as I haven't a chance of making them myself, without visiting casualty). Once again, try Australian liqueur Muscat, you'll love it – just try to stop when you've got through the first batch and bottle, otherwise you'll be drunk, fat and lock-jawed in one easy move.

Bread and butter pudding

Liqueur Tokay

You need wines with a bit of power and acidity for a traditional B & B pudding (so we are told, as this dish is really not our scene). Enter youthful Aussie liqueur Tokay. Otherwise, weightier Muscat-based wines are just the job – Moscatel de Setúbal from Portugal and Moscato or Passito di Pantelleria from the volcanic island off the south of Sicily would be there or thereabouts. Take it steady, though, as these are addictive, gloriously moreish and hugely alcoholic. Buckle up for a late night.

Cakes

Liqueur Muscat

What's wrong with a cup of Earl Grey? Well, quite a lot, really, when you could be enjoying an elegant glass of cream sherry (with your vicar) or a schooner of Aussie liqueur Muscat with *coffee cake* (and the ladies' guild), Bual or Malmsey Madeira with *Dundee* or *Battenberg* (and your grannie), Maury or Banyuls (the mega, port-like sweet Grenache wines from the south of France) with *brownies* (and the Brownies) or a traditional *fruitcake*, or demi-sec Champagne with *Victoria* (Beckham) or *lemon sponge*. For the perfect sugar hit try *doughnuts* (no lip-licking) and ice cold Asti (with Homer). Mmmmm.

Cheesecake

Botrytis Semillon
Botrytis Riesling

Whether it is baked or unbaked, cherry or any other style, the 'cheesiness', not the fruit, controls the choice of wine. Botrytised Semillon and Riesling from the New World, Coteaux du Layon and other sweet Loire wines, Austrian

Beerenauslese, and Alsatian Vendange Tardive Riesling and Tokay-Pinot Gris all work. The trick is to keep the sweetness intense and fruit-driven, without resorting to heavyweight styles of high alcohol/fortified wines.

Cherries

In *pie* form, cherries behave like berries and prefer the company of mid-weight sweet wines. Cherries served with *chocolate* in a *marquise* or *Black Forest gâteau*, though, can handle a much richer wine. Try fortified wines with plenty of sugar, port-styles and juicy vintage ports (or whatever they're called now that the Portuguese have reclaimed their name). Amarone, the wickedly intense red Valpolicella from Veneto in Italy, Maury or Banyuls from Roussillon (France) or really juicy Californian Zinfandel for a bizarre match. Your guests might think you're a course late with the red, but it works, honest.

> Late Harvest Muscat
> Botrytis Semillon
> Tawny Port
> Vintage Port

Chocolate

A deluxe *choccy cake* can, if it's not too intense, retreat into botrytised Rieslings and lighter Muscats or Tokays. Chocolate mousse (knock off the antlers), *petits pots au chocolat* and chocolate *soufflé* all head towards Orange Muscat, with its wonderful pervading aroma and flavour of orange blossom. This is one of the finest food and wine combinations of all, as orange and chocolate are natural partners. Australia and California make two examples that we know of, so well done Brown Bros (see **The Best Wines of 2009** on page 161 – you'll be delighted by the price!) and Andrew Quady respectively, your places in the choccy hall of fame are guaranteed. If these wines are too hard to find, then you could even twist our arm to open a bottle of Asti Spumante! Chocolate *croissants*, the single most decadent dish in the dessert repertoire, need unctuous fortified wines with a touch of burnt nuttiness – liqueur Muscat and liqueur Tokay (look to

> Botrytis Riesling
> Liqueur Muscat
> Liqueur Tokay
> Orange Muscat
> Pedro Ximénez
> Botrytis Semillon
> Tawny Port

Rutherglen in Victoria – the Muscat and Tokay centre of the universe!), Banyuls or Maury (Roussillon, France). Match any of these ridiculously insane dishes with the following list of galactically serious wines – Passito di Pantelleria (for its mind-boggling orange zest aroma), Tokaji, black Muscat (space-age – careful, get ready for re-entry), liqueur Muscat, liqueur Tokay, PX (short for Pedro Ximénez, the boozy, black, teeth-rottingly sweet turbo-sherry), botrytised Semillon, Maury and Banyuls (both French) and, finally, young, punchy, underrated, tawny port.

Christmas pudding

Tawny Port
Liqueur Muscat
Liqueur Tokay

During the festive period, it is useful to have a wine that lasts well once opened – you've got to make it all the way from Christmas Eve to New Year's Day, after all. Top-quality tawny port and liqueur Muscat or Tokay from Australia, as well as heady Malmsey Madeira, all fit the bill. You can squeeze twelve glasses out of a bottle without short-changing anyone. Not bad, hey, and these are not expensive wines by any stretch of the imagination. See **The Best Wines of 2009** for this year's worthy versions.

Cinnamon rolls

Liqueur Muscat

A heavenly creation – but ever so wicked. You need considerable levels of sweetness and toffeed aromas in the wine to cope with the intensity of sugar. Liqueur Muscat, Vin Santo, Hungarian Tokaji, and old oloroso sherry would be stunning.

Crème brûlée

Botrytis Semillon

As we only like the crunchy, caramelised bit on top, as opposed to the silky, creamy bit, we have asked some mates which wine is the best match. The general consensus is that you need to aim somewhere between our almond tart and cheesecake wines. As Loire sweeties, made from Chenin Blanc, appear in both sections, they must be spot on – Coteaux du Layon (and that extended family), Vouvray Moelleux, Bonnezeaux (pronounced

'Bonzo') and Quarts de Chaume are your choices. Australian botrytis Semillon also slots in perfectly, and you have full license to seek out more serious examples. You could always look for some South African Chenin Blanc sweet wines, as the grape is widely planted over there and they are stunning value for money.

Crème caramel
Late Harvest Riesling
Late Harvest Muscat

Sadly this is another dessert that you won't get us near (we've got a real texture issue with this dish – too slippery), but we have it on good authority that light, delicate sweeties are required. German Auslese Rieslings from the Mosel and youthful, fairy-light Muscats are apparently spot on.

Crêpes Suzette
Asti
Demi-sec Champagne

Asti (Italy's frothy Moscato) or Clairette de Die, the little-known sparkling wine from the Rhône, would be cheap but worthy options, with demi-sec (medium sweet) Champagne being the grown-up, expensive choice. These can be a little hard to track down in Oz, but once you've landed a bottle, save it to share only with your very best friends.

Croissants see 'Chocolate'

Custard
Liqueur Muscat
Liqueur Tokay

As soon as you start waving custard around on, say, a Christmas pudding, you are giving your palate much more to think about. Intense creaminess craves acidity in a wine. With custard being the ultimate in eggy creaminess, the big guns like Malmsey Madeira, liqueur Muscat and Tokay must be let out of the cellar.

Doughnuts see 'Cakes' (and 'Elephants')

Figs We're feeling too naughty to concentrate on this one, so you'll just have to flick forward to botrytis and cordon-cut Rieslings in **The Best Wines of 2009** and choose for yourself (not that you'll go wrong with any of them).

> Botrytis Riesling
> Cordon-cut Riesling

Fruit Australia is blessed with one of the most delightful selections of fresh fruit in the world, so make the most of it (and your waistline will thank you for it later). *Raw* fruit of any kind has a much lighter flavour than you would expect when pitted against a sweet wine. So stay

> Late Harvest Riesling
> Late Harvest Semillon
> Late Harvest Muscat
> Late Harvest Gewürztraminer
> Cordon-cut Riesling
> Liqueur Muscat

with fresh, clean dessert-style Rieslings, Semillons, and Muscats, dainty Asti, German or Austrian Spätlese demi-sec Champagne, Italy's Recioto di Soave, Spain's Moscatel de Valencia or very light, young Sauternes. Oh, if you fancy a *lychee*, then find a sweet Gewürztraminer, as it has remarkable lychee characteristics on the nose and palate. *Poached* fruit, like *peaches* or *apricots*, picks up sweetness from the added sugar and can be pretty intense, so tread carefully. You may need a rich Coteaux du Layon from the Loire to see you through. *Dried fruit* (the most heavenly snack of all – Tyson) is a notch up in intensity but not necessarily in sweetness. Cordon cut or late harvest Riesling is our favourite match. If you're munching on *raisins,* liqueur Muscat is decadently well-suited and one of the few wine-food matches that shares the same ingredient.

> Sweeties are some of the only wines you can gauge on **colour** before you open the bottle, so for a light, fresh, lively option, search through the shelves for the lightest colour you can spot.

Fruitcake see 'Cakes'

Gingerbread A wonderful creation that, along with *ginger*
Liqueur Muscat *cake* and *ginger biscuits,* is made even better
when accompanied by a glass of liqueur
Muscat at entry or classic level (not grand or rare), good-quality
cream sherry, Bual or Malmsey Madeira.

Ice cream If you want to play safe then *vanilla, chocolate,*
Pedro Ximénez *rum and raisin, coffee, toffee* and *cookie-*
Liqueur Muscat *dough* ice creams (naughty naughty!) all love
Pedro Ximénez (PX), the intensely coffee-and-
raisin-drenched sweet sherry. You could always try sweet Aussie
liqueur Muscats as well. If you have a *fruity* ice cream or *sorbet,*
just leave it alone – you need a few minutes without a goblet in
your hand occasionally. If you want to ignore us – go crazy and
experiment, but you're on your own. PX makes good body paint
– apparently!

Jam tart You have to find a very sweet wine. This is the only
Icewine rule, as you can't get sweeter than jam. Icewine
(made from pressing grapes that have frozen on the
vine) from Canada might be a relatively inexpensive way of
tackling this dish. Other than that, you are looking at a
monstrous price tag (with Trockenbeerenauslese from
Germany) and, you have to ask yourself, is the tart worth it?

Jelly Light, sweet German Riesling should not interfere too
Late Harvest Riesling much with jelly. Hang on a sec! Are you
seriously thumbing through this chapter
looking for the 'wine with jelly' entry?!

Kiwi Fruit A heavy, oleaginous sweet wine would trample all
Botrytis Riesling over this refreshing, palate-primping fruit.
Botrytis Semillon What you need is young, fresh botrytised
Riesling from Marlborough or a botrytised

desserts 239

Semillon, like Sauternes, Saussignac, Monbazillac or Loupiac, or Asti or demi-sec Champagne. Try to keep the price down, as more expensive wines will usually taste finer and more intense. Or grab a bottle of fresh, young, Riesling Auslese (Mosel, Germany) for a fruit-cocktail-style, grapey flavour – it will also be much cheaper.

Lamingtons

Moscato

Continuing with the theme from jelly, don't spend too long thinking about what to serve with your sweet little choc-dipped, coconut encrusted temptations. Moscato will keep things alive (including your finances).

Lemon meringue pie

Botrytis Chenin Blanc
Late Harvest Riesling
Late Harvest Semillon

German or Alsatian Riesling would work well here, but make sure it's sweet but not too cloying. Recioto di Soave (Italian) or youthful sweet Loire Chenin Blanc (Coteaux du Layon) would also handle this citrus theme very well if you can track one down. *Tarte au citron*, our preferred choice in the lemon/pastry arena, is also stunning with Coteaux du Layon. Your backups are Aussie botrytis Chenin Blanc and good ol' sweet Semillon or Riesling.

Meringue

Flying solo, meringues are virtually tasteless and often a bit dusty, so if served with fruit (*pavlova*), it's the fruit that you need to worry about – see 'Fruit'.

Mince pies

Tawny Port
Liqueur Muscat

We generally follow the Christmas pud/Christmas cake lead of rich, sweet Madeira, youthful tawny port and blindingly brilliant Australian liqueur Muscats. It will save you another trip to the shops and all of these brews are big enough to wrestle with a four star brandy butter.

Pastries

Belonging in the same school as tarts and cakes, we are not really convinced you need a wine recommendation for

Botrytis Riesling this family of buns and so on. Are you really going to crack open a bottle of wine for a *pain au chocolat*? If you are in the mood though, then don't let us stop you – Demi-Sec Champagne, Coteaux du Layon, Muscat de Beaumes-de-Venise, Saussignac and Monbazillac are France's best efforts. Botrytised Riesling from Australia and New Zealand, or sweet Muscat from California might also work well. Otherwise, try a German Spätlese Riesling but remember to keep the price down – and do wait for midday!

Pavlova Pav is the big brother of meringue, and similar rules

Late Harvest Muscat
Moscato
Late Harvest Riesling

apply for wine matching. Look to what you are serving on or around it. If it's doused in cream, look to light Muscats or Moscato – nothing too heavy. Riesling is the way to go if it's covered in strawberries. For chocolate pav, see 'chocolate'.

Peach melba Botrytised Riesling does the peachy thing

Botrytis Riesling
Late Harvest Viognier

well, as you should be able to detect peach notes in the wine – and Australia has a great line up to choose from, as do New Zealand and Germany. Alternatively, a late-picked Viognier from the Rhône would be stunning, but they are hard to come by and mightily dear, so you're best to stick with an Aussie rendition. If all else fails, grab a bottle of Sauternes, as it is the most multi-talented of all sweet wines.

Pecan pie A great dish, which craves the company of

Liqueur Muscat
Liqueur Tokay

Australian wines. Not sure why but this is exactly the right fit and you should search for a liqueur Muscat or Tokay. If you have a hankering for globe-trotting, hunt down a posh-tasting, but inexpensive Malmsey Madeira.

Pineapple upside-down pudding This deserves a

Botrytis Semillon mention as one of the classic and most irresistible menu items of all time. The caramel and pineapple team up to form a supremely exotic partnership and smart Sauternes would give a real result here. If you are keeping an eye on expenses, then Australian botrytised Semillon would also work wonders.

Plum crumble
Of the crumble family, plum is up there with **Icewine** blackberry and apple (90% of the Jukesy repertoire) as one of the mightiest. A degree of concentrated sweetness is needed here, so head off to Canada for decadent Riesling Icewines, Hungary for sexy Tokaji, or Italy for heroic Vin Santo.

Rhubarb crumble
A relative lightweight next to the plum **Late Harvest Riesling** crum, rhubarb crumble takes it easy on **Cordon-cut Riesling** the wine front. Exotically sweet Riesling **Botrytis Riesling** from just about anywhere has rhubarby notes on the nose and palate, so this is the one and only grape to follow with rhubarb–based desserts (including *fool, compote* and *ice cream*).

Rice pudding
No comment. Nothing has changed since last year's entry. Neither of us has eaten rice pudding since school, and don't intend to.

Rum baba
By the very nature of the beast, a rum baba has **Tawny Port** a bit of a kick to it. Underneath the mild, genial **Liqueur Muscat** exterior, a sweet-wine-thumping freak is itching to get out. Rum baba is the Hannibal Lecter of the dessert world and you have to go for a fortified wine to stand a chance of survival. Our SWAT team are tawny port, Bual or Malmsey Madeira and liqueur Muscat – night sights on... go get 'em boys.

Shortbread
see 'Biscuits/Biscotti'

Sorbet see 'Ice cream'

Steamed puddings We are devout fans of steamed puddings. The greatest syrupy, toffeed, old-fashioned ones (*treacle sponge* and *suet pudding* included) deserve the most regal sweet wines. We don't care that suet is a beastly ingredient and that these recipes don't involve any tricky cooking techniques. To us they are culinary utopia. All of these wines have been mentioned before, but they all do the business, so here we go – top-flight botrytised Semillon (from anywhere), decadent Madeira, Tokaji (spend up by as many puttonyos as you can afford), Vin Santo (see our recommended producers) and liqueur Muscat (from any one of our top Victorian or South Australian specialists).

> Botrytis Semillon
> Liqueur Muscat

Strawberries Top quality strawberries love Asti and Moscato d'Asti (Italy), demi-sec Champagne and Clairette de Die (Rhône, France). These are all fizzy or frothy, with the faintest touch of grapey sweetness.

> Asti
> Moscato
> Demi-sec Champagne

Strudel see 'Apple'

Tarte au citron see 'Lemon meringue pie'

Tarte tatin This is another of the greatest dishes of all time. We haven't put it into the apple section, and not because these days tatin is made with pear and all manner of other fruit (and savoury ingredients – we've seen a beetroot one! Why?), but because the tatin method of cooking is the influencing factor. The rich, toffee/caramel gooeyness is what preoccupies the palate and, for that reason, honeyed Loire sweeties like Coteaux du Layon are right on the money. Aussie botrytised Semillons are

> Asti
> Moscato
> Demi-sec Champagne

great, as well, and Sauternes would be a real treat.

Tiramisù

Vin Santo
Marsala

A strangely unappetising dish, in our opinion, as coffee, mascarpone, chocolate and brandy are frighteningly odd team mates. If you must eat this sickly dish, stay accurate with Vin Santo (to knock the flavour out) or Marsala (to knock yourself out).

Treacle tart

Liqueur Muscat

Treacle tart, particularly if you have included lemon zest in the recipe, is not as stodgy as you might expect. You could try Sauternes but, if in any doubt, Hungarian Tokaji, Vin Santo or youthful liqueur Muscat would probably be safest.

Trifle

Late Harvest Riesling
Cordon-cut Riesling
Botrytis Riesling
Botrytis Semillon

The grand old English creation, adorning vicarage sideboards up and down the country, must be delighted to have so many options on the wine front. German Riesling Beerenauslese is our top choice but any sweet Riesling would be lovely. Likewise, Sauternes and the family of worldwide sweet Semillons all love this dish. If you are going to pour in a bit of booze (sherry is traditionally used), a good quality cream sherry is probably best. Whatever you choose, do avoid the trifle jokes, and we'll each have a large glass of dessert wine please and politely refuse the trifle.

Zabaglione

Marsala

Passito di Pantelleria, from an island off Sicily, is the only wine to accompany this creamy concoction – unless the Marsala you use in the recipe is of sufficient drinking quality. If it is, then you can cover two bases with one wine – and that must be the epitome of food and wine matching.

cheese styles

cheese

Matching great cheese with the perfect wine can be one of the most satisfying experiences in the art of wine and food matching. It can also be one of the most challenging, and this is why this little chapter is one of the most vital in this book. It's not as simple as plonking any red wine on the table next to your favourite hunk of cheese. In fact, almost every style of wine has a place in this section – dry white, sweet white, red and fortified.

In order to nail some of the finer details of this game, we set about pulling off the mother of all cheese tastings. We headed down to De Bortoli in the Yarra Valley and filled a room with cheeses from around Australia, New Zealand and the world. Richard Thomas (the guru behind De Bortoli's fantastic cheese room) kindly offered to host the tasting for us. He's a naughty-sheriff-like character (like Deputy Dawg) who won't take any bullshit on his plate or in his glass. Richard has been making cheese in this country since before we were born (literally!) and has been named Australia's best cheese maker. The cheeses he's had a hand in developing read like a roll call of Aussie greats: Bries at King Island and Kangaroo Island, Sheep's Cheese at Meredith, Washed Rind at Milawa, Blues at Gippsland (now Tarago River), Clotted Cream and Goat's Cheese at the Yarra Valley and his latest creation – a great little Persian style Feta preserved in oil, garlic and herbs.

Before we got started, the naughty sheriff said, "Right, boys, the first thing to do is to group our cheeses into wine friendly and wine unfriendly." He then set about making a "friendly" group of Goat's cheeses, Cheshire, Cheddar, mature Buffalo cheese and Gruyère. He explained that the salty and acidic flavours in these cheeses make them easy to partner with wine.

Cheese and wine matching can be an immensely complex issue, but if you follow our guidelines you will whip together some incredible combinations in no time. You will also be amazed at what you can do with a little creativity. Our mate Stuart Knox, who runs the hip little restaurant and wine bar 'Fix St James' in Sydney, was daring enough to serve an aged Parmigiano-Reggiano with a sparkling white from the Yarra Valley – and the combination won him a place as a finalist for the *Hot Sommelier of the Year*! The naughty sheriff reckons a similar trick can work with some triple cream styles as well.

Blue Cheeses, White Mould and Washed Rind Cheeses fall into the **wine unfriendly** category because their alkaline nature and flavours resembling garlic and cauliflower can clash with wine. The secret to bridging these cheeses with wine is to introduce a third party that brings sweetness to the mix. This is why it's clever to serve accompaniments like **quince paste**, **muscatel clusters**, **figs**, **pears** and **honey** with your cheese platter.

The following entries list the main categories of cheese and mention the highlights from our tasting with the naughty sheriff as well as some of our favourite examples. Keep your mind open and your eyes peeled – there are many exciting cheeses to be discovered.

Blue cheese

Blue Brie
Danish Style
Gorgonzola Style
Roquefort
Stilton

Blue cheeses are packed with the strongest, most tangy flavours of all. It's going to take an intensely-flavoured wine to rise to the challenge of this explosive palate action. Big reds are totally out because the tannins are likely to have a bad reaction with the cheese. The answer is to reach for a sweet wine. Some

Botrytis Semillon
Tawny Port
Vintage Port
Botrytis Riesling

cleverly placed accompaniments like quince paste, muscatel clusters and figs will also help things along.

For a true blue flavour combo, look no further than Australia's very own Semillon-based sweeties. These are a treat with the smooth textures of our favourite Aussie Blues like *King Island Dairy Roaring Forties, King Island Dairy Discovery Ash* and *Lactos Tasmanian Heritage Signature*. For an even more palate-thrilling experience, step up to the nutty complexity of *King Island Dairy Bass Strait Blue, Glenmaggie Blue* or *Stilton* with a rich, nutty Madeira, tawny port or vintage port. The perfect partners to New Zealand's incredible *Kapiti Kikorangi Blue* are Marlborough's exotic Botrytised Rieslings. *Roquefort*, in contrast, prefers sweet Sauternes, Monbazillac or Saussignac; and Gorgonzola likes Amarone della Valpolicella.

Always taste a cheese prior to purchasing when you can. Judge it 30 seconds after you've chewed it because it's the aftertaste that's most likely to present any flaws. Bitterness is the last thing to hit your palate.

Eye cheese

Semi-soft Cheese

Eye cheese is named after the 'eyes' that form by bubbles during its creation. Its satin-like texture and sweet, nutty flavours align it best with white wines. With *Raclette*, try light, aromatic whites or flick back to our cooked cheese section on page 187 for some Pinot Noir action.

Edam
Emmenthal
Gouda
Gruyère
Jarlsberg
Raclette
Swiss Style
Tilsit

Riesling
Semillon
Sauv Blanc
Pinot Noir

Edam is not fussy, serve it with whatever light whites or reds you fancy. *Heidi Gruyère*, with its subtle, elegant complexity of flavours, would also work well with a wide range of lighter whites or reds.

Fresh unripened cheese

Soft White, Unripened or Fresh Cheese

These cheeses usually pop up in salads or simple cooking, and their flavours are not dominant, so drink what you fancy. Whites would be best and make sure they have some cleansing acidity on board. *Meredith Dairy Marinated Goat Cheese* is one of the best cheeses in this style at the moment, and there's only one wine to drink with it, but you'll need to wait, little fork in hand, for the next section.

Cottage Cheese
Cream Cheese
Feta
Frais
Fromage Blanc
Mascarpone
Neufchatel
Quark
Ricotta
Stracchino

Serve cheese at cool room temperature. Take it out of the fridge at least half an hour before you plan to serve it.

Goat's cheese

Sauv Blanc
Sparkling White
Sauv Blanc Sem
Botrytis Semillon
Late Harvest Riesling
Rosés

Right at the top of our list of wine friendly cheeses, billy goats are a wine's best friend. The simpler, inoffensive, salty flavours of most Australian and NZ examples make them suitable with a broad variety of wines, but particularly with white wines. There is one variety above all others that is a magic match with Goat's Cheese, and that's Sauvignon Blanc. The stunning wines from Sancerre in the Loire Valley are the benchmark (Chavignol is one of the finest wine villages in Sancerre and the home of the famous Crottin de Chavignol cheeses). This is one of the finest food and wine pairings that exists, but short of Sancerre, we have lined up an arsenal of great Aussie and NZ SBs among **The Best Wines of 2009**. Try them with *Meredith Pyramid Goat's Cheese* or any of the non-matured styles made by *Holy Goat*. With its silky, textural frame, *Woodside Cheese Wrights Goat Curd Goat Milk Cheese* would also work with sparkling wine or any cold white because the temperature of the wine won't coagulate the fat in this cheese. For aged goat's cheese such as *Gympie Aged Goat's Cheese* or any of the matured styles in the *Holy Goat* range, look for the most intense and complex Sauvignons or Sauv Blanc Semillons. The most likely contenders in **The Best Wines of 2009** come from Logan (page 65), The Lane (page 74) and Dog Point (Section 94, page 76). *Tarago River Mature Goat's Cheese*, one of Australia's best Goat cheeses, has the complexity to work with softer, older red wines and lighter botrytis or late-picked dessert wines. If you can't stand SB (some people can't, let's face it) then chances are you're not eating Goat's cheese, either – but if you are, try any dry, fresh, unoaked white or one of our fuller-bodied rosés.

A wine's temperature is an important consideration when serving it with cheese. Make sure it's not too cold. Hitting a soft cheese with an ice cold wine can make the fats coagulate in your mouth. Yuk!

Hard cheese

Grana Manchego
Parmesan
Parmigiano-Reggiano
Pecorino
Pepato
Romano

Australia and New Zealand produce and import all manner of cheeses that fit this category, ranging from mild to extra-strong flavours. Generally, the longer the cheese is matured, the more intense its flavours. As a starting point, get an idea of the strength and age of your chosen cheese (a small taste in the shop is recommended) and this will guide your wine selection. From wines for mild cheese all the way to wines for the extra strong: whites – Hunter Semillon, Aus or NZ Chardonnays; reds – Margaret River Cabernet, Shiraz from Frankland (WA), Barossa Valley, McLaren Vale and Clare

Semillon
Chardonnay
Cabernet
Shiraz
Tawny Port
Oloroso Sherry
Late Harvest Riesling
Late Harvest Semillon

Valley (all SA); fortified – tawny port or Australian port equivalents and old oloroso sherries. Lighter late-picked sweet wines can also work here, particularly with the nutty complexity of *Pecorino style* cheeses like *Shaw River Annie Baxter Mature Buffalo Cheese*. When in doubt, go for sweetness, either in a sweeter wine or introduced as a third party in the arrangement.

When to serve cheese? Should you serve cheese before dinner, during main course, before dessert or after dessert? Our answer is, "Yes, please!" It all depends on the style of the cheese, but we'll happily hoe in at any stage in the proceedings. Build up in flavour throughout the meal, leaving the strongest cheeses until last.

Semi-hard cheese

Cheddar and Cheddar Style

Cheddar
Cheshire
Club Cheese
Colby
Gloucester
Lancashire
Red Leicester

The most popular cheese style in Australia, Cheddar and its merry band of like-minded types fill every spot on the flavour intensity spectrum. The principles for wine matching closely follow those for Hard cheese (left). Cheeses with simpler flavours such as *Maffra Cheshire* leave the door wide open for a wide range of white and red wine matching possibilities. The more intense, complex flavours of *Maffra Matured Cheddar*, on the other hand, present the possibility of jeopardy with red wines, so a solid white or dry, soft rosé is a safer bet. In a different style again, the

See Hard Cheese
(previous page)

Use sweet accompaniments like quince paste, muscatel clusters, figs, pears or honey to link Washed Rind, White Mould and Blue cheeses with wine. Avoid chutney – its pungent flavour tends to trip wines up.

zesty white wine action

exceptional *King Island Dairy Cloth Matured Cheddar*, with its salty, medium matured flavours, would be just the thing for the boys with a few decent reds. Another of Australia's best Cheddars, *The Piano Hill Cheese Company Ironstone Extra Mature Cheddar*, has a touch of inherent sweetness. This makes it very friendly on the wine front – white, reds and sweeties are all options.

> Whenever you can, buy cheese **freshly cut** from a larger wheel rather than shrink-wrapped.

Stretched curd cheese

Pasta Filata, Spun Curd or String Cheese

> Bocconcini
> Haloumi
> Mozzarella
> Mozzarella di Bufala
> Pizza Cheese

Stretched curd cheese has a stringy texture and characteristic stretch when melted. Chances are you'll be eating it hot on a pizza, so flick back to page 187 to swot up on our

> Muscadet
> Fino Sherry
> Manzanilla Sherry

cooked cheese section. *Haloumi*, on account of its saltiness, works best with a simple dry white like Muscadet, with its salty tang, or fino or manzanilla style sherries. Buffalo Mozzarella appears in dressed salads, so pop back to our Fresh Unripened Cheese section on page 254 for some zesty white wine action.

> Keep your cheese board action simple by limiting the number of flavours and, therefore, wines needed. One or two great cheeses are always better than a smorgasbord of mediocrity.

Washed rind cheese

Washed rind cheeses rank among the strongest-smelling

cheeses of all, with aromas and flavours ranging from sweet, earthy, nutty characters through to some of the most pungent, ferrel aromas you could imagine. Any bottle of wine thrown into this cacophonous mix must surely fear for its life, and you should always have some sweet accompaniments on hand, ready to bail it out.

Munster
Reblochon
Red Square
Semi-Soft Washed Rind
Stormy
Wine Washed Rind

Cabernet
Merlot
Chardonnay
Riesling
Gewürztraminer
Pinot Noir
Grenache Blends
Viognier
Roussanne
Marsanne

Milder examples need nothing more than dry, fruity reds – Cabernets, Merlots or Cabernet Merlot blends from Hawke's Bay, Coonawarra or Margaret River, light Loire examples, or inexpensive red Bordeaux. Smellier cheeses like *Jensen's Red Washed Rind* (one of our leading lights in this category) really enjoy Chardonnay, particularly white Burgundy (from Chablis in the north all the way down to Mâcon in the south), Alsace Riesling or Tokay-Pinot-Gris, and other controlled (not too oaky) Chardonnays from Australia or New Zealand. Alsatian Gewürztraminer and Pinot Noir, red Burgundy, Beaujolais and lighter Grenache/Shiraz/Mourvèdre blends or red Rhônes are also able partners for the stronger flavoured cheeses in this category. France's delightful *Pont l'Evêque* is so rich and complex that it's difficult to find a wine up to the challenge, but we would reach for a Viognier from the Adelaide Hills or the Rhône. *Morbier*, with its brilliant intensity and ethereal texture, needs Roussanne, Marsanne or Viognier to do it justice, either from Australia or their home in the Rhône. *Reblochon* likes Pinot

Do you eat the rind? It's really up to you, but texture and flavour experiences will vary, and if there's an off flavour anywhere in the cheese, it's most likely to be in the rind.

Noir, much richer Gamay (smart Cru Beaujolais) and red Burgundy.

White mould cheese

Brie
Camembert
Double Brie
Triple Cream Brie

Once again, Sauvignon Blanc works terrifically well here. If you want the most palate 'oomph', head to Marlborough (NZ), Adelaide Hills (SA) or Elim (South Africa). Remember that the richer the cheese, the bigger the white, so Chardonnay can be considered, too. For reds, try Pinot Noir (Aussie, Kiwi or lighter red Burgundies), fresh young Shiraz/Syrah from McLaren Vale (SA) or the Rhône (France), or rosé Champagne. We've been disappointed to find white mould to be the most lacking cheese category in Aus, but *Jindi Triple Cream Brie* is our perennial favourite. *King Island Black Label Brie* is another delight that you must track down. Make sure that it's fully ripe and serve it with a late-picked Riesling or Semillon with a good dose of residual sugar – or go all the way and pull out a Madeira.

Sauv Blanc
Chardonnay
Pinot Noir
Shiraz
Rosé Champagne
Late Harvest Riesling
Late Harvest Semillon

T H E
WHO'S
W H O
OF WINE PRODUCERS

the roll call of heroes

This crucial chapter is your key to the best estates in Australia and New Zealand. We've been ruthless with the list this year, taking **The Who's Who of 2008**, added brand new finds that we've discovered and subjected the roll call of heroes to a thorough inspection – kicking out any who are not performing at the highest level and downgrading those who have slipped a little in recent years. This is the Who's Who of wines that you should be drinking when **The Best Wines of 2009** are out of reach or when it's time to experiment for yourself.

Occasionally you'll spot a producer or winery whose name is in **bold**. These are specially selected estates that are truly outstanding and every wine in their entire portfolio is first class. We've upgraded quite a few producers to bold who have really lifted their game this year, as well as downgrading a decent number who have slipped. If a producer is both in bold and has a $, it means that its wines are on the expensive side. The bold estates without a $ make more affordable wines, so keep an eye out for them – this is where we do virtually all of our everyday drinking.

Along with the top producers you'll also find our hot-list of the best vintages in every region, so stick with these when you're lining up that perfect bottle.

australia

We make no apology for the fact that we consider Australia to be the most exciting wine producing country in the world today. Granted, there are a few wild cards that Australia cannot pull – prestige Champagne, the very best red Bordeaux and red Burgundy, top end Port and Sherry – but you can't have everything, and you have to admit that our makers have done a tremendous job with what they've got. Gone are the days of sweaty, oaky Chardonnays – welcome fit, new-style, lithe, balanced Chardonnays. If you put a handful of top white Burgundies on the bench against a run of Aussie Chardonnays, you will be nothing short of amazed. High alcohol, monstrous reds are on the way out, too. Our Shiraz and Shiraz blends give the very best Rhône varietals a run for their money (and often a lot less money in our case). Red blends are well-judged, sparklers are looking great, Sauvignon Blanc is closer to perfection this year than ever, Semillon is already there, and if you are serious about Riesling then you are in for a memorable ride. Our list of **The Best Wines of 2009** is evidence yet again that we believe that Australian Riesling is one of the strongest categories in the world.

The place where this country is really excelling is in the $20 to $40 bracket. With the exception of very few grape varieties, Australian wines are shoulder to shoulder with the very best in the world at this level, and it is these wines that you should be embracing. Next time you reach for a

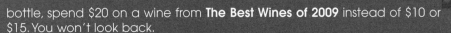

finger on the pulse

bottle, spend $20 on a wine from **The Best Wines of 2009** instead of $10 or $15. You won't look back.

We spend more time visiting Australian wine regions than any other place on earth. We get a buzz out of taking the time to absorb these beautiful places, to experience the depth of their wines, to take in the stories that go with them and, most of all, to come to an understanding and appreciation of the delightful people behind them. We urge you to take the time to do the same. You will be amazed over and over again, as we are, at the human energy and passion that you will discover – the determination, excitement, wherewithal and sheer finger-on-the-pulse-of-modern-society mentality that defines wine communities across this remarkable country. But at the same time, don't let this glamour distract you from the fact that these are vulnerable rural communities, farmers at the mercy of the elements, genuine Aussie blokes and gals who share a mateship and a loyalty that will drive them to help out a neighbour at any cost, time and time again. We saw this again this year as the 2008 vintage rocked the industry to the core. The drought dug its heels in further, and a record heat wave at the peak of vintage in many regions made for one of the most challenging seasons in history. Emerging from this turmoil is an industry more united than ever.

It is exactly this that not only differentiates Australia from every other wine-producing country on the planet, but indeed defines our success over the past decade. Australians work together. Neighbours share equipment for growing grapes and making wine, regions share promotions and marketing through generic industry bodies, and states share knowledge in conferences and journals. The profound impact of the Australian wine industry internationally has been a tangible and direct result of the momentum of tens of thousands of players committing to working together. This is one of the reasons why Italy, Spain and France have lost out to Australia in recent years. Australian winemakers understand something that they don't: that your best ally in any market is the guy next door.

We work night and day to find the greatest wines on the planet. We love our job and don't mind wading through hundreds of duff bottles if a good one pops up eventually. Working from the UK, I (Matthew) taste some 35 000 bottles from around the globe every year. I have a higher hit rate of stunning bottles in Australia than in any other country in the world. This is an irrefutable fact. And I also drink more Aussie wine at home than any other country, too.

There is an entire world of wine to be discovered right in our own back yard. We have so many regions and styles at our fingertips, and the following pages are your first step to unlocking them. Not one of these producers will let you down.

australia

western australia

Our tour of Australia begins in the west and works its way around this great continent. With a superb climate, somewhat cooler than the rest of Australia, but warm in European terms, Western Australia is a wine drinker's paradise, and a very important region to follow. Split into four main regions, the hottest and driest is the **Swan Valley/Perth Hills/Peel area.** Situated above, below and inland of Perth, several wineries make good value wines here, with Houghton's being our favourite.

The top producers in Greater Perth are – Houghton, Millbrook, Peel Estate and Talijancich

The best vintages in the Perth Hills and Peel are – 2008 2006 2005 2004 2003 2002 2001

The best vintages in the Swan District are – 2008 2006 2005 2004 2002 2001 1999 1998 1993 1991

Drive 150 kilometres south from Perth and you'll reach a relatively new region,

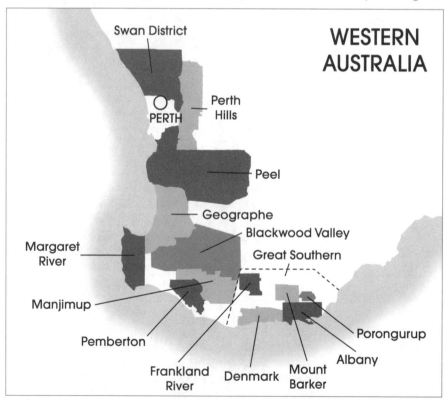

Geographe, which sits atop its more famous neighbour, Margaret River. Home to a handful of wineries, this region is centred on Bunbury, with Shiraz and Semillon being our picks of the grapes planted.

The top producers in Geographe are – Killerby and Willow Bridge

The best vintages in Geographe are – 2008 2005 2004 2003 2002 2001

World class wines rear their heads in **Margaret River**, (300 kilometres south of Perth, abutting Geographe). With a unique climate on account of its curious oblong shape which juts out into the ocean, this is the place to be in WA. With bodies of water on three sides, the microclimates here range from positively hot in the north to chilly and windy in the south. This supposedly cool region is warm enough to make some of the nicest Cabernet Sauvignons in Australia. With over 100 wineries in Margaret River, it still only makes up less than 1% of Australia's wine production. Having said that, in quality terms this is up there with some of the finest and most beautiful wine regions in the entire wine world. First planted in the early 1970s, most of the wineries are situated within 8 kilometres of the coast, around the various brooks that flow into the sea. As far as whites are concerned, Semillon (and Sem/Sauv blends) and Chardonnay do extremely well. Pierro, Cullen and Leeuwin make some of Australia's top Chardonnays and in world terms these are fantastic value wines. Cabernet is the main red focus in Margaret River and these wines are very highly sought after. The flavours cover all of the bases that Bordeaux manages, but with the warmer climate the vintages tend to be more reliable and, accordingly, the wines are more approachable in their youth. Dripping in class, the top few estates make Cab that stands shoulder to shoulder with anything the New World can offer and all but the very top echelon of red Bordeaux. Merlot and Cabernet Franc appear as well, but in much smaller quantities and only really serve to offer some variety, while Shiraz is showing some promise in good sites.

The top producers in Margaret River are – Amberley, Ashbrook Estate, Brookland Valley, **Cape Mentelle,** Catching Thieves, **Cullen $,** Deepwoods, Devil's Lair, Evans & Tate, Fermoy Estate, Hay Shed Hill, Howard Park, Juniper Estate, **Leeuwin Estate, Moss Wood $,** Pierro, Redgate, **Suckfizzle Augusta (Stella Bella),** Umamu, Vasse Felix, **Voyager Estate,** Watershed, Wine by Brad, Woodlands $, Xanadu and Zinful

The best vintages in Margaret River are – 2008 2007 2006 2005 2004 2003 2002 2001 2000 1999 1997 1996 1995 1994 1992 1991 1987

The **Great Southern** area of WA encompasses five particularly interesting sub-regions – **Mount Barker, Frankland River, Porongurup, Denmark** and **Albany.** With around fifty wineries, this is a busy part of WA, and while there has been very little volume here in the past, increased plantings look set to ramp up production for this region into the future. We have tasted some very impressive Riesling and Chardonnay from this area, and Cabernet and Shiraz are also performing well in some parts. Sauvignon Blanc is looking good, too.

The top producers in Great Southern are – Alkoomi, Castle Rock Estate, Ferngrove, Forest Hill, **Frankland Estate,** Galafrey, Garlands, Goundrey, Phillips Brook Estate, Plantagenet, West Cape Howe, The Yard (Larry Cherubino) and Wignalls

The best vintages in Great Southern are – 2008 2005 2004 2002 2001 1997 1996 1995 1994 1992 1991 1990

There are two other regions of note on the south-western tip of Australia. **Manjimup** has a slightly more continental climate than Margaret River and it is also a little higher. Chardonnay, Cabernet and Merlot all perform well but perhaps with less overt quality and vintage reliability than, say, Margaret River. Recent years have been more stable, with **2008, 2005, 2004, 2002 and 2001** the vintages to look out for.

Pemberton, nestled within the great Karri forest south of Manjimup, is cooler and has more rainfall than its neighbour and is better suited to Pinot Noir and Chardonnay, as well as the ever-present Bordeaux varieties. Treated with care, Shiraz can also shine here.

The top producers in Pemberton are – Blackwood, Gloucester Ridge and **Picardy.**

The best vintages in Pemberton are – 2008 2005 2004 2002 2001

south australia

Nearly half of Australia's wine production comes from South Australia. The headquarters of most of Australia's largest wineries are based here as well. The climate varies from region to region, with Riverland being at the hot end of the scale and Coonawarra and Adelaide Hills, among others, being much cooler.

The **Clare Valley** (120 kilometres north of Adelaide), is our starting point. With over 150 years of continuous vine growing, Clare has a warm, sunny climate and refreshingly cool afternoon breezes. This, coupled with good altitude (around the 400m-520m mark) and cold nights, makes Clare home to some of the finest wines in Australia. Clare does not have the starry profile and glitzy tourist allure of the Barossa Valley or the Mediterranean, hippy chic of McLaren Vale, and being a bit of a hike from Adelaide it doesn't have the footfall of visitors either. In essence, Clare has an agricultural feel, with only a handful of hotels and restaurants. Having said this, it is a wonderful wine region where the people are close to the soil and work extremely hard at what they do. Cellar Door tastings are, more often than not, hosted by family members and not corporate employees and this authenticity, commitment and skill shows in the wines. Home to Australia's most famous and awesome value dry Rieslings, Clare wines are a cornerstone in our wine diets. Magnificently balanced and age-worthy and crackling with limejuice and verve, they drink beautifully in their youth, but run and run if you let them – ten years is a doddle for these stunning wines. We also adore Clare Shiraz (and Cabernet for that matter) as it shows control, balance and complexity – this can't be said for your average Aussie Shiraz! This may be a region that flies under the radar, but is an integral and essential part of any serious wine list or collection. Clare wines are fantastic value for money, exceptionally age-worthy and totally and

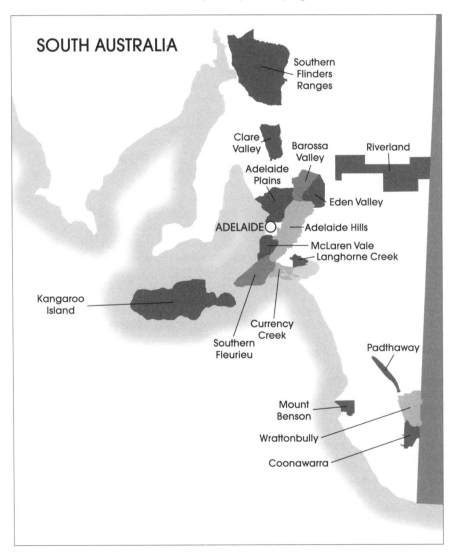

SOUTH AUSTRALIA

Southern Flinders Ranges

Clare Valley

Barossa Valley

Riverland

Adelaide Plains

Eden Valley

ADELAIDE

Adelaide Hills

McLaren Vale
Langhorne Creek

Kangaroo Island

Currency Creek

Southern Fleurieu

Padthaway

Mount Benson

Wrattonbully

Coonawarra

utterly unique in the world of wine.

The top producers in the Clare Valley are – Annie's Lane, Cardinham, Clos Clare, **Eldredge**, Fireblock, **Grosset**, Jeanneret, **Jim Barry, Kilikanoon, Kirrihill, Knappstein, KT and the Falcon, Leasingham, Leo Buring**, Mitchell, **Mount Horrocks, Neagles Rock, O'Leary Walker, Petaluma, Pikes**, Reilly's, Sevenhill, **Skillogalee, Tim Adams**, Two Fold, **Wendouree \$** and Wilson.

The best vintages in the Clare Valley are – 2008 2006 2005 2004 2002 2001 1999 1998 1997 1996 1994 1992 1991 1990

The **Barossa Valley** is one of the most famous wine regions in Australia. It's a warm region that produces powerful, spicy red wines with a good capacity for ageing. The favoured grapes here are the meaty trio of Shiraz, Grenache and Mourvèdre. Ancient bush vines (many are well over 100 years old and unirrigated) abound in Barossa and it is these grandfathers of the wine world that have made these wines so intense and sought after. Cabernet Sauvignon is also widely planted and while the spotlight is on the Shiraz wines and its SGM blends, Cabernet is responsible for some stellar wines, too. Most estates make a Riesling and Semillon as well, so it is not all blockbuster reds, and these can be either sourced from the Valley itself or, more often than not, from the neighbouring, high altitude region of Eden Valley. The inky, rich, high alcohol Barossan reds, typified by the wines from Penfolds, Peter Lehmann and Yalumba, are legendary. But things are changing. There is a move to lower alcohol levels, by judicious viticulture; taking the foot off the oak a little to allow the fruit to be heard; and there is more blending – after all, Shiraz loves the company of Grenache, Mourvèdre and Cabernet! This all looks good for the future, and with a run of cracking vintages so far in the 21st Century, the Barossa Valley is set to continue in its position as King of Oz.

The top producers in the Barossa Valley are – Barossa Valley Estate, Bethany, Burge Family Winemakers, Charles Cimicky, **Charles Melton**, Colonial Estate, Craneford, **Dutschke**, Elderton, First Drop, **Fox Gordon, Glaetzer, Grant Burge, Greenock Creek \$, Haan,** Heartland, **Heritage, Hobbs, Kaesler, Kalleske**, Langmeil, **Leo Buring**, Massena, McLean's Farm, Murray Street Vineyards, **Orlando (Jacobs Creek), Penfolds, Peter Lehmann**, Rockford, Rolf Binder Wines, Rusden, Saltram, **St Hallett**, Schwarz, Seppelt, Sorby Adams, **Spinifex, Standish Wine Co,** Tait, **Teusner**, Thorn-Clarke, Tin Shed, **Torbreck \$, Turkey Flat**, Two Hands, Willows, Wolf Blass and **Yalumba**.

The best vintages in the Barossa Valley are – 2006 2005 2004 2003 2002 2001 1998 1997 1996 1994 1993 1992 1991 1990 1988 1986

The **Eden Valley**, which rubs shoulders with the Barossa and actually falls under its jurisdiction, is geographically a completely different proposition. Much cooler than the Barossa on account of its altitude (380m at the warmer north end and 500m at the southern cooler end) Eden is, as the name suggests, a lovely place to grow grapes. Riesling (running a close second to Clare's supremacy with this variety) favours the higher ground and its cooler evenings. The reds (mainly Shiraz and Cabernet) are grown further north in the warmer areas around Keyneton, where Henschke's Hill of Grace vineyard resides. The big names in this pretty part of SA making stellar reds are Henschke, Irvine and Yalumba. Yalumba's own labels Heggies and Pewsey Vale are both top Rieslings along with Barossa-based Orlando's epic Steingarten and Penfolds' heavenly Leo Buring Leonay.

The top producers in the Eden Valley are – Irvine, Mesh (Grosset & Hill Smith) and **Yalumba (including Heggies and Pewsey Vale).**

The best vintages in the Eden Valley are – 2006 2005 2004 2003 2002 2001 1998 1997 1996 1994 1990

There are very few wine regions in the world as beautiful as the **Adelaide Hills**. Only twenty minutes out of downtown Adelaide, climbing up to a height of between 400m and 500m, with vines clinging to some of the steepest slopes in the country, this is cool climate viticulture at its sexiest. Adjoining Eden Valley to the north and running into the northern tip of McLaren Vale in the south, and with views of the ocean and/or rolling hills from every vantage point, this is heaven. The difference in temperature between downtown and the 'Hills' can be over 10 degrees C! This means that more sensitive varieties can be grown up here – Sauvignon, Chardonnay, aromatic varieties, like Riesling and Pinot Gris, and Pinot Noir are the prime candidates. Warmer vineyard sites can handle Shiraz and even Cabernet – and they result in wines with elegance, herbal lift and definition. These are European-shaped wines with fine, minerally acidity, and they inevitably find their way onto the smartest wine lists in the country. With Chardonnay and Pinot Noir in the ground, it is no surprise that fizz is made up here, too. With over fifty small operations crammed into the folds in the Hills, and only a short hop from the vibrant city of Adelaide, this is a wonderful place for a wine tasting holiday.

The top producers in the Adelaide Hills are – Arrivo, **Ashton Hills, Barratt**, Chain of Ponds, **Geoff Weaver, The Lane and Off the Leash**, Longview, **Mike Press, Nepenthe, Petaluma, Riposte by Tim Knappstein, Shaw & Smith** and **Tapanappa.**

The best vintages in the Adelaide Hills are – 2006 2005 2004 2003 2002 2001 1999 1998 1996 1995 1992 1991 1990 1988

North-west of the Hills, heading toward the Gulf of St Vincent, are the **Adelaide Plains.** Home to a handful of lesser-known estates, this is a hot temperature, low rainfall region which generally makes rather ordinary wine. Primo moved to McLaren Vale this year.

The top producer in the Adelaide Plains is – Wilkie.

The best vintages in the Adelaide Plains are – 2005 2004 2002 2001 1997 1996 1995 1994 1992 1991 1990

Like Clare, **McLaren Vale**, keeps a relatively low profile considering its awesome quality wines. Half an hour south of Adelaide city and bounded on the east by the Adelaide Hills, McLaren Vale has a wonderful, moderating maritime climate (and some of the most beautiful beaches in South Australia). Shiraz, Cabernet and Grenache are responsible for the best reds, and this is very much a premium red wine region. Sauvignon, Semillon, Chardonnay, Riesling and Viognier (in the coolest sites) do quite well, too. With wonderful balance and less heat and power than most Barossa reds, McLaren Vale's finest really register on our Richter scale. The chassis is more European and the fruit more New Worldy and it is this wicked balance which ensures that we drink a load of these reds over the course of the year. Still underrated (price-wise), follow our list of estates below and you will be in for a real treat.

The top producers in McLaren Vale are – Anvers, **Bosworth**, Cascabel, **Chalk Hill**, **Chapel Hill**, Chateau Reynella (Hardys), Clarendon Hills $, **Coriole**, **d'Arenberg,** Fonthill Estate, Fox Creek, **Gemtree**, Geoff Merrill, **Hardys Tintara, Hastwell & Lightfoot,** Hoffmann's, **Kangarilla Road, Kay Brothers Amery**, Koltz, **Linda Domas, Mitolo**, Noon, Oliver's Taranga, Parri, Pertaringa, Pirramimma, Possums, **Primo Estate**, Richard Hamilton, Rosemount (McLaren Vale), Samuel's Gorge, Scarpantoni, Simon Hackett, Tatachilla, **Ulithorne**, **Wirra Wirra** and Woodstock.

The best vintages in McLaren Vale are – 2006 2005 2004 2003 2002 1998 1996 1995 1994 1993 1992 1991 1990 1988

Heading further down the Fleurieu Zone (60 kilometres from Adelaide), you come across four more wine sub-regions – Langhorne Creek, Currency Creek, Southern Fleurieu and Kangaroo Island. Langhorne is stuffed with big company money grinding out Shiraz and Cabernet to blend into varietal wines. There are also a few smaller operations making quality wines, with the highlights being intense, concentrated Shiraz and Cabernet Sauvignon. Currency Creek, surrounding the holiday destinations of Goolwa and Port Elliot, is a mini version of Langhorne. The Southern Fleurieu, Kangaroo Island and Wrattonbully are relatively new wine-producing areas which are still defining their specialties, with SF Shiraz and KI Cabernet showing promise.

Miscellaneous estates of quality are – Ballast Stone (Currency), Bleasdale (Langhorne), **Bremerton** (Langhorne), Brothers in Arms (Langhorne), **Heartland** (Limestone Coast/Langhorne), **Lake Breeze** and **BullAnt** (Langhorne), **Tapanappa** (Wrattonbully) and Zonte's Footstep (Langhorne).

The best vintages in Langhorne Creek are – 2006 2005 2004 2003 2002 2001 2000 1999 1998

The best vintages in the Southern Fleurieu Peninsula and Mount Benson are – 2006 2005 2004 2003 2002

The best vintages in Kangaroo Island are – 2006 2005 2004 2003

Further afield, some 370 kilometres south of Adelaide, you'll find **Coonawarra** – the founding father (and big daddy) of the group of Limestone Coast regions. Famous for its "terra rossa" (red earth) soils and its terrific Cabernet Sauvignons, Coonawarra is a must if you are a fan of this noble red grape. Intense blackcurrant flavours and a eucalyptus and mint nose are the hallmarks of Coonawarra Cab. Shiraz is also grown to a very high standard in Coonawarra and there are even a few worthy whites down here as well. **Padthaway, Mount Benson**, **Robe** and **Wrattonbully** are the names of four other regions down here and each of them is championed, in some way, by a large company (Lindeman's, Stonehaven – Hardys, Yalumba etc) and a handful of smaller ones. There are only a few wines worth tracking down from these regions to date as a lot of the fruit goes into multi-regional blends.

The best vintages in Padthaway are – 2006 2005 2004 2003 2002 2001 2000 1999 1998 1996 1994 1991

The best vintages in Wrattonbully are – 2008 2006 2005 2003 2002

The top estates in Coonawarra are – **Balnaves**, Bowen, Brand's, DiGiorgio, Highbank, **Hollick**, Jamiesons Run, **Katnook**, Ladbroke Grove, **Leconfield**, Lindemans, **Majella**, Orlando, **Parker**, **Penley**, Punters Corner, Redman, **Wynns, Yalumba** and Zema.

The best vintages in Coonawarra are – 2008 2005 2004 2003 2002 2001 2000 1999 1998 1996 1994 1993 1991 1990

Riverland is worthy of a short mention as the baking hot region on the banks of the Murray River, 230 kilometres inland from Adelaide. This is the workhorse of the Australian wine industry where tons of bulk wines are made, accounting for a phenomenal 30% of the country's production. Angoves, Banrock Station and McPherson are here, among others, and it's no surprise that Chardonnay, Shiraz and Cabernet are the most planted varieties.

The best vintages in Riverland are – 2006 2005 2004 2003 2002

victoria

Extraordinarily complicated and with more wineries than South Australia, Victoria takes a while to get your head around. To add to the confusion, its wine-growing regions cover most of the diverse and exciting pockets of the state, from cool coastal hills and baking inland plains to the extremes of its upper Alpine reaches. The list of our favourite wineries tacked onto each of these regions should ease the pain. This is the best way to discover the joys of this wonderful state!

Starting in the **Yarra Valley**, just 40 kilometres from Melbourne, where Pinot Noir and Chardonnay are king and queen, the Yarra is a very popular tourist destination for city daytrips. With a climate somewhere between France's Burgundy and Bordeaux, this is regarded as a cool climate region. The variation in altitude and microclimate between the hills and the valleys provides opportunity for success with Shiraz and Cabernet as well. The Yarra also makes some great fizz and a wide range of other varieties (Roussanne, Marsanne etc), usually championed by artisanal, perfectionist wineries.

The top producers in the Yarra Valley are – **Coldstream Hills, De Bortoli,** Diamond Valley Vineyards, **Domaine Chandon (Green Point)**, Giant Steps, **Gembrook Hill**, Hillcrest, Hoddles Creek, Lillydale Estate, Luke Lambert, Métier Wines, **Mount Mary**, Oakridge, **PHI**, Punt Road, Rochford, Seville Estate, Train Trak, **William Downie,** Yarra Burn, **Yarra Yering**, Yarrabank, **Yeringberg** and **Yering Station**.

The best vintages in the Yarra Valley are – 2006 2005 2004 2003 2002 2001 2000 1998 1997 1996 1994 1992

Mornington Peninsula is a very chichi region, packed with massive houses and helicopter landing pads. This is where loaded Melbournites head for the weekend – being a peninsula it is very pretty. Once again, this is a cool climate region and so Pinot Noir, Chardonnay and Pinot Gris all do very well here. There is a slight element of Emperor's New Clothes about Mornington, as there are more than seventy producers packed into this small region, but only a short list make our top selection.

The top producers in the Mornington Peninsula are – Allies, Craig Avon, Dromana Estate, **Kooyong, Main Ridge**, McCrae Mist, Merricks Creek, Ocean Eight, Paradigm Hill, **Paringa Estate**, Port Phillip Estate, Scorpo, **Stonier**, Ten Minutes by Tractor and **Yabby Lake**.

The best vintages in the Mornington Peninsula are – 2006 2005 2004 2003 2002 2001 2000 1999 1998 1997 1994 1993 1991

It's just a short ferry ride across the water from the Mornington Peninsula to the Bellarine Peninsula and the **Geelong** wine region. This region is the other 'jaw bone' that makes up Melbourne's mouth – Port Philip Bay. On a clear day you can see the city glinting in the distance. Not surprisingly, this is another windy, maritime-influenced wine region. Once again, being cooler, Chardonnay and Pinot Noir are the grapes of choice. Shiraz (and even Cabernet) does much better here than in Mornington, particularly in sheltered vineyards and warmer vintages.

The top producers in Geelong are – **Bannockburn**, By Farr, Curlewis, Farr Rising, Provenance and **Scotchmans Hill**.

The best vintages in Geelong are – 2006 2005 2004 2003 2002 2000 1999 1997 1996 1995 1994 1992 1990

Fifty kilometres northwest of Melbourne and you find the Macedon Ranges. Famed for Chardonnay and Pinot Noir, and in particular for its sparkling wine production, this is a hilly, relatively high altitude region and it is peppered with interesting, small, boutique wineries. As always, Shiraz pops up and this time makes a Rhôney, peppery style.

The top producers in the Macedon Ranges are – Bindi, Cobaw Ridge, Curly Flat, **Domaine Epis**, Hanging Rock and Virgin Hills.

The best vintages in the Macedon Ranges are – 2006 2005 2004 2003 2002 2001 2000 1999 1998 1995 1994 1993 1991 1990

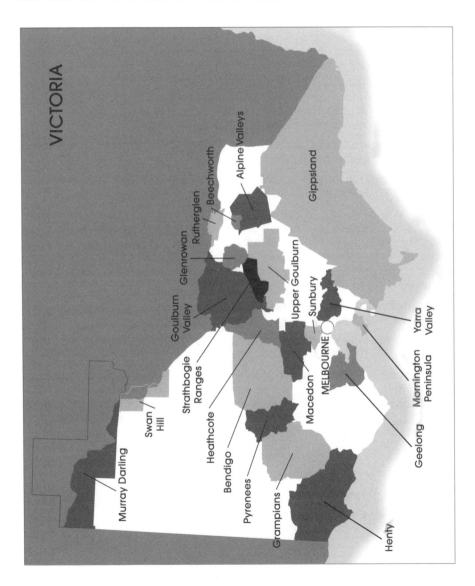

The tiny region of **Sunbury** is about fifteen minutes past the airport (Tullamarine) on the way out of Melbourne – it is the closest wine region to the city centre. There is only one winery here that has rocked our world – **Craiglee**. With a superb Chardonnay and a stunning Shiraz, Pat Carmody leads the pack, showing that fully ripe, totally complex, age-worthy wines can be made at moderate alcohol levels.

The best vintages in Sunbury are – 2006 2005 2004 2003 2002 2001 2000 1999 1998

In the Western Victoria Zone, **Grampians** is the new name for Great Western. This is a beautiful region with three amazing wineries. Shiraz is the main deal here, but not big bold Shiraz, rather peppery, herbal, black fruit soaked wines. Best's, set up in 1867, is one of Australia's iconic wineries. The original plantings still produce wine today and we're amazed at the ancient cellar, where the wines still age today like they did back then.

The top producers in the Grampians are – **Best's Great Western, Mount Langi Ghiran** and **Seppelt Great Western**.

The best vintages in the Grampians are – 2006 2005 2004 2003 2002 2001 2000 1999 1998 1997 1996 1995 1994 1993 1992 1991

Just to the east of the Grampians is the **Pyrenees** region. Small, perfectly formed and blessed with some star estates, this is a cool, but sunny red wine region, focusing on Shiraz, Cabernet Sauvignon/Merlot and Pinot Noir. For the record, Dalwhinnie ranks among our favourite estates in the world – small, dramatic amphitheatre-shaped vineyard, an awesome, one room, space-age winery and sensational wines!

The top producers in the Pyrenees are – **Dalwhinnie**, Redbank, Summerfield and **Taltarni**.

The best vintages in the Pyrenees are – 2006 2005 2004 2003 2002 2001 2000 1999 1998 1996 1995 1993 1992 1991 1990

Henty is a region we have not yet visited, but tune in for an update soon because this region is one of the most impressive quiet-achievers in this country today. In the far south-western corner of Victoria, with Coonawarra over the border in SA not that far away, the plantings are tiny, but it is clear that the potential is enormous. If Crawford River's dry and sweet Rieslings, Tarrington's Pinot Noir and a number of whites from the Seppelt stable are anything to go by, we have only just seen the beginning of what this region can do at the very top end. Stay tuned.

The top producers in Henty are – **Crawford River**, Seppelt and Tarrington

The best vintages in Henty are – 2006 2005 2004 2003 2002 1997 1996 1995 1994 1993 1992 1991 1990

Bendigo is situated to the east of Pyrenees and it has in the past happily surfed along nurturing a growing reputation for fine wines. That was until Heathcote was granted its own autonomy and a few of the star estates were lost. Balgownie, Passing Clouds, Pondalowie and Water Wheel remain, holding the fort, and making Shiraz, Cabernet, Chardonnay and Riesling to a high standard. Next door, stand alone Heathcote has been the proud owner of some serious street cred since 2003, when it broke away from Bendigo, and a few very smart wineries now carry the banner for this region by making wondrous, peppery, moreish styles of Shiraz.

The top producers in Bendigo are – Balgownie, Passing Clouds, Pondalowie and Water Wheel

The best vintages in Bendigo are – 2006 2005 2004 2003 2002 2001 2000 1999 1998 1997 1996 1994 1992 1990

The top producers in Heathcote are – Heathcote Winery, **Jasper Hill**, Mount Ida, Paul Osicka, **Shelmerdine**, Tyrrell's (Heathcote Shiraz) and Wild Duck Creek $

The best vintages in Heathcote are – 2006 2005 2004 2003 2002 2001

The **Goulburn Valley** and its **Nagambie Lakes** sub-region are home to some superstar estates. Here Tahbilk has its world famous 1860 vineyard, which looks in great nick to us – and the wine is phenomenal, too. Shiraz, Cabernet, Chardonnay, Riesling and the Rhôney white varieties Marsanne, Roussanne and Viognier are all thriving here. The vast majority of these wines also remain very good value as they haven't attracted the label hunters as much as the likes of the wines from Heathcote.

The top producers in Goulburn, Upper Goulburn and Nagambie Lakes are – Delatite, David Traeger, McPherson, **Mitchelton, Tahbilk** and Tallarook.

The best vintages in the Goulburn Valley are – 2006 2005 2004 2003 2002 2001 2000 1999 1998 1997 1992

Rutherglen is a north-eastern Victorian wine region that gives us goosebumps just thinking about it! It is home to the most hypnotic of after dinner tipples – Liqueur Muscats and Tokays. There are four levels of fortified wine in Rutherglen – Rutherglen Muscat/Tokay, Classic, Grand and Rare. You simply must taste these wines. They make port, sherry and Madeira look positively sheepish. With phenomenal power and length on the palate and very good value for money, bearing in mind just how old some of these wines are, this is a name to remember. **Glenrowan** is a separate region to Rutherglen but it does exactly the same thing (all bar the obvious one below are from Rutherglen).

The top producers in Rutherglen are – **All Saints, Baileys of Glenrowan**, **Campbells, Chambers Rosewood, Morris**, Rutherglen Estates and **Stanton & Killeen**.

The best vintages in Rutherglen and Glenrowan are – 2005 2004 2003 2002

2001 1992

Just a quick drive up the range from Rutherglen, the historic township of **Beechworth** is another world away. Up here, the temperature has dropped significantly from the hot plain below, and a dramatic variation in altitude across the region from cool, high slopes to warmer, sun-drenched valleys, makes it friendly to almost every grape that its dynamic band of producers cares to throw at it. The superstar estate Giaconda first put it on the map with one of Australia's finest Chardonnays. They also make a stellar Pinot, an awesome Cab, a frighteningly good Shiraz and a very sexy Roussanne! Just up the road, Sorrenberg makes excellent Chardonnay, too, and one of Australia's funkiest Gamays. Battely's and Castagna's Shirazes and Savaterre's Chardonnay and Pinot Noir are another four great Beechworth wines which we can heartily recommend. Oh, by the way, all of these are at the expensive end of town!

The top producers in Beechworth are – Battely, **Castagna**, **Giaconda $**, **Savaterre** and Sorrenberg

The best vintages in Beechworth are – 2006 2005 2004 2003 2002

The **King** and **Alpine Valleys** to the west of Beechworth in north-east Victoria are home to one very famous name, Brown Brothers. These areas are also a great source of fruit for sparkling wines by virtue of the altitude of some of the vineyards.

The top producers in the King Valley are – Brown Brothers and Gapsted (Buckland Gap, Tobacco Road)

The best vintages in the King Valley are – 2006 2005 2004 2003 2002 2000 1999 1998 1992

We have almost completed our clockwise (albeit disjointed) circuit around Victoria, and the giant area of **Gippsland** is the last of the main regions worthy of a mention. It is here that the delightful Phillip Jones, of **Bass Phillip**, fashions the most extraordinary and collectable Pinot Noirs.

The best vintages in Gippsland are – 2006 2005 2004 2002 1997 1995 1994 1991

The only other region is way up in the north west corner of Victoria, straddling the state boundary with New South Wales. **Murray Darling**, centred on Mildura, is another huge area, and combined with **Swan Hill** to the east, makes up nearly 40% of the country's crush. Names like Andrew Peace, Deakin Estate, Hardys, Lindemans' Karadoc winery, McWilliams, Mildara Blass, Simeon, Trentham and Zilzie are all up here. This might not be a beautiful part of the world, but it is a very important one.

The best vintages in the Murray Darling are – 2006 2005 2004 2002

tasmania

Split into two distinct regions – **Northern Tassy** around the delightful town of Launceston and **Southern Tassy** surrounding the main city of Hobart. Chardon-nay and Pinot Noir are the stars here, with Riesling, Pinot Gris and Gewürz also doing a good job. Tasmanian sparkling wines are doing extremely well in the world market – clean, dry, complex and very affordable. The big companies know it, and a good percentage of each of the top sparkling wines made in Australia come out of Tassie. Impressive though they may be, it is the Pinots that we are obsessed with. Victoria does a good job with this variety and so do a handful of winemakers in the Adelaide Hills, but with the chilly Tasmanian climate, ample rainfall and fleeting moments of sunshine, Pinot must think it's back home in Burgundy, it is performing so well! For every rule there is an exception raring to be set free. The Coal River area in the south is home to Domaine A and they make awesome Cabernet and Merlot – just to prove you can do anything if you select the correct site and work like a demon!

The top producers in Southern Tasmania are – Apsley Gorge, **Craigow, Domaine A (Stoney Vineyard), Domaine Chandon**, Elsewhere, **Hardys (sparkling)**, No Regrets, Spring Vale, **Stefano Lubiana** and Touchwood.

The best vintages in Southern Tasmania are – 2008 2006 2005 2004 2003 2002 2001 2000 1999 1998 1997 1995 1993 1992 1990

The top producers in Northern Tasmania are – **Bay of Fires**, Chatto, **Clover Hill, Freycinet**, Grey Sands, **Jansz, Pipers Brook (Ninth Island)**, Pirie, Providence and **Tamar Ridge** (including **Devil's Corner**).

The best vintages in Northern Tasmania are – 2008 2006 2005 2003 2002 2001 2000 1999 1998 1997 1995 1994 1992 1991

Northern Tasmania   LAUNCESTON

Southern Tasmania

HOBART

TASMANIA

new south wales

The **Hunter Valley**, 130 kilometres north of Sydney is NSW's most famous region. For decades, the Hunter has been a massive tourist destination and New South Wales' more important wine producer. But there are a few other very smart areas that are rapidly challenging Hunter's divine right for the limelight. But before we tell you about these, let's get stuck into the venerable old dear herself.

The **Lower Hunter** is a bizarre place. It is a very marginal wine region – bloody awful weather more often than not! But with a string of great vintages in recent years, it appears that climate change might be a blessing! This region is responsible for one of Australia's most famous and multi-award-winning wine styles – dry Semillon. There is some useful Shiraz here, particularly when the rain holds off at harvest time, as it has done recently. A few other grapes (Chard and Cab) are planted, too, with varying success. Now golf courses, hotels, restaurants, some of the world's most important studs (horses!), and a mandatory weekend onslaught of Sydneysiders all rub shoulders with acre upon acre of picturesque vineyards. Rise above the hype: Hunter Semillon is a must in you wine diet. It is more often than not unoaked, a delight in its youth and eminently age-worthy. Think nothing of opening up a ten year old wine!

The top producers in the Lower Hunter Valley are – Allandale, Audrey Wilkinson, Benwarin, Bimbadgen, **Brokenwood**, Chateau Pato, **Chatto, De Iuliis**, First Creek, Glenguin, **Keith Tulloch,** Krinklewood, **Lake's Folly,** Lindemans, Margan, **McWilliam's/Mount Pleasant,** Meerea Park, Scarborough, SmithLeigh, **Tempus Two, Thomas, Tower Estate, Tyrrell's** and Wandin Valley Estate.

The best vintages in the Lower Hunter Valley are – 2007 2006 2005 2004 2003 2002 2000 1999 1998 1997 1995 1992 1991 1990 1987

The **Upper Hunter Valley** is famous for one winery only, and it is a biggy – Rosemount. We could not believe the size of the tank farm at Denman when we first visited Rosemount – they took us for a tour by car!

The top producers in the Upper Hunter are – Arrowfield, Pyramid Hill and Rosemount (Hunter Valley),

The best vintages in the Upper Hunter Valley are – 2007 2006 2005 2004 2003 2002 2000 1999 1998 1997 1996 1995 1992 1991 1990

In **Mudgee,** where Rosemount also sources grapes (actually they take them from all over Oz), there are a load of smaller wineries. Not surprisingly Chardonnay, Semillon, Shiraz and Cabernet are responsible for the main action, with the reds receiving the most attention. Huntington Estate and Simon Gilbert are our two picks from this 'nest in the hills' – the aborigine translation of Mudgee. High in the hills south-east of Mudgee, producers in the vicinity of the historic township of Rylstone are beginning to come up with some enticing cool-climate styles. Louee sources Riesling, Pinot Gris and Pinot

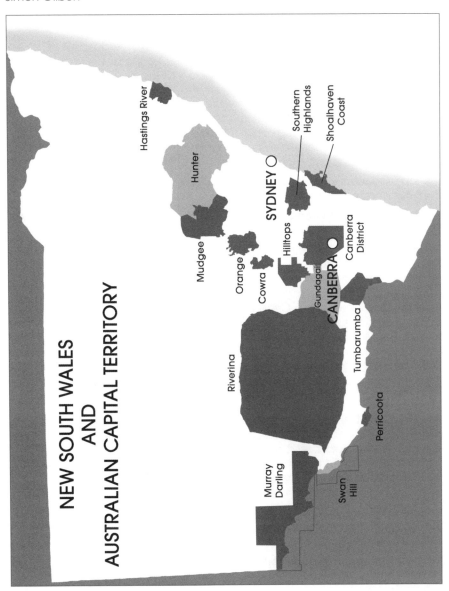

Noir from the highest vineyard in Australia (1100m), as well as a refined, spicy Shiraz from a lower site.

The top producers in Mudgee are – Abercorn, Huntington Estate, Louee and Simon Gilbert

NEW SOUTH WALES
AND
AUSTRALIAN CAPITAL TERRITORY

Hastings River

Hunter

Southern Highlands

Shoalhaven Coast

SYDNEY ○

Mudgee

Orange

Cowra

Hilltops

Gundagai

Canberra District

CANBERRA ●

Riverina

Tumbarumba

Perricoota

Murray Darling

Swan Hill

The best vintages in Mudgee are – 2006 2005 2004 2002 1998 1997 1996 1994 1990

We will rather rudely jump over **Cowra** as we have never been particularly wowed by any of the wines from this region, but if you're keen to give them a go, stick with 2005, 2003 and 2002 .

One region which is causing a huge stir is **Orange.** This is high altitude winemaking – between 600m and 1000m. As the expression goes, 'Orange starts where Adelaide Hills stops'. This is what the Orange dwellers are singing, anyway – insinuating more than just the idea that the region is closer to God. Chardonnay, Sauv Blanc, Shiraz, Cabernet and Merlot are all looking smart up here. The higher you go the less likely the reds will ripen, but if you push the vines and have a magical touch, the resulting wines will be more edgy and elegant. This is a beguiling region which we are following closely. Certainly, top end restaurants in Sydney are snapping up small estate wines like smarties. Our favourite producers really impress our palates, and represent good value.

The top producers in Orange are – Bloodwood, Brangayne, Canobolas Smith, **Cumulus** and **Logan Wines**

The best vintages in Orange are – 2006 2005 2004 2003 2002 1998 1997 1996 1992

Riverina, also known as **Griffith** and the **Murrumbidgee Irrigation Area (MIA)**, is 600 kilometres southwest of Sydney, 300 kilometres west of Canberra and 500 kilometres north of Melbourne (i.e. it's in the middle of nowhere!) and this is where a load of the big companies make some of their largest volume wines. Casella, McWilliam's and Orlando all hang out here. There are only two smaller companies to send a search party out for – Lillypilly Estate, and their superb Tramillon (a Traminer/Semillon blend) and De Bortoli's sensational, Sauternes-style, botrytised Semillon – Noble One. This is one of Australia's most celebrated and finest sweeties.

The best vintages in the Riverina are – 2005 2004 2003 2002 1997 1996 1995 1992

The **Canberra District** follows the pretty, rolling hills from the outskirts of the nation's capital and into the hills of surrounding New South Wales. This is a cool district, with the upper reaches producing tight, defined Chardonnay, Pinot Noir and Riesling and the lower, warmer stretches better suited to Shiraz. Three stunning estates in particular are making sensational wines – Clonakilla (Shiraz and Viognier experts), Brindabella Hills (Riesling) and Lark Hill (Pinot and Chardonnay).

The top producers in the Canberra District are – Brindabella Hills, **Clonakilla** and Lark Hill

The best vintages in the Canberra District are – 2006 2005 2004 2003 2001 2000 1998 1997 1996 1995 1991

Heading toward Victoria from Canberra, the region of Tumbarumba is nestled in the foothills of Mount Kosciusko. It goes without saying that this is a cool place, and as such it produces some of the best Chardonnay in Australia. Most of it is snaffled away by the big companies for sparkling wine base, but some of it also makes its way into their super-cuvée Chardonnays. There aren't any small producers here that have hit our list yet, but watch this space as we have seen some samples in the pipeline which point to great things to come.

The best vintages in Tumbarumba are – 2006 2005 2002

queensland

The Queensland wine industry is growing at pace, with production increasing ten-fold in five years from some 180 producers distributed across the **Granite Belt**, **South Burnett** and **Queensland Coastal** regions. Almost all of these are small and boutique and rely on the thriving wine tourism industry from the burgeoning populations of Brisbane and the Gold Coast to keep their small estates alive. The vast majority have no need to promote their wares beyond their cellar doors and mailing lists.

Regrettably, vine age and winemaking expertise have not always kept pace with the rapid growth in the Queensland industry, and we look forward to the quality of these wines continuing to rise as experience reveals the varieties that are best suited to each of the regions. Verdelho appears to be showing some promise.

The top producers in Queensland are – Ballandean Estate, Boireann, Robert Channon and Symphony Hill

The best vintages in the Granite Belt are – 2006 2005 2004 2003 2002 2001 1996 1995 1994 1993 1991 1990 1989

The best vintages in South Burnett are – 2006 2005 2003 2002

We are not finished yet, but in a way we have already covered the bases, because **Gundagai**, **Hastings River**, **Hilltops**, **Perricoota**, **Shoalhaven Coast** and **Southern Highlands** are all up and running, but they don't trouble the scorers, at the moment. There are murmurings that the next big thing is around the corner, and who are we to say no to that? This country is moving at such a pace that we are blown away at every turn. This is what makes Australia such a wondrous wine producer and vital player in the international market.

new zealand

We have given New Zealand wines a lot of attention this year, and they deserve the same in your own drinking calendar. A cursory glance of **The Best Wines of 2009** will make it clear that these wines are not only top quality, great value and readily available, but our friends across the ditch are creating some unique wine styles that deserve a place in your wine diet. With their championing of screwcaps (the best thing to happen to winemaking in the last decade), brilliant viticulture (the growing side) and inspirational vinification (the making side), they are justifiably winning friends far and wide.

south island

Nelson, on the northwest tip of the South Island, is where Neudorf Vineyards makes fabulous Pinot Gris and stunning Chardonnay. It is cooler and wetter here than around the corner in **Marlborough.** Marlborough is situated on the north-eastern tip of the South Island, and this region is the Sauv Blanc capital of the southern hemisphere! Centred around Blenheim, Marlborough is split into two main areas. The **Wairau Valley** is by far the biggest of the two and all of the famous names are based here. The main style is what we would call 'classic Kiwi Sauvignon', as demonstrated by icon estates such as Hunter's, Jackson and Cloudy Bay.

The other main region is the **Awatere Valley** (pronounced Awa-tree). This is a smaller, cooler region and its Sauvignons tend to be more linear and racy. These wines often taste tighter and more youthful than the neighbouring Wairau styles. Many estates blend the two area's harvests in order to build complexity in their wines.

The other main varieties grown in Marlborough are Chardonnay (very good from the top estates), Riesling (usually forward in style and showing promise) and Pinot Noir (just starting to rival Martinborough on the north island at the top end). Gewürztraminer and Pinot Gris are both made in fresh, forward, lighter styles (which we adore) and some very good sparklers are made, too. There is a new fashion for hillside plantings and some Pinots and other reds look pretty good. We suspect this movement will gather momentum. There is, not surprisingly, a large roll call of recommended estates here.

The top Marlborough producers are – Allan Scott, Astrolabe, **Auntsfield**, Babich, **Blind River**, **Cloudy Bay**, The Crossings, **Dog Point**, **Forrest Estate**, Foxes Island, Framingham, Fromm, Giesen, Gravitas, Grove Mill, Hawkesbridge, Highfield, **Huia**, **Hunter's**, **Isabel Estate**, **Jackson Estate**, Kathy Lynskey, **Lawson's Dry Hills**, Montana Mount Vernon, Brancott, Mud House, Nautilus, **Saint Clair**, **Seresin**, **Spy Valley**, **Te Whare Ra**, **TerraVin**, Tohu, **Vavasour**, Wairau River and **Wither Hills**.

The best vintages in Marlborough are – 2008 2006 2005 2004 2003 2002 2001

2000 1999 1998

Canterbury and **Waipara,** on the eastern side of the South Island, are cooler and dryer, with Pinot Noir and Chardonnay the most planted varieties. Sadly, very few of these wines are exported, but of the few, **Mountford Estate**, **Pegasus Bay** and **Pyramid Valley** are our clear favourites. Just when we thought that every great wine region had already been identified, a brand

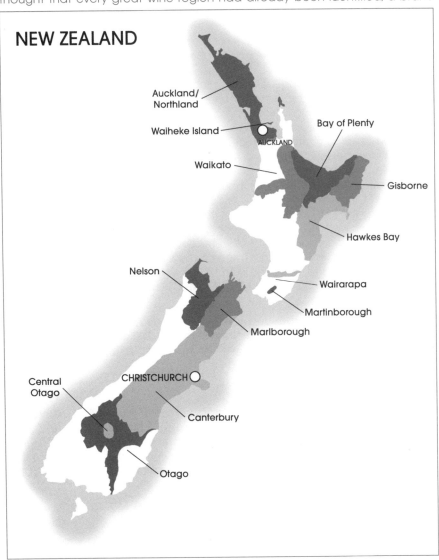

NEW ZEALAND

Auckland/
Northland

Waiheke Island

AUCKLAND

Bay of Plenty

Waikato

Gisborne

Hawkes Bay

Nelson

Wairarapa

Martinborough

Marlborough

Central
Otago

CHRISTCHURCH

Canterbury

Otago

new one comes along. **Waitaki,** situated north of Dunedin and some 65k inland on the banks of the great river of the same name, is just such a place. With only 400 or so hectares of vineyard-suitable land this is only ever going to be a boutique region. Having said that, the examples of Pinot Noir and Pinot Gris that we have tasted (admittedly off only four- and two-year-old vines respectively) were very impressive indeed. Stay ahead of the pack and hunt down some bottles from wineries such as Craggy Range, Forrest, Lake Hayes, Valli and Waitaki Whitestone, who all source fruit here.

The last main NZ region is in the south of the south island (two hours drive from Waitaki), and it is one of the very best – **Central Otago.** Home to the world's most southerly grapevines, this is where Pinot Noir, and to a lesser extent Chardonnay, Pinot Gris and Riesling, are really setting people's palates alight. There are a handful of cracking wineries here and a load of Johnny Come Latelys trying to cash in on this stunning viticultural landscape. Winemaking is often seen as a wonderful lifestyle option for wealthy businessmen as they wind down their careers. This could not be further from the truth. As one famous Otago personality put it, downscaling into winemaking is as ridiculous as downscaling into helicopter design! The result is a load of Pinots which imitate the brilliance of the wines made by the following list of overachievers. This is one of the most exciting wine regions in the world, not least because we are Pinot freaks, but we must admit that we really don't want to see it dragged down by half-hearted attempts to tackle the world's most beguiling grape variety. In the year 2000 there were around fifteen different recognised wine producers in Central Otago. There are now over one hundred, and while they have, on average, lifted the bar this year, there is still work to be done! This is one reason for **The Great New Zealand Pinot Noir Classification** (see page 25).

The top Central Otago producers are – Akarua, Amisfield, Bald Hills, **Carrick**, Chard Farm, Cornish Point and **Felton Road, Mt Difficulty,** Mount Edward, Mount Michael, Olssens, **Peregrine,** Pisa Range, Quartz Reef, Rippon, Rockburn, Sleeping Dogs, **Two Paddocks** and Valli.

north island

Matakana, north of Auckland, is a well-trodden tourist route, with a handful of small, boutique wineries – Ascension Vineyard and **Matakana Estate** (great Pinot Gris) are our two picks here. **Auckland** and its environs, just below Matakana, is still a little too cool for full-on reds, but aromatic white varieties and Chardonnay work very well. Syrah (as the Kiwis call Shiraz) is also creeping into vineyards, making cooler, peppery styles of wine.

The top Auckland estates are – Collards, **Kumeu River,** Matua Valley, Soljans, West Brook and **Villa Maria.**

Take a forty minute ferry ride from downtown Auckland and you arrive at

Waiheke Island, a stunningly beautiful ex-hippy colony, which is now one of the most chic addresses to holiday on (and grow vines). Interestingly, the Cabernet Sauvignons, Merlots and even Malbecs look good here, as do the classy Chardonnays.

The top Waiheke Island estates are – Cable Bay, Goldwater Estate, Passage Rock and **Stonyridge Vineyard**.

Waikato and the **Bay of Plenty** have very few wineries but a special mention must go to the exceptional Mills Reef. **Gisborne,** on the east coast, is Chardonnay territory and here it picks up a creamy, tropical fruit texture and flavour, with a luscious character that is almost uniquely Gisborne's own. Montana has a large outfit here, and there are loads of smaller producers. **Hawke's Bay** is next on the list and it is from here that, in recent years, some of the meatiest Kiwi reds come – Gimblett Gravels is the name of a new appellation where Cabernet, Merlot and increasingly Syrah is planted to great effect. Sauv Blanc here has a fatter, fleshier feel than the more classic areas like Marlborough, and Chardonnays often lack the richness of Gisborne and come in a leaner shape.

The top Hawke's Bay estates are – Alpha Domus, **Bilancia**, Braided River, **Craggy Range** and **Wild Rock**, **Esk Valley**, Gunn Estate, Kim Crawford, Ngatawara, Sacred Hill, Sileni, Southbank, **Stonecroft**, Te Awa, Te Mata, **Trinity Hill**, **Unison** & **Vidal**.

The best vintages in Hawke's Bay are – 2008 2006 2005 2004 2003 2002 2001 2000 1999 1998 1994 1991 1990

Wairarapa and its most famous sub region **Martinborough** sit at the southern end of the North Island, near Wellington. Fantastic Chardonnay, Riesling, Sauvignon and, most importantly, Pinot Noir is made here. Ata Rangi's Pinot Noir is one of New Zealand's finest.

The top estates of Martinborough are – Alana Estate, **Ata Rangi**, Borthwick Vineyard, Escarpment, **Dry River,** Martinborough Vineyards, Matahiwi, Murdoch James, **Palliser Estate**, Solstone, Te Kairanga and Voss Estate.

who's who

DIRECTORY OF
AUSTRALIAN
W I N E
RETAILERS

This directory is **your personal guide** to the best places to buy wine in 2009. You'll find national chains and online retailers first, then flick to your state for our hand-selected list of the top stores in your area. We've marked our favourite shops in **bold** – don't miss these in your buying rounds this year.

If your favourite wine store isn't listed, of if you're a retailer and we haven't found you yet, please let us know by emailing **taste@winepress.com.au**. Subject to a thorough grilling, we'll give you a place in **Taste 2010**. If you're listed in our directory but haven't got your name next to any wines in **The Best Wines of 2009**, check your email (we did ask).

the recommended national retailers

1st Choice Liquor Superstores (1st)

Open every day
Ph 1300 308 833

www.1stchoice.com.au
customerservice@1stchoice.com.au

1st Choice represents the Coles Group's most serious chain store network in Australia. Not only has the number of stores mushroomed again this year but 1st Choice continues to roll-out innovations like in-store plasma screens and touch-screen information kiosks. Each of the stores is supermarket-proportioned, with a focus on wines from its home state. They all offer a wide range from all over Australia, as well as imports from Italy, Germany, Spain, South Africa, Hungary, Argentina, New Zealand and France (including a great range of Champagne). Across the stores, a whopping 160 wines from our **Best Wines of 2009** are stocked. This represents more than half of our list, which makes 1st Choice a great place to find some of the best wines in the country. Weekly specials are good, and this is the place to go when you need a decent Champagne fix (which, let's face it, we all need from time to time)! Pricing is very keen and price-matching is offered on current competitors' specials. Free delivery is offered on straight cases to Melbourne, Sydney, Adelaide, Brisbane and Canberra.

BWS

www.beerwinespirits.com.au

With more than 600 stores nationwide, BWS has more locations on the ground than any other wine shop in the country. The range varies between stores, but expect to find at least a good commercial range, and some stores also offer a reasonable selection of boutiques, premiums, some back-vintages and basic imports. We pop into BWS stores frequently and we still find their prices to be too high and their range to be too limited, so it's worth driving a little further to find a Dan Murphy's instead. Otherwise, be sure to stick with weekly specials and make the most of 10% off any six bottles.

Dan Murphy's (DMs)

Ph 1300 723 388   www.danmurphys.com.au

The fine wine arm of the Woolly network, Dan Murphy's offers a rapidly growing chain of large, well-presented stores across Australia. The range is big, and focuses on low- to mid- range wines but includes some premiums, top-shelf imports and selected cheaper foreign wines imported directly by Dans. This year, you'll find 144 wines from our **Best Wines of 2009** across Dan Murphy's stores, which represents a great selection of the best wines in the country. Pricing is very competitive and good discounts are offered on mixed six-pack buys. Dan's regular discounting cycle is worth watching, as is its "Aged Cellar Release Program." Here you will come across some premium mature wines from some of the better vintages at very reasonable prices.

Liquorland (Lland)

Open every day (except NT)   www.liquorland.com.au
Ph 1300 888 913   customerservice@liquorlanddirect.com.au

Liquorland is a great first stop on your hunt for that perfect bottle, because with more than 500 stores across Australia, there's a good chance there's one near you. If you're looking for something a bit more unique, step up to Vintage Cellars, the fine wine arm of the same network. Liquorland offers a standard range of wines and fortnightly promotions like 10% and 20% off, fuel vouchers and bonuses on 6-pack buys. Regular pricing tends to be on the steep side, so make sure your purchases take advantage of these specials.

Vintage Cellars (VCs)

Open every day   www.vintagecellars.com.au
Ph 1300 366 084   customerservice@vintagecellars.com.au

VCs is the fine wine arm of the Coles network, and with close to 100 locations nationwide, and more opening this year, it is growing into an impressive network. The range is extensive and well-selected, offering everything from standard commercial lines to boutiques and back-vintages. Across all stores, you'll find some 190 wines from our **Best Wines of 2009**. This represents the biggest selection from this list of any retailer in the country – well done VCs! There is also a selection of imports in every store, with some locations offering a stronger range of top-shelf goodies. VCs sources wines directly from around the world and you will spot a number of thier exclusives among our **Best Wines of 2009**. We are promised an ever-widening range of imports, so look out for new additions. The group also offers tastings, dinners and other events for members as well as an active (free) wine club and rewards program. Be sure to buy on special, take advantage of 10% off mixed dozens or time your purchasing to coincide with 20% off weeks.

Wine Selectors
Ph 1300 303 307   www.wineselectors.com.au

Wine Selectors offers a wide range of wine services including the impressive *Selector Life Food Wine* magazine (which is well ahead of its time), member privileges at cellar doors, accommodation and restaurants, wine education opportunities and member events. The range of wines that Wine Selectors offers through its wine club is second to none, covering a comprehensive variety of value-for-money commercial wines through to hard-to-find boutiques. The secret to the standard of its wines is that it employs some of the best palates in the country in its tasting panel, and only wines deemed to be of medal-winning standard make the cut. We have given Wine Selectors a thorough going-over at every level – writing for the magazine, tasting with the tasting panel and visiting its headquarters in Newcastle. The switched-on team behind this organisation is going places at a rapid rate, and our advice is that you get on board.

Woolworths Liquor Stores
www.woolworths.com.au

Selected Woolworths stores (Safeway Liquor in Victoria) offer a standard range of wines. Look for specials.

the recommended retailers in ACT

1st Choice Liquor Superstore (1st)
170 Melrose Dr Phillip   www.1stchoice.com.au

The former Theo's / David Farmer store has been significantly re-vamped and upgraded to have a large range of wines, spirits and beers in the "barn store" style. Like all 1st Choice stores, the best buys are from the weekly advertised specials, especially the NV champagnes at sharp prices, which seem to be an enticement to up-market and special occasion buyers. Can't argue with that! 1st Choice also has a store at the Belconnen Retail Markets, 15 Lathlain St (Ph 6217 8100).

the recommended online retailers

Auscellardoor
Ph 1800 088 022

www.auscellardoor.com.au
simon@auscellardoor.com.au

Australian Wine Centre (Aus)
Ph 08 8272 7248

www.auswine.com.au
gtrott@auswine.com.au

Boutique Wineries

www.boutiquewineries.com.au
customerhelp@boutiquewineries.com.au

D'Or to Door (DOr)
Ph 08 8563 1551

www.dortodoor.com
jeremy@dortodoor.com

Discount Wines (DW)

www.discountwines.com

Frontier Wines

www.frontierwines.com.au
info@frontierwines.com.au

International Fine Wines (IFW)
Ph 03 8415 0206

www.ifw.com.au
orders@internationalfinewines.com.au

Intervino
Ph 02 9690 0888

www.intervino.com.au
info@intervino.com.au

Liquor King

www.liquorking.com.au
lk@lk.com.au

Liquorland Direct
Ph 1300 300 640

www.liquorlanddirect.com.au
customerservice@liquorlanddirect.com.au

Organic Wine
Ph 03 9387 0500

www.organicwine.com.au
info@organicwine.com.au

Oz Liquor Mart

www.ozliquormart.com.au

Porter's Liquor

www.portersliquor.com.au

The Boutique Wine Company

www.boutiquewineco.com.au

The Tasting Room
Ph 03 9583 1944

www.tastingroom.com.au
service@tastingroom.com.au

WineSale

www.winesale.com.au

WineStar
Ph 03 9379 9119

www.winestar.com.au
shop@winestar.com.au

Campbell Liquor Discounts
4 Blamey Pl Campbell   Ph 6247 1366

A tiny, cramped shop with an interesting range of wines and some back vintages which look like they've been sitting on the shelves for a while. CLD seems to have a loyal local clientele and pick up trade from local shopping centre visitors and restaurant-goers.

Canberra Cellars
Cnr Luxton & Josephson Sts Belconnen (Ph 6251 9410)   www.canberracellars.com.au
and 21 Lonsdale St Braddon (Ph 6262 8599)   Open 10am-11pm daily
                                                    canberracellars@optusnet.com.au

Canberra Cellars has had a facelift on the outside, but inside you'll still find an eclectic store boasting a wide range of wines including many commercial "standards" and a great range of boutiques. The other news this year is a second outlet at Braddon (ex Australian Wine Brokers). Close to half of the reds are the product of small makers all over Australia, including a strong representation of Canberra District wines. This would have to be the only place in Canberra to find many of these, so call in if you are looking for something unusual.

Candamber
4 Oatley Court Belconnen   www.discountwines.com   Ph 6251 4247
                                                    john@discountwines.com

If you're looking for a great place to buy wine at competitive prices from friendly and helpful staff, we've found just the place. One of the original local discount wine stores, established in 1976 and still under its original ownership, Candamber competes with the chain stores by offering "case prices" on single-bottle purchases. The store boasts a large range of wine, although much of it is displayed standing up on crowded shelves in a non-air-conditioned store (so stick with recent vintages, or trade up to the premium and museum wines in refrigerated storage). They have two other outlets besides the large home store in Belconnen, one in the City Centre (cnr Bunda St and Garema Place, Ph 02 6248 6522) servicing the passing and restaurant trade and another in the Weston Creek shopping precinct (17 Brierley St, Ph 02 6288 9429). Promotional specials are kept up to date on a simple but effective web site.

Criss Cross Cellars
Ph 6286 5230   Southlands Shopping Centre Mawson

A small shop crammed with a smallish range of wines, but featuring some interesting wines that you won't find in the chain stores. Prices are fairly standard, but there are plenty of spot specials on display all the time.

Georges Liquor Stable   Ph 6285 3075
17 Dundas Court Phillip and James Court Braddon

George's is the place to head if you are looking for unusual and hard-to find wines. This is a family-owned and run business, with a large outlet in the Phillip Commercial area and another store on the edge of the city. George sources and stocks a wide range of premium wines and stacks them in apparently random order around the Phillip shop (which can make it a pain to browse, but we enjoy a good treasure hunt!). There's some fancy new display racking to be discovered this year. Single bottle prices are fairly standard (high) but case prices are negotiable.

Jacks Liquor
See local phone book for locations

A small chain scattered throughout small suburban shopping centres with a basic range of wines.

Jim Murphy Airport Cellars   Ph 6247 7921
7 Mustang Ave Majura (Canberra Airport)   jcellars@bigpond.net.au

When we first saw the new barn-type outlet in a stark business park on the edge of Canberra Airport we thought Jim was being rather brave. But with a Brand Depot warehouse nearby and a busy stream of cars passing by daily, this actually makes a lot of sense. It follows the original Jim Murphy (and Dan Murphy) format, with low and mid-range wines on long shelves, cases underneath and a dedicated premium wine area. There's something here for everyone.

Jim Murphy Market Cellars
19 Mildura St Fyshwick
Open M-F 8-6, Sat 7:30-6, Sun 8:30-6
jcellars@bigpond.net.au
Ph 6295 0060

Located next to the Fyshwick retail markets, Jim Murphy's store is a big brick shed with a tin roof, but you'll be pleased to know that it is insulated and air conditioned. You'll find a big range of wines on the floor and a special section with long verticals and back vintages of selected wines (just be cautious with old vintages if they're standing up). This is the place to go for John's Blend or a special old-vintage red. Jim holds regular small and some very large-scale tastings and hosts dinner tastings for regular buyers.

Kingston Hotel Wines
Cnr Oxley & Giles St Kingston
Ph 6232 6174

Tucked in behind the drive-thru outlet at the Kingo Hotel, this smallish shop is crammed with a large range of wines, spirits and cigars. Weekly specials are advertised by email list and include some sharp prices and discounts for case buys.

Kippax Cellars
Shop 4, Kippax Fair, Hardwick Crs Holt
Ph 6254 5754

A small shop competing with Woolworths Liquor in the same shopping centre, Kippax Cellars boasts a useful range of wines that you won't find in the chain stores.

Local Liquor
www.localliquor.com.au

Local Liquor has mushroomed this year to more than 130 locations across the ACT and NSW. As the advertising and buying brand for the IGA chain of independent supermarkets (and some hotel bottle shops), it offers a fair range of mainstream wines.

Supa-Barn
Bunda St Canberra City
www.supabarn.com.au/liquor
Ph 6257 4055

One of a local chain of medium-sized supermarkets, this one is in the Civic shopping precinct and has a large wine section. As well as the standard commercial lines there is a fair sprinkling of more interesting (and expensive) wines. See the web site for full list of locations and open hours.

The Wine Shed
Belconnen Markets Belconnen
Ph 6251 1777

Located at the Belconnen Retail Markets, this shop has a good selection of wines including some premiums and many local wines. Standard pricing, but there is a discount for case buys.

Vintage Cellars (VCs)
Manuka and Woden
www.vintagecellars.com.au

These are two small stores with much of the standard VC range plus some interesting discretionary stock (particularly at Manuka) at the usual VCs prices. Manuka has a sizeable cellar underneath for super-premium and back vintage stock. As always, look for specials.

Vintage Cellars
4 McEwen Ave Oaks Estate
Ph 6297 2278

This isn't the chain store. Housed in an old Nissen/Quonset hut, this store gets pretty hot in summer and cold in winter, but you never know what you may find if you spend a bit of time browsing through the stock. The locals tell us that something interesting will sometimes catch their eye.

the recommended retailers in NSW

Sixty Darling Street Fine Wines (Sixty)
60 Darling St Balmain East
Open M-W 9-7:45, T-Sat 9-8:30, Sun10-6:30
Ph 9818 3077
suzi.hamilton@swiftdsl.com.au

Here's a shop worth poking around. There are plenty of premium and interesting wines at fair to good prices, although not many imports. You'll notice some back-vintages and a good supply of well-priced magnums, but watch the provenance – it was sweltering last time we visited in summer! Stick with new releases and buy in the cooler months. Look for specials, and buy by the case if you can. Free delivery in Sydney. Give them a call to be added to their mailing list.

Amato's Liquor Mart

267 Norton St Leichhardt
Ph 9560 7628

www.amatos.com.au
Open M-Sat 9-8, Sun 10-6
amatos@amatos.com.au

A big store with a large commercial range, speckled with the odd boutique and imported wine at fair prices.

Avalon Fine Wine

35 Avalon Pde Avalon

Ph 9918 3207
finewine@bigpond.net.au

A great variety of Aussie, New Zealand, French and Italian wines are crammed into the narrow aisles of this inviting corner store in the heart of Avalon. You'll find interesting options at every price point. Mixed dozen prices are competitive.

Best Cellars NSW

91 Crown St East Sydney

www.bestcellars.com.au
Open M-F 9-9, Sat 10-9, Sun 1-8
Ph 9361 5454

A great range with plenty of interesting, hard-to-find Aussies and imports. There are also some bargains to be had at the top end if you buy wisely. It's nice to see a cleverly assembled range at refreshing prices.

BWS Gladesville

235 Victoria Rd Gladesville

www.beerwinespirits.com.au
Ph 8732 5667

This is Sydney's BWS flagship store, and it's a huge shop with a great variety of Australian and New Zealand wines, top shelf back-vintages and all sorts of high-end boutiques (mostly Aussie) that you won't find at other BWS outlets. Prices are fair if you take advantage of 10 percent off on mixed six-packs.

CBD Cellars City (CBD)

36 Carrington St Sydney
Open M-W 8.30-7, T-F 8:30-7:30, Sat 10:30-7

www.cbdcellars.com.au
john.bellis@cbdcellars.com.au
Ph 9262 4522

A slick inner-city store with a big range of Aussie boutiques, imports and a selection of back-vintages. CBD Cellars is a longstanding corporate beverage supplier and prides itself on tailor-made gifts, boardroom tastings, cellar management, storage, special events and wine education. You would expect to pay a premium at a location like this – and you will – but you're getting more than just a bottle off the shelf at CBD Cellars.

David Jones

Sydney Centrepoint
Ph 9266 5544

www.davidjones.com.au
contactus@davidjones.com.au

When we visited DJs at Sydney Centrepoint we discovered an interesting range with 20% off imports and 10% off 6-packs at the time. The standard deal across the stores is 10% off 6 wines and 20% off 12. We're told that 30% off wine sales come up a couple of times a year, not widely advertised, but worth snapping up some bargains. DJs operates seven liquor departments across Sydney, Newcastle, Melbourne, Adelaide & Perth.

Elizabeth Bay Cellars

76 Elizabeth Bay Rd Elizabeth Bay
Ph 9358 1688

www.ebaycellars.com.au
ebaycellars@bigpond.com.au

Swing by EBay cellars, rent a DVD to go with your latest drop and choose from a good variety of wines at average prices. When you're after more than a DVD wine, check out the ultra-premium, back-vintage wines and large-format bottles in the climate-controlled room at the back – gotta love that space-age door! The sky's the limit in there (in more ways than one)!

First Estate at Figtree Cellars Lane Cove

231 Burns Bay Rd Lane Cove
Toll free 1800 808 408

Ph 9418 9666
mleahy@firstestate.com.au

This is the last standing First Estate store in the Woolworths empire, and it's worth a visit. You'll find a great range of interesting boutiques, top shelf back-vintages and the odd import at keen mixed or straight case discounts (15%).

Five Ways Cellars

4 Heeley St Paddington

Ph 9360 4242

Ian Cook knows his stuff, and he'll look after you with a variety of Aussie wines (downstairs) and imports (under climate control upstairs). Just beware of anything in the reach of direct sunlight through those front doors. There's a good selection of Italians here (and no shortage of Italian wines, either!). Fair prices and good service.

George's Liquor Nest
95 Willoughby Rd Crows Nest   Ph 9437 6688

George's offers a good range of commercial and domestic boutique wines at average to high prices, plus some imports tucked away at the back.

GPO Cheese & Wine (GPO)
Lower ground floor, 1 Martin Place Sydney   www.gposydney.com
Open M-W 10-6, T 10-8, Fri 10-9   mail@gposydney.com
Ph 9229 7701

A well-thought-out range of Aussie and Kiwi boutiques and a selection of affordable Frenchies. Don't miss the wall of international cheeses while you're here. Matched cheese and wine tastings are offered and don't miss the new cheese and wine room. Prices are to be expected at such an address.

Kemeny's (Kem)
137-147 Bondi Rd Bondi   www.kemenys.com.au
Open M-Sat 8am-9pm, Sun 9am-8pm   orders@kemenys.com.au
Ph 138881

A bustling supermarket of food and wine on the busy Bondi drag, Kemeny's is a fun, must-visit wine shop, albeit a bit chaotic at times. There are bargains to be had at every turn amid a wide range of Aussie, NZ, French and Italian wines, with mixed dozen discounts. Kemeny's strong relationships with many of Australia's better producers are reflected in its "Kemeny's Hidden Label" range of premium wines bottled under Kemeny's own label and sold at bargain prices. We've had some fun trying to find the winemaker's name hidden in the label, but somehow it disappears after a glass or two! It's worth the trip to the beach to stock the cellar (and grab the groceries while you're at it) but if you're not in range, check out their online wine store instead, or phone 13 88 81. Kemeny's operates one of the most efficient wine delivery systems in the country. Last time we ordered a case it arrived in Bris less than 24 hours later! All up, this is one of the best wine stores in Australia. Congratulations to Andrew and his team.

Leura Cellars
169-171 The Mall Leura   www.leuracellars.com.au
Open M-T 10-8, F-Sat 10-9, Sun 10-7:30   sales@leuracellars.com.au
Ph 4784 1122

Leura cellars is the back-vintage capital of Australian wine retailers. You can browse the range on their web site, but it's much more fun to poke around the historic cellars, so pack up the kids for a Sunday in the Blue Mountains and make this your one mandatory, self-indulgent stop for the day! You might not discover any bargains, but you will find big verticals of virtually every decent Australian label. A unique and remarkable store.

Liquor Prince
8 Princes St Turramurra

www.liquorprince.com.au
Ph 9449 8550
enquiries@liquorprince.com.au

A compact store with an eclectic array of Australian wines at good case prices and the occasional bargain. Liquor Prince is your party and function specialist and will deliver everything you need for eats and drinks.

North Sydney Cellars
189 Miller St (cnr Berry St) North Sydney
Open M-F 9-8, Sat 10-8

Ph 9954 0090
www.northsydneycellars.com
shop@northsydneycellars.com

The inimitable Jules and his enthusiastic team are taking their excellent and interesting hand-selected range of wines at NSC to the next level. The emphasis is on small, quality-focused Aussie producers and good value imports from Italy, Spain and France. We're big fans of the old store and we can't wait to check out the new joint. Standard prices tend to be inflated but 20% off by the dozen makes for good value. Free national delivery on dozen purchases.

Palm Beach Wine Company
1109 Barrenjoey Rd Palm Beach

Ph 9974 4304
www.palmbeachwineco.com
sales@palmbeachwineco.com

You're in for a fun weekend at the beach after a stop at this exciting store, boasting an outstanding range of local and imported boutiques and plenty of gourmet goodies for a picnic in the sun! You'll discover an extensive stock of interesting wines here that you won't find elsewhere. Matt Maunz directly imports an impressive French and Italian range Pricing is fair, with keen mixed dozen discounts and free delivery to Sydney on mixed dozens. Enthusiastic buyers drive up from Sydney to buy here, and it's not hard to see why.

Summer Hill Wine shop (Sum)   Ph 9798 7282
7a Lackey St Summer Hill
www.winebizz.com.au

Open 10-8 every day
info@winebizz.com.au

A fair range of premium Aussie wines that you won't find in the chain stores, plus the odd import. Dozen prices are good (so buy in bulk), and service is friendly and helpful. Staff are happy to track down any obscure wines that they don't have in stock.

The Lambton Fridge   Ph 4957 1274
86 Elder St Lambton

lambtonfridge@optusnet.com.au

Damien Hogan is the passionate and knowledgeable name behind this great wine shop in Newcastle. He keeps his shelves well-stocked with a great range of interesting boutiques from around the country, and a few from far shores. Don't miss his Regional Exhibitions – a great way to learn about our best regions. Case buy discounts are worth taking advantage of.

The Oak Barrel
152 Elizabeth St Sydney
Ph 9264 3022

www.oakbarrel.com.au
Open M-F 10-8:30, Sat 11-10
info@oakbarrel.com.au

The Oak Barrel is under new ownership this year, and we're told that plans are afoot to significantly upgrade the range of imported wines. The staff are helpful and friendly and there are loads of interesting back-vintage, boutique and hard-to-get Aussie wines at fair prices for this part of the world. There's also a healthy selection of vintage ports and a decent cross-section of imports with a focus on Champagnes. If beers or spirits are your thing, you'll also be a happy chappy here. Free delivery is offered within 5km of Sydney's CBD. Locals tell us that The Oak Barrel is relatively unknown but one of the best. You know about it now, so you have no excuse!

Ultimo Wine Centre
Shop C21/99 Jones St Ultimo
Open M-W 9-7, T-F 9-8, Sat 10-8 Ph 9211 2380

www.ultimowinecentre.com.au
info@ultimowinecentre.com.au

Is this Sydney's best wine shop? You be the judge, but there is certainly no question that this is a premium wine store in every way, with an outstanding range of wines and books. It's the place to buy your imports at all price points, with one of the best ranges in the country and a keen team constantly scouring the planet to broaden its range. A climate-controlled shop, refrigerated storage and warehouse mean that you can confidently do your shopping here for Vintage Port back-vintages as well as older Aussie wines (but prices increase with age, so look for specials). A good range of half-bottles is also stocked. Ultimo prides itself on an ongoing program of wine education, monthly dinners and great tastings every Saturday.

Victoria Cellars Gladesville
122 Victoria Rd Gladesville   www.victoriacellars.com.au
Ph 9816 5277   victoriacellars@bigpond.com.au

A small VC store with a good boutique range at keen case prices. There are also some top-shelf imports to discover. Ask Joe to show you the interesting stuff "out the back."

the recommended retailers in QLD

Best Cellars QLD
Shop 18 Central Brunswick Centre Martin St   Ph 3257 2862

There's a better range than you might expect to find in a shop of this size, largely a consequence of the refreshing absence of bottom-end commercial lines. Instead you'll find a well-chosen range of premium and imported products. Four stores across Brisbane.

Chalk and Cheese (Chalk)
Shop 3/75 Hardgrave Rd West End (Ph 3255 2322) and   www.chalkncheese.com.au
29 Florence St Teneriffe (Ph 3252 1608)   talk@chalkncheese.com.au
9am-11pm daily

Chalk and Cheese presents a good range of premiums and top boutiques from Australia and New Zealand, but look for specials. The West End store is a handy place to grab a bottle to let loose on the restaurant strip that surrounds it.

Cru Bar & Cellar
22 James St Fortitude Valley   www.crubar.com
Ph 3252 1744   cellar@crubar.com

Flowing into Brisbane's ultra-hip Cru Bar (one of our favourite hangouts), Cru Cellar is stacked from floor to very high ceiling with a great range of wines from all over the world. You'll find a good selection of Aussie boutiques at reasonable prices and you'll get 10% off case buys if you ask nicely. There's an unabashed focus on premium wine and a refreshing absence of budget quaffers. The bar always offers something interesting by the glass, so sidle up for a drink while you're here. Or – better – choose a bottle from the shop and they'll open it for you at the bar. We set another long lunch record here this year after judging **The Great Australian Red** (into double figure hours this time!) Did we say we like it here?

Drinx at Central
Under Central Station, Ann St Brisbane   Ph 3216 0655   www.drinx.com.au
sales@drinx.com.au

The team at Drinx Central are switched on to wine, and the range of great booze packed into this little store is proof. They've tracked down a shop full of great labels, many of which you won't see in most other outlets, and stuck "buy me" prices on them. Considering the central location, the value afforded here is pretty smart. There's an unashamed Barossan bias to the range and Whisky is also a specialty but their policy is that they will stock anything that the customer requests that's available in the country. Boardroom deliveries and tastings are offered by a passionate team. Ten stores across Brisbane.

Festival Cellars
Shop 7 Festival Towers 108 Albert St Bris (entry via Charlotte)   Ph 3012 9880
Open M-W 9-8, T-F 9am-10pm, Sat 10-10, Sun 10-8   www.festivalcellars.com
info@festivalcellars.com

Festival Cellars is still Brisbane's newest, hippest wine shop. A very clever range is hand-selected by a switched-on team, and every base is well-covered. From a remarkably drinkable range of Festival-Cellars-branded cheapies, through commercial premiums, hard-to-find boutiques and some imports, you'll have no trouble finding just the right bottle in this fun little shop. But the biggest surprise still awaits you, because when you front up to pay for your stash, you won't believe how little you pay. With weekly tastings and approachable staff, "Festy" Cellars is making wine accessible to a new generation.

Friday's
Riverside centre 123 Eagle St Brisbane   info@fridays.com.au
Ph 3832 2122

Steve has been in the wine retail game in Bris for a long time, and takes pride in his hand-selected range at Fridays. He also has a well-developed network of sources for back-vintage and interesting wines, as a quick glance around the store will reveal. Current vintage wines are fairly priced.

shake the sand off your feet

McGuires Paddington Tavern

186 Given Tce Paddington
www.mcguireshotels.com.au

Open 10-8 every day
Ph 3217 5093
paddo@mcguireshotels.com.au

The Paddo boasts a specialist fine wine section with a strong range of Oz and some overseas wines, including some premiums and back-vintages. It's climate controlled and offers good specials. This group runs a serious of great tastings across the year, which are not to be missed. There are nine stores in the McGuires group across Brisbane and the Gold Coast.

Stewarts Wine Company

Eagle St Pier 1 Eagle St Brisbane (under Vinos)
www.stewartswineco.com.au
swc.city@stewarts.net.au

Ph 3220 1286
Toll free 1300 138 838

Ted Stewart, Steve Knight and their team are passionate about wine and their expertise spans a longstanding line of key restaurants, function rooms and wine shops in Brisbane. Their four Stewarts stores showcase a great range of boutique and exciting Oz wines as well as a small but well-chosen shelf of imports and a climate-controlled rooms for premiums. Some prices are high, but there are some great specials to be snapped up as well as competitive case buy discounts. They also run a serious program of wine events throughout the year.

Sunshine Cellars

Hastings St Noosa

Ph 5474 9480

Shake the sand off your feet and duck into any of Sunshine Cellars' four locations in Noosa to discover a good range of commercial and boutique wines at reasonable prices. The Noosa Heads store is right in the hub of the action and the perfect spot to grab a bottle to take to a BYO on the esplanade. Or, even better, buy a case for your holiday weekend and take advantage of mixed dozen discounts.

The Wine Emporium (Emp)

Shop 47 Emporium Traders 1000 Ann St Fortitude Valley
Open M-Sat 10-8, Sun 10-6

Ph 3252 1117
ww.thewineemporium.com.au
traviswatson@thewineemporium.com.au

We have again this year spent a lot of time and money at The Wine Emporium! This team holds between them the most intensive knowledge of wine retail in the state, and it shows in every facet of this outstanding shop. The range ranks among the best-assembled in Australia, with every base covered at every price point. Pricing is generally reasonable, with some lines particularly attractive. Not only are the shop and storage area fully climate-controlled, but the provenance of all back-vintages is guaranteed. Imports are a specialty, and make sure your name is on their list for Bordeaux and Burgundy en-primeur and special shipment announcements. The store also hosts a comprehensive education program and many dinners throughout the year. They describe themselves as "all round top chaps" and it's not a bad assessment!

The Wine Room
480 Waterworks Rd Ashgrove (Ph 3366 5381) **and 3/33 Lytton Rd East Bris** (Ph 3891 2959)
Open 10-10 every day

A commercial range with a few interesting boutiques along the way. Prices are up there so you'll want to take advantage of 10% off on 6-packs.

Urban Cellars
525 Boundary Rd Spring Hill   Ph 3227 1999

A large but now relatively sparse store displays some good lines at the right price. A climate-controlled room at the back guards top-shelf and back vintage wines. Don't miss the micro brewery while you're here.

Wineaway
Unit 3, 276 Abbotsford Rd Bowen Hills
Open T-F 12-6, Sat 9-1

www.wineaway.com.au
Ph 3852 1891
email@wineaway.com.au

Much more than a storage facility, Wineaway is a fine wine destination with a growing emphasis on events and retail. Scott, Felicity, Jody and Chris have their finger on the pulse when it comes to wines that are highly sought after, difficult to procure or just great value. If you're in QLD and you're seriously interested in fine wine, make sure you're in the Wineaway circle.

WINE @ Era
102 Melbourne St South Brisbane
Open M-W 10-8, T-Sat 10-8, Sun 10-6

www.erabistro.com.au
wine@erabistro.com.au
Ph 3255 2009

The Era precinct is a revolution in wine and food in South Brisbane, with a restaurant, café, market and wine shop connected in a delightful same-place-but-not-really kind of way. WINE @ Era is a new addition to our list this year, and if you haven't discovered this shop yet, get on over and check it out. The wall of wines featuring nearly 4000 bottles is worth the visit in its own right. While you're here, have a fossick through the great range of imports. The selection is focused on the $20 to $40 market, with a particular emphasis on wines from South America, Spain and Italy. If you're into beer, they've lined up more than 130 for you to choose from. Dave Cross and Steve Powell are so excited about Taste that **if you mention this book when you visit WINE @ Era they'll give you 20% off any wine** that isn't already discounted. Great deal!

the recommended retailers in SA

1st Choice Liquor Superstore (1st)
Cnr Unley Rd and Clifton St Unley

www.1stchoice.com.au
Ph 1300308833

1st Choice offers a huge range and good weekly specials. In this outlet you'll find some top shelf and hard to find back-vintages chained (literally) to the shelf at the back (no chain store jokes, please!). Pricing is keen, and there are discounts on mixed-dozens. This is an average 1st Choice store but nonetheless huge!

Booze Brothers Norwood
97 The Parade Norwood

Ph 8366 5100
www.boozebros.com.au

This is BB's central SA store, and it's one mother of a shop with an extensive range of boutiques, imports, back vintages and oddments. Watch what you pay when you reach for the top shelf, but there are good specials and discounts for six bottles.

Cellarbrations Strathmore Cellars
Shop 18, 19 Bank St Adelaide

Ph 8238 2900 www.strath.com.au/cellars.htm
info@strath.com.au

A small store with a range of commercials and some interesting boutiques. Prices are good for an inner-city store.

East End Cellars (EEC)

22-26 Vardon Ave Adelaide
Ph 8232 5300

www.eastendcellars.com.au
Open M-T 9-7, W 9-8, T 9-9, F 9-20, Sat 10-8, Sun 12-6
wine@eastendcellars.com.au

Michael Andrewartha describes his EEC store just off Rundle St as "a hobby, not a business." This is one serious hobby – a producer, wholesaler, importer and exporter in one – and he sells wine as well! Needless to say, EEC has more than its share of expertise behind the counter, and it shows in shelf after shelf of wine . Expect to find an outstanding hand-selected range of everything from everywhere, with a focus on premium wines from small producers, at very keen prices. A climate-controlled room houses floor-to-ceiling super-premiums, back-vintages and top imports. The store also hosts Friday night tastings and a large annual tasting event. We enjoy visiting Mike and his team whenever we're in Adelaide, and we always emerge with something interesting. Last time it was two dozen Ashton Hills Salmon Brut (the most we've ever seen of this cult wine in any shop!).

Fassina Liquor Merchants

37-39 Oaklands Rd Somerton Park

Ph 8376 1848
somerton@fassinaliquor.com.au

Fassina is a big store in the Adelaide suburbs with a wide range of commercials and South Australian boutique wines. The big surprise for a store of this size is a great selection of back vintages at not much more than current retail prices in the back of the store. And it's not just the dud vintages, either! You'll also find a clever "try before you buy" tasting system on some current specials - although there are only plastic thimbles to drink from. Fassina carries and impressive range at very competitive prices and offers ten percent off on six bottle purchases. Fassina has recently opened a new store on Anzac Highway in Morpheville.

Goodwood Cellars

125 Goodwood Rd Goodwood

Ph 8271 7481
goodwoodcellars@toucangroup.com.au

A good selection of predominantly SA wines is on display here. You'll also find a small range of back vintages and imports in the store. Buy on special whenever you can.

Hutt St Cellars

253 Hutt St Adelaide
M-W 9am-10pm, T 9am-11pm, F-Sat 9am-12am, Sun 10-9

Ph 8232 1570
www.arabsteedhotel.com.au
mark@huttstreetcellars.com.au

Described by its staff as a quaint store, its homely arrangement of small rooms boasts a range of mainly SA wines with some top-shelf back-vintages and selected imports. You will discover some interesting boutiques here that you won't find in the chain stores. Pricing is fair.

Melbourne Street Fine Wine Cellars

93 Melbourne St North Adelaide

Ph 8267 1533

This is a terrific spot in Adelaide to lose yourself between the bottles. Melbourne Street is brimming with boxes of everything from everywhere, representing one of the bigger and better ranges in the state. Pricing is keen and air conditioning keeps the store cool in summer. If we lived in Adelaide, our credit cards would often find their way here!

Parade Cellars Sip 'N' Save

Shop 15, 161 The Parade Norwood

Ph 8332 0317
paradecellars@optusnet.com

A small shopping complex store with a good selection of boutiques and some imports. Pricing is reasonable, but buy on special whenever you can.

Southern Cross Cellars Bottle O

14 James Place Adelaide
Open M-T 9-6, F 9-7, Sat 11-5

www.southerncrosscellars.com.au
Ph 8231 2271
marrakesh@internode.on.net

Southern Cross Cellars offers a commercial and premium range with the occasional boutique wine. Pricing is fair, and there are some bargains to be found.

Tanunda cellars

14 Murray St Tanunda
Ph 8563 3544

www.tanundacellars.com.au
tanundacellars@ozemail.com.au

This is back vintage heaven in the heart of Tanunda in the Barossa, showcasing a great range of Barossa's best of all ages. It's appropriately located in an 1853 heritage listed building. Prices are generally fair for what they are, but look for specials. The shop is air conditioned and free freight is offered to Australian capital cities.

The Edinburgh Hotel and Cellars (Ed)

7 High St Mitcham
Open M-Sat 9am-10pm, Sun 10-8

www.edinburgh.com.au
Ph 8373 2753
cellars@edinburgh.com.au

Housed in a grand historic building, The Ed is the best presented wine shop in South Australia. Living up to its motto that "Its all in your ED," its huge range (2750 wines at last count!) is neatly organised into logical varietal sections. There are loads of premiums and boutiques to tempt you in this big shop, as well as a great variety of imports. The Ed's specialty is small, independent and artisanal makers. Pricing is keen, and there are good specials to snap up. Don't miss a poke around the back-vintages in the (real) cellar underneath. Take advantage of 10% off six or more bottles and 15% off two dozen. Log on to the web site to join the mailing list and be informed of regular tastings and events. The Ed prides itself on being able to arrange delivery "to most countries in the world, even Australia!"

West Lakes Cellars (WLC)

141 Brebner Dr West Lakes
Open 9am-10pm
www.mycellars.com.au

Ph 8356 4444

gpriest@lakesresorthotel.com.au

A premium drive-through boasting a to-be-expected commercial range and then – WHAT THE?! – Greenock Creek, Rockford, Mollydooker, Torbreck, Majella, Kalleske, Giaconda... at great prices. Ten percent off on mixed half-dozens. West Lakes Cellars is now linked with mycellars.com.au.

the recommended retailers in TAS

Aberfeldy Cellars BWS

124 Davey Street Hobart

Ph 6211 6633

Aberfeldy Cellars is a BWS store with a reasonable range of wines in the centre of Hobart.

Gasworks 9/11 Bottle Shop

Shop 3, 2 Macquarie Street Hobart
Open 9am-11pm every day

Ph 6214 7525
info@911.com.au

Gasworks is an award-winning bottle shop with a good range, including a

strong selection of our **Best Wines of 2009.** Be wary of the provenance of older vintages and stick with specials wherever possible.

Just Add Wine
339 Elizabeth Street North Hobart

www.justaddwines.com.au
Open M-Sat 12:30-9
Ph 6234 7220

A small, homely wine shop that specialises in a growing list of Tasmanian wines and a large range of cleanskins. An easy-to-navigate web site is set up for shopping from home, and the more than 600 wines, spirits and liqueurs listed are in stock. Pricing is competitive.

The Tasmanian Wine Centre (TWC)
201 Collins Street
Open M-F 9-6, Sat 9:30-5

www.tasmanian-wine.com.au
sales@thetwc.com.au
Ph 6234 9995

An epicentre for Tassie wine, with events, tours and retail sales coordinated under one roof. Look out for the annual Tasmanian wine fairs. You'll find a good range of wines at competitive prices and knowledgeable staff.

the recommended retailers in VIC

1st Choice Liquor Superstore (1st)
Tooronga   Village   Shopping   Centre   Tooronga   Road
www.1stchoice.com.au   Ph 1300 308 833

1st Choice is Coles' liquor barn superstore. The large Toorak store combines "by the box" retailing with a very broad range of premium wines. It offers aggressive price matching, particularly on dozen purchases. Visual merchandising features such as the Champagne corner break up the size of the store. The excellent Information kiosks scattered throughout the store provide printable details for the wines on range. You can even use them to plan your next party!

Boccaccio Cellars (Boc)
1030 Burke Rd Balwyn
Open M-F 9-7, S-S 9-5

Ph 9817 2257
www.boccaccio.com.au
sales@boccaccio.com.au

The outward appearance of the shop suggests that the store is a mere supermarket offshoot, but don't be deceived – Boccaccio is a significant size,

With a large range to match, the only thing that's small about the store is the pricing, with some of the best specials in the country. A good mainstream Australian range is supplemented with a very nice selection of imports with a building emphasis on Italian and Spanish fine wines. Boccaccio boasts a very strong mailing list and online presence, fuelled by its competitive pricing strategy. The new Boccaccio Café is the venue for a range of food and wine events.

Cellarbrations
295-297 Clarendon St South Melbourne
www.cellarbrations.com.au
Ph 9686 8967

Cellarbrations has exploded to a whopping 400 stores nationwide! The South Melbourne store has a good range of wines at keen prices and a nice range of specials. They also know how to stage a smart tasting.

Cloudwine Cellars (Cloud)
317 Clarendon St South Melb
Open M-Sat 11-8, Sun 1-7
Ph 9699 6700
www.cloudwine.com.au
sales@cloudwine.com.au

A small store on the Clarendon St strip with an eclectic selection of Australian and New Zealand wines and international beers. The focus is firmly on smaller producers in Australian and New Zealand – there is no place for big company wines here. Wines are organised by price brackets to suit the casual browser. The range isn't huge, but neither are the prices, and there's an additional 10% off mixed dozens and 5% off straight 6 packs. A themed fortnightly newsletter advises of special discounts, regular winemaker dinners as well as releases of some of Australia's hardest-to-get labels. It's little wonder that mailing list sales are as active as they are! Also at 34 Church St Brighton (Ph 9553 8416) and 766 Burke Rd Camberwell Camberwell (Ph 9882 0954).

Dan Murphy's Melbourne City (DMs)
QV Building Lonsdale St Melbourne
Open M-W 9-8, T-F 9-9, Sat 9-8, Sun 10-6
Ph 1300 723 388
www.danmurphys.com.au

Big discount retailing has returned to the Melbourne CBD with the opening of a new Dan's store in the lower level of the QV Complex. As you'd expect, it's more compact than the typical Dan's, but it carries the same main mix of bulk and fine wines, along with beers and spirits. The commercial section is arranged by grape variety rather than the more typical winery order seen in other stores.

Dan Murphy's Newtown (DMs)
155 Pakington St Newtown

www.danmurphys.com.au
Ph 1300 723 388

Geelong is proud of its status as a wine producing region and it's good to see that it's not only the independent retailers who are offering a good selection of local wines. The large store on the Pakington St strip reflects the typical DMs layout, with volume wines up front and premiums at the back. The Geelong West store also boasts a very good selection of local wines and the fine wine staff are as knowledgeable and passionate as a boutique retailer. Tastings on Friday and Saturday.

Neuschafer's Bottle Shop
90 Mercer St Geelong

Ph 5229 8871

Neuschafer's is as much an experience as it is a liquor store. From the handwritten adverts on the windows and the pumpkins and sacks of onions that flank the doorway, to the amazing jumble of boxes and bottles inside, this is an experience you've got to have. Poke around and you'll discover some order to this seeming chaos, with a distinct Australian focus to its broad range of wines. There's a good selection of fortifieds, and occasional back vintage treasures can be found lurking among the piles. Pricing is as mixed as the store.

Nicks Wine Merchants Malvern (Nicks)
1219 High St Armadale (Open M 9-6, Tues-Sat 9-7) and
10-12 Jackson Crt Doncaster (Open M-Sat 9-7, Sun 10-5)

Ph 9822 9100
Free call 1800 069 295
www.nicks.com.au
sales@nicks.com.au

Nick's inner suburban store is a compact storefront among the High Street art galleries and fashion stores, featuring a very well selected range of local and imported wines. The labels that Nick is associated with, including Tatiarra and Journey's End, represent a level of value well above most store's 'house' labels. A very strong mailing list is centred around a Vintage Direct newsletter and online store and free delivery is offered on orders over $200. A "Vintage School Online Wine Course" is also run through the web site. You'll regularly see Nick in the store and it's worth taking the time to say "g'day" to one of the long-standing names of the Victorian Wine Industry.

Prince Wine Store (PWS)

Ph 9686 3033

177 Bank St South Melbourne (Open M-T 10-8, F-Sat 10-9)   www.princewinestore.com.au
2a Acland St St Kilda (Sun-Thurs 12-10, F-Sat 12-11)   pws@theprince.com.au
and Clarendon Centre 269 Clarendon St South Melbourne

The Prince now comprises three of the slickest wine shops in the country, with fit outs and sound systems as hip as their extensive, premium range. You will find everything decent from all over the world, including 100 of our **Best Wines of 2009** at fair prices – but value is not merely about price. The centrepiece of the South Melbourne store is a room with premium wines and a long table for tastings, tutorials and dinners. The store also offers an extensive program of wine education courses and tastings, including free tastings every Saturday between 12 and 2. Join the mailing list on the web site for details of special offers and events. A knowledgeable team ensures that this store sets the standard for fine wine retailing in the state. The new store is now fully operational in the Clarendon Centre in South Melbourne.

Prospect Wines

www.prospectwines.com.au

Ph 9877 1099   sales@prospectwines.com.au

A retail chain with eight stores in Melbourne and one in Hobart. The focus is on buying unlabelled wine and selling it under their own label. See the web site for store locations.

Randall The Wine Merchant Newtown (Rand)

www.randalls.net.au

324 Pakington St Newtown   Ph 5223 1141   newtown@randalls.net.au
and 186 Bridport St Albert Park   Ph 9686 4122   albertpark@randalls.net.au
Open M-W 10-8, T-F 10-9, Sat 9-9, Sun 11-7

Randall Pollard has long been at the forefront of wine retailing in Geelong, from establishing and building Bannockburn Cellars to setting up a store under his own name at the "Paris end" of Pakington St. The large store offers a very good range (although the dominance of cleanskins tend to overwhelm the front half of the store). Don't let this slow you down, because there is also a deep range of premium and imported wines on offer. Pricing is generally on the premium side, but specials are worth looking out for. Tastings on Saturday and occasion wine events. The locals tell us that the staff is knowledgeable and on a first name basis with many of their clients. Nestled in the Middle Park shopping centre, Randall's boasts a good selection of imports reflecting Randall's Burgundian leanings. Knowledgeable staff, regular tastings and dinners.

Randall The Wine Merchant Hawthorn (Rand)
Troubadour Centre (rear), 673 Glenferrie Rd Hawthorn   www.randalls.net.au
Ph 9818 6194   hawthorn@randalls.net.au

The latest addition to Randall's stores is this huge new outlet in Hawthorn, due to open in the same week that this book hits the stores. We are told that it promises to take the Randall's wine experience to hitherto unprecedented heights! A total refit of an old second-hand furniture store will provide space for a massive range of wines including many imports as well as a dedicated tasting room. With our mate Stew Plant of Brisbane fame at the helm, this will be one store not to be missed (although we do miss you, Stew!).

Strathmore Cellars
305 Napier St Strathmore   Ph 9379 3353
www.winestar.com.au   shop@winestar.com.au

Tucked away in a small suburban shopping strip, Strathmore Cellars has an unexpectedly broad range for its location. Premium Australian brands and Champagnes are very well represented, and a growing range of imported wines are coming on board. Pricing is very good on most products, and look out for excellent specials and offers. The inimitable Bert and Pierre Werden inject tremendous knowledge and passion into their business. Bert is the unsung hero of online wine retailing in this country, having developed Strathmore Cellars as the base for a stratospherically successful 'WineStar' store. This is one of the cheapest places in the country to buy great wine. But its service and professionalism are everything but "cheap." Little wonder, then, that it has quickly mushroomed into the hub of a thriving online wine community with a weekly online newsletter that has become an institution in itself (celebrating its tenth birthday last year).

The Grape Unknown
221 Clarendon St South Melbourne   Ph 9699 4433
info@thegrapeunknown.com.au   www.thegrapeunknown.com.au

The Grape Unknown is a small store exclusively focused on its own labelled wines and discounted estate labelled wines. But don't confuse this great little shop with generic cleanskin outlets, because all of the wines sold are available as estate labelled products. Derek Carter is passionate about wine, and he tells us that he rejects fifty wines for every one that he accepts for the store. He presents the whole range for tasting on a rotating basis and offers a money back guarantee. Pricing is slightly above standard cleanskin rates, but for this you get a more reliable product and production quality labels with good regional and winemaking information. The business is on an upward spiral, with a growing online presence and a new store just opened at 2 Station Rd Cheltenham.

The Victorian Wine Centre
20-22 Armstrong St Middle Park

Ph 9699 6082
www.victorianwinecentre.com.au
info@victorianwinecentre.com.au

Grab a coffee as you browse a compact but well-selected range of boutique Aussie and top French estates at fair prices.

Vintage Cellars Melbourne CBD (VCs)
215 Little Bourke St Melbourne

Ph 9639 4198
www.vintagecellars.com.au

The Melbourne CBD only has a few wine retailers of note, and this is one of them. VCs features a decent range of mainstream premium wines and some imports. Pricing tends to be premium, but look for gems in their advertising cycle. The Cellar Shares program rewards regular shoppers. We have found staff to be knowledgeable and enthusiastic.

Wine House - Old & Rare Wines (WH)
133 Queensbridge St Southbank
Open Tues-Fri 11-7, Sat 11-5

Ph 9698 8000
www.winehouse.com.au
sales@winehouse.com.au

Wine House specialises in old and rare wines, although there are also many current vintages available. Ten percent discount is generally offered on dozen orders and free delivery is available on orders over $300. Monthly wine dinners feature super-premium and cult names and don't miss the weekly wine education courses, tailored wine events and free Saturday afternoon tastings.

the recommended retailers in WA

Chateau Guildford
124 Swan St Guildford

Ph 9377 3311

Chateau Guildford offers top shelf and boutique Australian wines at reasonable prices. There is also a good cross-section of French wines and some keenly priced back-vintages.

De Vine Cellars
909 Beaufort St Inglewood

wine@devinecellars.com.au
Ph 9271 9197

The emphasis at De Vine is on Aussie wines, but you'll find a selection of imports under $30. Make your way to the air-conditioned premium room at the back for some great back-vintages at very competitive prices. Look out for specials and discounts on six bottle buys.

Grand Cru Fine Wine Merchant
Downstairs at Liquor Barons 654 Beaufort St Mt Lawley

Ph 9271 0886
grandcru@iinet.net.au

A good range of Australian and NZ boutique and hard to get wines. Lots of back-vintages and collectors wines, but virtually no imports. Make sure you know what it's worth before you buy here, and make good use of 10% discount on 6 bottle buys and 15% on mixed dozen purchases.

Harborne & Cambridge Cellars
Cnr Harborne & Cambridge Sts Wembley

Ph 9388 3033
www.hc-wines.com.au
enquiries@hc-wines.com.au

H&C presents a decent range of Australian wines alongside some Italian, NZ, German and French imports. A climate-controlled room houses an extensive range of top Aussie, Italian, Spanish, French, NZ and US wines and the occasional back-vintage. Look out for six-bottle buy deals.

La-Vigna Liquor
302 Walcott St Menora

Ph 9271 1179
lavigna@lavigna.com.au

La-Vigna is the home of a big range of affordable and premium imports including an extensive line up of French, Spanish and Italian wines. We nearly got lost browsing here! Good prices and the occasional back-vintage wine make the fossicking all the more exciting.

Sexton Cellars
30 Sexton Rd Inglewood

ingewinestore@yahoo.com.au

Ph 9370 4111

Sexton is a small corner store with an interesting, albeit petite, collection of current and back-vintage wines from Australia and the world. Look for specials and take advantage of 10% off any 6 wines and 15% of dozens. A friendly staff will order that special wine that you can't track down.

Stephen McHenry Wine Merchants (SMWM)
Ph 9386 3336
171 Broadway St Nedlands
bottleshop@steves.com.au
Open Sun-Thurs 10-8, F-Sat 10-9
www.stephenmchenrywinemerchant.com.au

We feel right at home in shops like this. James Majer and Michael Hartley have clearly put a lot of thought into assembling an eclectic and extensive range of boutique wines from every corner of the globe. These are showcased in a downstairs climate-controlled cellar packed to the roof with interesting and reasonably priced cult wines, back vintages, and imports. You'll find more than 160 of our **Best Wines of 2009** here. It's a well laid-out shop in a historic building, which is exactly the vibe of the outstanding range of wines that it houses. After undergoing extensive renovations we're looking forward to visiting the brand new store!

The Re Store Liquor and Gourmet Foods
Ph 9444 9644
231 Oxford St Leederville
restore231@hotmail.com

Between the rows of Italian smallgoods you'll discover an interesting and extensive range of Australian wines and a strong selection of (mostly) Italian and French imports. If you're into spirits, this is your spot, too. Prices are keen, and look for specials.

The Wine Store
www.thewinestore.com.au
48 George St East Fremantle
Ph 6424 9500
qjones@thewinestore.com.au

In this quaint, well-presented store in East Fremantle, Quentin Jones has assembled a great range of wines from around the world, including a good selection of WA boutiques.

Vintage Cellars Cottesloe (VCs)
Ph 9384 0777
504 Stirling Hwy Cottesloe
www.vintagecellars.com.au

This is a VCs with an excellent, eclectic range of Australian wines and a good variety of imports, right up to the very top shelf French wines. Prices aren't cheap, so look out for specials and buy by the dozen.

Vintage Cellars Shenton Park (VCs)
Ph 9381 6555
95 Nicholson Rd Shenton Pk
www.vintagecellars.com.au

This VCs store stocks a good range of Australian collector wines, back vintages and imports from Bordeaux and Burgundy. This is your spot if you're chasing top shelf labels (but at a price). There's also a good selection of hard-to-get boutiques and back-vintage wines.

DIRECTORY OF
NEW ZEALAND
WINE
RETAILERS

There are a few vital tips to arm yourself with before setting out to buy a bottle of wine in New Zealand. We drove the length and breadth of the country and visited every bottle shop worth walking into between Invercargill and Auckland. The following pages summarise the highlights of our discoveries, with national chains first, then local stores in alphabetical order of city.

The first thing that we have to point out (because we're too excited to leave it until later) is that there are a handful of retailers in NZ who leave the rest for dead in every way – range of local wines, imports, competitive pricing and helpful, knowledgeable staff. You'll find the names of these world-class operations in **bold**. You simply must visit them at every opportunity you can make.

On the whole, we found that many of New Zealand's commercial chain stores are presenting a better range of wines at more competitive prices than we had expected – well done to you! Against this competition, independent stores must provide a point of difference by sourcing a special range of wines that aren't available in supermarkets.

Sadly, many of New Zealand's more specialist wine retailers clearly haven't risen to this challenge. New Zealand is blessed with scores of artisanal winemakers whose wines deserve pride of place in these smaller shops. You'll find dozens of these wines lurking among our **Best Wines of 2009**. Every independent retailer in New Zealand should be scrambling to secure an allocation of these wines and then scouring Australia to do the same with Aussie boutiques (again, our **Best Wines of 2009** includes all of the names you need to know).

We have sat down in the past with New Zealand retailers and given them secret lists of the best Aussie boutiques for them to track down. We hope that they will act on these so that we can include their names with **The Best Wines of 2009** next year. In the meantime, there is no more need for secret lists because we are shouting it from the rooftops in this very book!

Make the most of this directory of the best places to buy wine in New Zealand.

hooray

the recommended national retailers

Liquorking
Ph 0800 746 762

www.liquorking.co.nz
webmaster@liquorking.co.nz

Liquorking may be a large chain (43 stores between Kaitaia and Dunedin) but don't expect just an average chain store range. You'll find a good selection of mainstream and boutique wines from Australia and NZ, with a particular emphasis on top shelf Aussies. There is also a small selection of imports from France, Italy, South America and South Africa. Pricing is keen and specials are competitive. See web site for locations.

Liquorland

www.liquorland.co.nz
Ph 0800 560 560

With more than seventy stores across the country, Liquorland is New Zealand's largest specialist liquor retailer. Unrelated to Liquorland in Australia, this chain offers a strong range of Aus and NZ wines with a good selection of top shelf products. You'll find some impressive boutiques in stock as well. Pricing is reasonable and look for specials. You'll find a store finder on the web site.

New World Supermarkets
Open 8am-10pm every day

www.newworld.co.nz

New World Supermarkets offer a big range and aggressive discounting (hooray for supermarket prices!). This is the place to shop for big brands and any NZ and Aussie wines under $20. There is also a good selection on the top shelf from the big boys, balanced by a pretty good line up of wines from nearby regions in most stores. Some locations also stock super premiums including Grange and prestige Champagne. European imports are limited but there are some exciting surprises to be discovered.

Super Liquor
Ph 09 272 4781

www.superliquor.co.nz
enquiries@superliquor.co.nz

With nearly 100 stores from Kerikeri to Invercargill, there's sure to be a Super Liquor near you, offering a good range of main-stream New Zealand and Australian wines. The emphasis here is on the sub-$30 sector at aggressively discounted prices. See the web site for store locations.

The Mill (Mill)
Ph 06 769 9304

www.themill.co.nz
feedback@themill.co.nz

Next time you're in need of a quick quaffer, pop into The Mill. This is NZ's largest independent discount liquor chain with 41 stores throughout the country (predominantly on the north island) offering a reasonable range of commercial NZ and Aussie wines and cleanskins. The focus is on sub-$20 wines as well as spirits, pre-mixers and beers. See web site for locations.

The Wine Importer
Ph 09 412 8542

www.wineimporter.co.nz
info@wineimporter.co.nz

The Wine Importer is Paul Mitchell, and he brings in a big range of affordable and premium wines from (mainly) France, Germany and Spain.

Woolworths
Ph 0800 404 040

www.woolworths.co.nz
onlineshop@progressive.co.nz

Woolworths stores offer a big selection of predominantly Australian and NZ wines at good prices with some great specials. The selection is largely commercial, but some premium wines, Champagnes and New Zealand boutiques are represented.

the recommended retailer in arrowtown

Allan Hamilton Wine Cellars
Ramshaw Lane Arrowtown
Open M-Sat 10-8, Sun 11-7

www.pinotcentral.com
Ph 03 442 1026
allanhamilton@xtra.co.nz

Allan Hamilton and his wife Barbara are the names behind this great little wine shop in Arrowtown. Have a poke around and you'll see that they've put some careful thought into assembling a good selection of local, NZ and Australian wines at good prices. There are plenty of interesting boutiques awaiting discovery, as well as some foreigners from France, Italy and Spain.

the recommended retailers in auckland

Accent on Wine
347 Parnell Rd Parnell Auckland
Ph 09 358 2552 or 0800 69 8466

www.accentonwine.co.nz
Open M-Sat 10-10
sales@accentonwine.co.nz

The accent here is on importing fine and rare wines from around the world. Miguel Frascione and Jean-Pierre Pasche have packed their corner store high with a great range covering small and large producers from Australia, New Zealand, France, Italy, Spain and Argentina. Of particular interest is a good selection of Aussie and NZ boutiques and some back-vintage French wines at pretty good prices. Top wines are stored in climate-controlled cabinets.

Caro's Wine Merchants
114 St Georges Bay Rd Parnell Auckland
Open M-F 9-6.30, Sat 10-6

www.caros.co.nz
wine@caros.co.nz
Ph 09 377 9974 or 0800 422767

John and Richard Caro have put a lot of consideration into assembling an

extensive but eclectic range covering Australian, New Zealand, French and other European wines. Some back vintage super-premiums are also stocked. Pricing is good and 10% discount is offered on 6 bottle buys.

Fine Wine Delivery Company

50 Cook Street Auckland
Open M-F 9-6:30, Sat 10:30-5
Ph 09 377 2300

www.finewineonline.co.nz
info@finewineonline.co.nz
Free call 0800 346 394

This is not just a wine shop – it's a fully functional, self-contained wine universe! You name it, it's going on in this huge multi-level tardis in the middle of Auckland. Private climate-controlled storage, tasting rooms, dinners, events, international wine trips – and we haven't even got to wine sales yet! When you have more than 4500 wines in stock, we believe you when you say that you specialise in everything! The range is massive, with one of the best selections of Aussie boutiques in the country, as well as a strong focus on all things Spanish and Argentinean. We had a great time in the climate-controlled room drooling over the stash of top French, Italian, back-vintage Aussie and other exciting goodies. Pricing is very competitive, with case discounts offered. While you're here, enjoy a tasting at any time of the day from a selection of 40 wines via an automated machine ($1-$3 per taste). Oh, and the store does live up to its name – international delivery is offered, and climate controlled shipping to Australia costs $150 per case. This is a brilliant store and about as serious as wine retail gets in New Zealand. Get into its orbit, and stay on board!

First Glass Wines & Spirits

5 Huron St Takapuna Auckland
Open M-F 9-6:30, Sat 9-6, Dec only Sun 9-6

Ph 09 486 6415
www.first-glass.co.nz
firstglass@clear.net.nz

First Glass focuses on local wines and an extensive range of NZ and Aus boutiques as well as a good selection from France, Italy and Spain. This is a big store with an outstanding range at competitive prices (and keen specials). Shiraz and Chardonnay are particular specialties here. Sam Kim and Kingsley Wood are close at hand, with a wealth of wine expertise to share. They tell us that their tastings every Wednesday night are some of the biggest in Auckland.

Glengarry (Glen)

Ph 0800 733 505

www.glengarry.co.nz
sales@glengarry.co.nz

A wine business doesn't get any more "family" than this. Glengarry was started by Joseph Jakicevich in 1940, and is currently owned and run by the family's 3rd generation, with six family members on staff, headed by, neatly enough, Joe. Eleven outlets around Auckland and three in Wellington stock a huge range of everything from everywhere based on monthly blind panel tastings.

The company runs its own importing and distribution business, which ensures an extensive range from Australia, Italy, France, Chile, America, Spain and virtually everywhere else on the planet. Climate-controlled rooms in many of the stores house the top wines. Very competitive specials. See web site for locations.

Herne Bay Cellars
Shop 8 In the Arcade 182 Jervois Rd Herne Bay Auckland www.hernebaycellars.co.nz
Open M-T 10-9, Sat 10-10, Sun 10-8 Ph 09 376 3497 trish@hernebaycellars.com

Michael and Trish Hudson are the faces behind Herne Bay Cellars. The store has been family owned and run for sixteen years, and the entire family is involved – when we visited last we were greeted and welcomed by their young children. This little store offers a good selection of mainstream and boutique NZ and Aus wines at good prices.

Kemp Rare Wine Merchants
143 Carlton Gore Road Newmarket Auckland Ph 0800 KEMPWINE
Open By appointment daniel@kemprarewines.com www.kemprarewines.co.nz

Daniel and Simon Kemp are passionate about wine and food, and when we visited them they were about to open the doors of their wine library on the mezzanine floor of Jones the Grocer in Newmarket. If you're after something rare, old or interesting from New Zealand, chances are they've got it. The collection reads like a "Who's Who" of NZ greats with all the usual suspects in attendance, back-vintages, large-format bottles and curios. They have also assembled many of the most collectable labels from Australia, France, Italy, Spain, Portugal and the US. Check out the full list on the web site – or, better, give them a call and drop in for a chat and a chance to see this impressive collection.

La Barrique
154 Remeura Rd Remuera (Ph 09 5246666) and www.labarrique.co.nz
31 Normanby Rd Mt Eden (Ph 09 6385000) Auckland Open M-W 10-8:30, T-Sat 10-9, Sun 11-7 admin@labarrique.co.nz

La Barrique offers a strong range of New Zealand and Australian wines, including a great selection of boutiques – some of which are not sold anywhere else in the country. Also a good selection of French, Italian and Spanish wines. A climate-controlled cellar houses a nice selection of top shelf and back-vintage wines, but choose carefully as some represent great value while others come at a price. Prices throughout the rest of the shop are quite good.

La Vino Wine and Spirit Merchants

16 Williamson Ave Ponsonby Auckland
Open M-W 10-10, T 10-10:30, F-Sat 10-11, Sun 12-9

Ph 09 360 0134
www.lavino.co.nz
wines@lavino.co.nz

Growing up on a vineyard and trained as a winemaker, Peter Ivicevich knows his wines. La Vino showcases a great range of specialist wines from across NZ, Australia, Franc and the world. The top shelf selection is a particular highlight, as is the range of local beers. Pricing is competitive.

Maison Vauron (MV)

5 McColl Street Newmarket Auckland
Open M-F 8-6, Sat 9-5

www.mvauron.co.nz
Ph 09 529 0157
scott@mvauron.co.nz

Sharing its premises with Pyrénées French Charcuterie & Epicerie, Maison Vauron is very French in every way. French wines (predominantly); French staff (mostly); even the atmosphere is French, in a vast, atmospheric, dimly lit room with a curved ceiling with the aromas of French cheeses wafting up the stairs from the shop below. As would be expected, everything from France is here, from everyday drinking wines to the very top domaines. Scott Gray, Jean-Christophe Poizat and Peter Ropati describe their specialty as exciting, high quality, good value wines and they claim to be NZs largest importer of small domaines from France. Everything is imported directly in climate-controlled shipping containers. C'est tres bien!

Milford Cellars

172A Kitchener Road Milford North Shore Auckland

Ph 09 486 1977
Open M-Sat 10-9, Sun 3:30-7:30

Milford Cellars is a little shop with a lot more to offer than its narrow street front suggests. A great range of hand-selected boutique and mainstream Aus and NZ wines are offered at good prices. It's clear to see that David & Dianna Carthew have set out to provide a point of difference to the two supermarkets directly across the road, and they have done a fine job about it.

Peter Maude Fine Wines

33 Coates Ave Orakei Auckland
Ph 09 520 3023

www.pmfw.co.nz
petermaude@pmfw.co.nz

If you're at all interested in top shelf wines, Peter Maude is a man you must get to know. New Zealand's longest established independent fine wine merchant (since 1976) now specialises in French wine and offers the best range of imports in the country. His shop has wine slotted into every corner, with floor to ceiling stacks of timber boxes of some of the finest wines in the world. There is a focus on the top estates of France, and Peter visits the country twice annually to stay up to date. He also deals extensively in New Zealand wines and some excellent wines from Australia (Mt Mary), California (Dominus),

Germany, Italy and Port (Quinta do Vesuvio). All wines are transported in temperature controlled containers. Make sure your name is on Peter's list for en primeur offerings, tastings and (epic) dinners.

Point Wines
141 Queen St Northcote Auckland
Open 11-7 every day

www.pointwines.co.nz
Ph 09 480 9463
orders@pointwines.co.nz

Pop in to Point Wines and say "g'day" to Aidan Hardy, one of the longest-standing independent retailers in the area. Taste some wines with him while you're there (he's always got a bunch of bottles open) and have a poke through his excellent, eclectic range. He focuses particularly on local wines and European imports at fair prices.

The Wine Vault (Vault)
453 Richmond Rd Grey Lynn Auckland
Open M-W 11-8, T-Sat 11-9, Sun 11-7

www.thewinevault.co.nz
Ph 09 376 3520
orders@thewinevault.co.nz

The Wine Vault is a great little shop with a range that belies its size. Don't tell anyone, but they also offer some of the more competitive shelf prices in the country on a great range of boutique Aus and NZ wines. There are always a few bottles open to taste.

Wine Direct
16 St Marks Rd Newmarket Auckland
Open M-F 9-6, Sat 10-4

www.winedirect.co.nz
Ph 09 529 5267
Free call 0800 660 777
sales@winedirect.co.nz

Wine Direct is tucked into an unlikely location almost under the highway next to Beaurepaires. But don't be fooled – this is a great wine shop. There is a strong focus on European wines (80%), all of which are imported directly from the producers. We're particularly impressed with the range of French wines. There's also no shortage of Aussie and NZ boutiques. Pricing is competitive, particularly on en primeur offers.

the recommended retailer in blenheim

Fresh Choice Springlands
133 Middle Renwick Rd Blenheim

Ph 03 578 6289
www.freshchoice.co.nz

This south island supermarket chain presents a good selection of NZ wines from across the country, with a particular feature on local brands. There is no shortage of boutique and commercial everything from all over NZ at supermarket prices. Also a good selection of Aussie wines including some great top shelf labels, vintage Champagne, a good little line up from Europe and loads of premium beer to match. We could camp out in here and still be having fun a week later! A big tick for Fresh Choice.

come in and get naked

the recommended retailers in christchurch

Hemingway Fine Wines
Ph 03 374 3344
51 Chester Street West Christchurch
www.hemingwayfinewines.co.nz
Open M-T 11-7, W-F 10-8, Sat 10-7
hemingwayfinewines@xtra.co.nz

From its central location in Christchurch, Hemingways offers an extensive range of local and imported wines from Australia, France, Spain and Italy. The selection of NZ and Aussie boutiques is strong, and pricing is fair. Premium and older wines are maintained in a 14 degree cellar.

Rare Fare
www.rarefare.co.nz
10 Winston Ave Papanui Christchurch
shop@rarefare.co.nz
Open M-Sat 9.30-6
Ph 03 352 9047

Rare Fare is a gourmet delicatessen with all variety of exciting goodies from the small food and wine producers of NZ. Bill Clousten and Kirsty Isaacson keep their wine section well-stocked with a good range of NZ commercials and boutiques at competitive prices. You'll also find some Aussie commercial lines and a Vintage Port or two.

The Grape Escape
Ph 03 332 0233
69 Centaurus Rd Hillsborough Christchurch
Open M-W 10-7, T 11-7, F 10-8, Sat 11-8

Before we even stepped through the door of The Grape Escape we were chuckling at a chalkboard sign which read, "Come in and get naked Sauvignon Blanc." Inside, we were greeted by hand-written shelf talkers with such statements as "the best fun your mouth had since its first snog", "more balls than a naked matador" and "big, seductive body (no – not me)." And that about sums up John Alexander. If you're going to get anything out of a visit to his little suburban store, it's going to be a good laugh. And while you're here, you might as well grab a bottle or 6 from his hand-selected range of imports and locals. His emphasis is on lines that the supermarkets and chains don't carry, and his prices are pretty good. Local delivery.

The Village Grape
41 Nayland St Christchurch
Ph 03 326 6306
Open M-W 10-8, T-Sat 10-9, Sun 12-7
grape@xtra.co.nz

Under new ownership this year, The Village Grape is a seriously impressive little shop at the beachside suburb of Sumner. It boasts an outstanding range of NZ and Aus wines covering both mainstream and more interesting labels. There's a great line up of imports from Germany, Chile, France and Italy, with a particular focus on the sub-$30 bracket. If you want it cold, there's a good chance they have it in a second fridge out the back, so be sure to ask. And they tell us that if you want it and they don't have it, they'll get it. To top it all off, the prices are pretty competitive. If it means a bit of a drive for you to get to this shop, take our word for it, it's well worth it. We drove from Brisbane and London respectively, so you've got nothing to complain about!

The Wine Ferret (TWF)

130C Montreal St Christchurch
Open M-T 12-5, F-Sat 12-6

www.wineferret.co.nz
Ph 03 379 1674
wine@wineferret.co.nz

The Wine Ferret is an online retailer with an excellent range of imports, specialising in wines from France, Spain, Italy, Germany and Austria. There is also a selection of Aus and NZ wines. Check out the web site or visit "The Ferret's Den," a shop front for the store in Christchurch.

Vino Fino Cellars (VFC)

188 Durham St Christchurch
Open M-Sat 9-6

www.vinofino.co.nz
Ph 03 365 5134
wine@vinofino.co.nz

Vino Fino is located right next door to a motor mechanic, but don't be put off by its glamorous location – this is the single largest retailer of fine wines in Christchurch, specialising in wines from NZ, Aus and around the world. A large and atmospheric shop on multiple levels, set off with antique furniture, is stocked to the gills with a wide and eclectic range of NZ wines (one of the best selections on the south island), commercial and boutique Australian as well as a strong line up from Italy, France, Germany, Portugal (Vintage port), Spain (Sherry) and California. The top wines are stored under climate control. Pricing is competitive, specials are worth snapping up and there's also plenty of value in bottom shelf wines. Vino Fino is also set up to look after your parties and gift needs with free glass hire, only pay for what you drink, free gift wrapping and free delivery in Christchurch. Sign up for weekly emails, monthly newsletters and twice yearly wine festivals. Dave Graham and Rex Ormandy each have over 20 years experience in the liquor retail trade, and they've used it to full advantage to create one of the top wine shops on the south island.

the recommended retailers in cromwell

The Big Picture Wine Adventure

Cnr of State Hwy 6 and Sandflat Road Cromwell
Open 9-6 every day

Ph 03 445 4052
www.bigpicturewine.com
info@bigpicturewine.com

The Big Picture Wine Adventure is an interactive wine and film experience, which makes it a very innovative place to taste and learn. The shop contains a small but well-selected range of local wine and various vinous paraphernalia. It's a unique experience and worth a visit next time you're in Central. The big news this year is that the Big Picture is getting even bigger. Around the same time that this book hits the shelves, a Big Picture Wine

Adventure will open in Hawkes Bay (Indulge Building, Napier) and before the end of the year in Auckland (Sanford's Precinct, Viaduct Basin, Freemans Bay).

Pembroke Wines & Spirits Cromwell (Pemb)

Cromwell Mall Cromwell
Open M-Sat 10-6

Ph 03 445 4480
pembroke.wines@xtra.co.nz

John Hallum runs this store Cromwell as well as in nearby Wanaka (read on), and both feature a great range of local wines as well as a fantastic line up of Aussie boutiques and a few imports. You'll also find an extensive Whisky range here. Prices are at the higher end, but there are good wines to be discovered. The store has been here for a few years now, but it's only just starting to be discovered, which is strange because it boasts a great hand-selected range. Stop by for a chat.

the recommended retailers in dunedin

Castle Macadam Wine

11 Mailer St Mornington Dunedin
www.nzwinespecialist.co.nz

Ph 03 4533327
darren@nzwinespecialist.co.nz

A small, humbly presented shop on the hill, but inside you'll discover a good little selection of Australian and NZ wines. Central Otago is rightfully given pride of place on its own shelf.

Meenan Wines & Spirits

750 Great King St Dunedin
enquiries@meenans.co.nz

www.meenans.co.nz
Ph 03 477 2047
Free call 0800 772 04

Despite its seemingly crazy personality on the surface, if you take a good hard look at Meenans you'll discover one of the best wine shops in town. Extensive and well-presented, the range features plenty of NZ wines from all over, with Central Otago gaining centre place. Australian wines focus on the big brands, and there is an extensive selection at competitive prices. The store imports a range of wines from Europe, with the back wall displaying a selection from France, Chile Germany, Spain and Italy. There's also an eclectic range of fortified wines – and don't miss the glass cabinet of vintage Scottish Whiskeys.

Munslows Fine Wines

338 George St Dunedin
Open M-W 10-7, T-Sat 10-8

www.munslows.co.nz
munslowswines@paradise.net.nz
Ph 03 477 1585

Munslows is a great store that oozes wine passion from its central location in Dunedin. It prides itself on an excellent range of New Zealand and Australian wines – and rightly so. Central Otago takes pride of place, but there is also a good range from throughout New Zealand, Australia, Spain, Italy, France,

South America and Germany. There isn't a huge emphasis on the very top shelf imports, but instead a great selection of wines in the more useful $20-$100 range. So as to distinguish itself from the competitive supermarket sector, the store focuses on the boutique and interesting, with an excellent, hand-selected range. Peter Munslow still has a hand in the operation, lining up a busy tasting schedule and winemaker visits throughout the year. Join the (free) mailing list and receive 7.5% off all bottled wine.

Rhubarb	Ph 03 477 2555
297 Highgate St Dunedin	Open M-T 7-5, F 7-7, Sat 8-6, Sun 9-4

Sitting proud in the trendy hill suburb of Roslyn, Rhubarb is about serious coffee, food and wine. Part of the café is a wine shop offering a small, eclectic range of NZ, Aussie wines and Champagnes at fair prices. There are some interesting cult wines in the mix that you won't find anywhere else in this part of the world.

the recommended retailers in hamilton

Primo Vino	www.primovino.co.nz
955 Victoria St Hamilton	Ph 07 839 3139
Open M-F 11-6, Sat 11-4	wine@primovino.co.nz

Primo Vino is a small, stylishly presented shop with a good range of Aus and NZ wines and some imports at keen prices. The well-designed range includes some smart boutiques, the best of which are stored in climate-controlled cabinets. Discounts on six bottle buys. The store also operates a wine club, winemaker events and Friday tastings.

The Hamilton Wine Company (HWC)	nick@hamiltonwine.co.nz
29 Hood St Hamilton	www.hamiltonwine.co.nz
Open M-W 6-10, T 10-7, F 10-8, Sat 10-7	Ph 07 839 1190

Nick Yeoman (yo man, wot up?) and the team at Hamilton are down-to-earth and clearly have a lot of fun in this shop. You will, too, when you discover their huge range of Aus and NZ wines with an outstanding selection of hard-to-find boutiques – not to mention one of the biggest ranges of beer in the country. Pinot Noir is the feature with a huge range of (particularly) New Zealanders. Check out the back wall for imports including some top-shelf French back-vintages. Prices are good and 12.5% discount is offered on case buys.

imposing

the recommended retailer in **invercargill**

Centrepoint Liquorland
252 Dee St Cnr Thames St Invercargill
Open M-T 9-7, W 9-8, T 9-9, F-Sat 9am-10pm, Sun 10-7

www.liquorland.co.nz
Ph 03 211 3650
centrepoint@ilt.co.nz

Centrepoint is a big store with an extensive mainstream range, commercial for the most part but with the occasional rare NZ boutique. The Aussie selection is strong, and includes some top-shelf, big-brand back vintages. A small selection of French, Italian and Spanish wines is also sold. Pricing is keen across the store.

the recommended retailer in **nelson**

Casa Del Vino (Casa)
214 Hardy St Nelson
Open M-Sat 10-6

www.casadelvino.co.nz
wine@casadelvino.co.nz
Ph 03 548 0088

Under new ownership under brother and sister team Mark and Ann Banks, Casa de Vino continues to offer a largely boutique range at pretty good prices in the heart of Nelson city. Local wines are given feature position, but the range also includes a good selection from across New Zealand, Australia and Europe. Aged and rare wines are stored under climate control.

the recommended retailer in **palmerston north**

The Village Wine Trader
350 Albert St Palmerston North
Open M-W 10-7, T-Sat 10-8, Sun 2-6

www.winetrader.co.nz
wine.trader@xtra.co.nz
Ph 06 357 0779

On the same street as an imposing line up of supermarkets and wine chain stores, TVWT needs a point of difference to distinguish itself, and this little shop has found it in an interesting range of New Zealand and Australian wines that aren't all found in the larger stores. Some of the great boutique labels that grace the shelves here are hard to find anywhere in NZ, for that matter. There's also a small selection of French, Spanish and Italian wines. Prices are quite good.

the recommended retailers in queenstown

The Wine Deli
2 Shotover St Queenstown

www.winedeli.com
Ph 03 442 4482
store@winedeli.com

Last time we were in town the old shop at 40 Shotover St was in the middle of a refit for an ice cream shop and plans for the new store were well under way. We're told that it's now open, so ignore the address on the web site and head across to 2 Shotover St for an extensive selection of New Zealand wines with a focus on Central Otago. The Wine Deli has joined forces with Pembrokes' stores in Cromwell and Wanaka, promising an even broader range of wines than in the past.

Wine Tastes Central Otago
14 Beach St (O'Connell's Pavilion) Queenstown
Open 10-10 every day

Ph 03 409 2226
www.winetastes.com
queenstown@winetastes.com

Moor the jet boat, hang up the skis and stash the safety harness because it's time to settle yourself in for a wine experience that's going to get the adrenaline pumping. Wine Tastes is more than just a wine shop – it's a full-on wine assault on the senses! More than 80 wines are on tasting at any time from a fancy machine that not only keeps them fresh and cool but also remembers what you've tasted and prints out a list when you've finished. Tastings vary from around $1.50 to $5 and cheese and antipasto platters are available. If you ever drag yourself out of there, there's a great selection of wines to take with you, but buy carefully because prices are high. Central Otago is the feature of the range, but top shelf wines from across New Zealand and a few Frenchies are available.

the recommended retailer in rotorua

Arawa Wines and Spirits
1106 Tutanekai St Rotorua
Open M-Sat 11-9, Sun 5-8

Ph 07 348 6590
mchorner@xtra.co.nz

Arawa is a small, homely shop boasting a good selection of wines with a focus on NZ aromatics and Aussie reds. New Zealand boutiques are chosen so as not to overlap with supermarket products and pricing is fair for this part of the world. Mick are Judy Horner are very welcoming and helpful.

the recommended retailer in taupo

Scenic Cellars (SC)
32 Roberts Street Taupo
Open Winter Sun-W 9-7, Thurs-Sat 9-8, Summer Sun-W 9-8, Thurs-Sat 9-9

www.sceniccellars.co.nz
info@sceniccellars.co.nz
Ph 07 378 5704

From the sweeping views of Lake Taupo and the mountains through wide front windows, to the vast atmospheric cellar downstairs, to an extensive selection of wines on tasting, this is a destination you just have to visit. When we called in they had Grange and d'Yquem on tasting for $20 a taste. What a great way to make these brilliant wines accessible! They claim a range of rare and fine wines larger than any other outlet in the country – and with more than 3000 different labels and some 100 000 bottles in stock, they just might be right! Don't leave without poking around the cellar, where you'll discover one of NZ's best ranges of top shelf imports, magnums and some back vintages. Scenic imports a wide selection from Australia, France, Italy, Spain, Chile and California. Considering all this, pricing is pretty good. What a great place to experience wine!

the recommended retailer in tauranga

Hillsdene Wines
673 Cameron Road Tauranga
Open M 9-8, T 9-8:30, W-Sat 9-9, Sun 11-7 winter, 11-8 summer

www.hillsdenewines.co.nz
Ph 07 578 7236
info@hillsdenewines.co.nz

Nestled into a bustling supermarket strip, Hillsdene offers a range which sets it apart. It's been family owned and operated for 48 years and today it offers an extensive NZ and Aussie range with a good balance of mainstream and smaller brands as well as a good selection of French and Italian wines at competitive prices.

the recommended retailer in te puke

McGregors Wholesale Liquor
120 Jellicoe St Te Puke
Open M 9-7, T-W 9-7:30, T-F 9-8, Sat 9-9, Sun 10-6

www.mcgregors-wines.co.nz
sales@mcgregors-wines.co.nz
Ph 07 5737570 or 0800 185030

The McGregors have been in Te Puke almost forever, with a wine shop close to fifty years old and a hotel twice its age. This is a big store in the heart of Kiwi fruit central, cram-packed with wines which overflow the shelves and spread onto the floor. A range of Aus and NZ lines are on show at keen prices. It's also a great place to fossick as there are some brilliant back-vintage premiums to be found at bargain prices – but some are post their peak so watch the condition (no climate control). There's also a good selection of Waiheke Island wines and a range of imports from South America, South Africa and Europe.

the recommended retailer in timaru

Highfield Liquor
Highfield Mall Wai-iti Rd Highfield Timaru
Open M-W 9-7, T-Sat 9-8, Sun 10-6
www.highfieldliquor.co.nz
Ph 03 688 4186
highfieldliquor@xtra.co.nz

Highfield stocks a big range of everything – commercials, boutiques, you name it, you'll find it here. There is a particular focus on Australia and New Zealand with a smattering of French wines. The best range in Timaru, and all at keen prices.

the recommended retailers in wanaka

Pembroke Wines & Spirits Wanaka (Pemb)
47 Helwick St Wanaka
Open M-S 10-9, Sun 3-8
Ph 03 4443 7818
www.pembrokewines.co.nz
pembroke.wines@xtra.co.nz

You must visit Wanaka at least once in your life (and you will certainly return!), and when you do, this great little shop will help you enjoy your stay. Tucked into the heart of one of the prettiest places on the planet, it features a strong range of Central Otago, some French and a fantastic selection of Aussie Boutiques including some surprises that you won't track down anywhere else. You'll pay top dollar for them but you won't mind. NZ wines are well-priced and there's no shortage to be found in this exciting little shop.

Wanaka Fine Wines (WFW)
19 Helwick St Wanaka
Open 9-9 every day
www.wanakafinewines.co.nz
henry@wanakafinewines.co.nz
Ph 03 443 7539

For a small town, this store has quite an extraordinary selection of Central Otago wines, a good mix of boutique and big brand Aussies and a few shelves of French and Italian. There are lots of top shelf products and a few back vintages along the way. Pricing is pretty good. Grab a bottle of local pinot (plenty to choose from) and get yourself down to Relishes Café.

the recommended retailers in wellington

Glengarry Thorndon
232 Thorndon Quay Wellington
Open M-W 9-7, T-Sat 9-8, Sun 10-5
www.glengarry.co.nz
thorndon@glengarry.co.nz
Ph 04 472 7051

Glengarry runs three stores in Wellington, and this is the biggest. It boasts a great range of everything including lots of imports from France and Italy, with a very active en primeur program. The climate-controlled room at the back holds the top wines. Competitive pricing and a comprehensive range make this an outstanding place to shop in Wellington.

Regional Wines and Spirits

15 Ellice St Mt Victoria Wellington
Open M-Sat 9-10, Sun 11-7:30

Ph 04 385 6952
www.regionalwines.co.nz
raymond@regionalwines.co.nz

This is one of our favourite wine shops in the country, and there is nothing south of it in NZ that compares. It's crammed with everything from everywhere, including the very top wines from France, Italy, Australia, Germany – oh, and New Zealand! It features a brilliant range at every price point – and those prices are very good. Regional imports a lot of French and Italian wine that it distributes to local restaurants and trade. The store runs comprehensive tastings and events as well as a longstanding education program which now runs 5 days a week for 9 months of the year. This is our kind of wine shop!

Rumbles Wine Merchant (RWM)

32 Waring Taylor Street Wellington

Ph 04 472 7045
rumbleswine@xtra.co.nz

Step underground for a wine shop with a different feel. Like a set from the Wombles, this is a rustic and interesting store. But what it lacks in polish it certainly makes up for in range. This is a serious wine shop with a great range of imports – the NZ section is only one-quarter of the shop. An eclectic range is set off by entertaining shelf talkers (worth a read just for a laugh). Top shelf back vintages are hidden away in a climate-controlled cabinet (behind a ladder when we visited!). Ask to see the fine wine list – the back vintage range is to die for! Keen, passionate staff and good pricing make this an essential place to shop.

Wineseeker (Seek)

86-96 Victoria Street Wellington
Open M-W 10-7, T-F 10-8, Sat 11-6

www.wineseeker.co.nz
Ph 04 473 0228
wine@wineseeker.co.nz

"Unique and boutique" is the philosophy at this great location in downtown Welly, and it's very much reflected in its range – you won't find any supermarket wines here. The well-presented selection features France, Italy and Spain, with the NZ range emphasising Martinborough and Nelson. Wines are organised into sections according to mouth feel. There's a real "no nonsense" approach, to make wine accessible to everyone and monthly courses are offered in "How to Taste Wine & Wine-Tasting Tricks". Husband and wife team Nicola and Carl say they specialise in "matching people with wine." Sounds pretty good to us!

SERVING WINE

WINE LANGUAGE

There's an alarming amount of **pompous ceremony** associated with the rituals of wine drinking. While some of the old practices are helpful in getting the maximum enjoyment out of your favourite bottle, there's also a lot of superfluous etiquette perpetuated by wine snobs who want to look like they are 'in the know'. This handy little chapter is here to help you **cut through the crap!**

Serving wine is like serving food. You wouldn't serve your guests cold steak for breakfast in soup mugs. You know that timing, temperature and utensils are all an important part of the dining experience, and the same principles apply to wine.

'How much should I spend?' is an important question. **The Best Wines of 2009** cover every-thing from $5 to $500, so you have every base covered. One rule that we use is to always aim to serve a better wine than your guests would expect. This doesn't necessarily mean spending more. If you stick with **The Best Wines of 2009**, you'll nail this every time. Another rule of thumb is that the fewer the number of people you're sharing the bottle with, the better the wine should be. Save your most exciting purchases for special moments with your nearest and dearest. No one will care if you spend less on that bottle for your extended family reunion BBQ.

Good **glassware** is essential for fully appreciating wine. An ideal selection to have on hand would be a white wine glass, a red wine glass, a Champagne glass and a smaller glass for sweet wines. If you're tight for options, one medium-sized glass would cover all bases except Champagne. All good glasses curve in slightly at the top. Ironically, the finer the glass, the less likely that it will break when polished and the better it will look on the table. Avoid cut, engraved or coloured glasses as these make it harder to appreciate the colour of the wine. It's most important that there is not the slightest residue of detergent in the glasses as this will destroy the taste and smell of the wine. When pouring, never more than half-fill a glass.

Opening a bottle of wine does not require some ridiculous ritual with a fancy napkin and elaborate corkscrew. It's not as hard as some people make it look. To remove a cork, your first objective is to get your hands on a good corkscrew. There are plenty of strange contraptions out there, but many are guaranteed to make for hard work before you even start. Our favourites are the straightforward "waiter's friend" and the up-market "Screwpull."

First, cut off the capsule (we prefer to remove it completely) and screw the corkscrew vertically, straight and all the way through the cork. Then lever or pull using constant pressure rather than a nervous jerk. This will prevent the cork breaking and you elbowing somebody into next week! Always taste the wine yourself first to check that it's not "corked" (musty/cardboardy).

To open a screw-capped bottle, hold the entire cap and sleeve firmly in one hand, and twist the body of the bottle with the other. If only every bottle were so simple! Screw caps are our favourite closure because they don't have the detrimental effect on wine that many corks have.

Opening a champagne bottle is pretty easy, but many people make such a fuss about it that they end up stuffing it up altogether. There are a few basic points to grasp before showering your friends with a bottle of fizz. First, ensure that nobody has shaken the bottle before you get hold of it (not funny!). Always have a target glass nearby to pour the first gush into, and hold the bottle at forty-five degrees. Check the firing range for chandeliers and unsuspecting passers-by and re-aim if anything fragile is within range. Remove the capsule, but keep your thumb over the end of the cork as you remove the wire, in case the cork attempts to fire out of the bottle and lodge itself into someone's eye. Twist the bottle (not the cork) slowly and ease the cork out gently. When the cork is almost out tilt it sideways to release the gas slowly. This maintains the maximum bead (bubbles) in the wine. It should make a gentle hiss like a fine lady's fart, not an ostentatious pop (unless you're in a particularly vulgar mood, in which case the record to beat is 41400km/h). Check that the wine tastes right, then pour half a glass for each drinker, and top them all up after the 'mousse' has subsided.

Timing is important and if you follow the guidelines in our **Food and Wine** section, you'll have this nailed. Start with Champagnes and lighter, unoaked whites and work your way up in colour and intensity through oaked whites and into reds, finishing with sweeties and fortified styles. There are, of course, exceptions to this progression, but we'll leave it to you to find these in our **Food and Wine** chapter.

Decanting is the process of pouring a wine from one con-tainer to another. It serves the dual purpose of leaving any sediment behind and allowing the wine to "loosen up" through contact with air. There are all sorts of exotic decanters available, but any glass jug will do the trick. We tend to use very cheap, plain decanters because we're terrified of breaking expensive glassware! To decant a red, stand it upright for a day to allow the sediment to settle, open it carefully without stirring it up and then pour it into the decanter slowly and evenly. Look through the neck of the bottle to watch the flow of the wine and stop pouring as soon as you see sediment creeping near the neck. Looking through the neck at a candle can make this easier, but any light will work (a Dolphin torch is great!). You can then pour from the decanter, or double-decant back into the bottle (after rinsing the sediment out of the bottle).

Serving temperature has a big impact on the aromas and flavours of wine. Whether it's white or red, the exact same wine poured at fridge, cellar or room temperature will taste completely different. Fridge-cold whites taste flavourless and acidic, while warm reds tend to become soupy and undefined. Our simple rule of thumb is to **take a white wine out of the fridge and leave it sit for a little while before you serve it, but put a red wine in the fridge for a little while before you serve it.** An hour might suffice, but it depends on a few things. Lighter, unoaked whites can be a little cooler, oaked Chardonnays a little warmer. Lighter, fruitier, young reds like rosés and some Pinot Noirs are content in the fridge for a little longer than big reds. Sweet whites are the only wines that should be served really cold, since even Champagnes benefit from a spell out of the ice bucket. If it's a hot Aussie summer day, serve everything a little cooler and it will soon warm up. Don't be afraid to order an ice bucket with your red wine in a restaurant (we do!). You might cop a strange look from the waiter, but trust us – it will be worth it.

Following these principles can seriously add to your enjoyment of wine. Stick with these basic rules, but don't be afraid to experiment a little, and do have plenty of fun along the way.

wine language

This section is your code-breaker for unlocking the language of wine. You'll find here all those weird and wonderful words that you've wondered about but never been game to ask.

Acidity A crucial, natural, balancing element that gives a wine freshness, vitality and life and a sharp, clean taste on the back palate (finish).

Aggressive A sensation resulting from an excess of tannin, acidity or both.

Alcohol The common name for "ethanol" measured as a percentage of the volume of the wine. Alcohol is the result of fermentation, when sugar is combined with yeast.

Alcoholic A "hot" feeling on the palate, from high levels of alcohol.

Angular A wine lacking in fruit and depth, without a smooth taste.

Aperitif A drink used to gets the taste buds humming before a meal.

Aromatic Wines from pungently smelly or strongly scented grapes like Riesling, Gewürztraminer, Muscat and Tokay.

Astringent A dry or sour sensation on the palate, usually from high tannin levels in a red or high acidity levels in a white. Generally an indication of youth.

Austere Quirky, or maybe a little too young. Wines that seem difficult to appreciate, perhaps "closed", atypical or "funky".

Backward A wine that still tastes young despite its age leading you to believe that it should be more approachable.

Balance A wine that is in harmony, with all of its elements complimenting each other – the Holy Grail in winemaking and something we look for in every wine we taste.

Barrel-fermented A white wine that has been fermented in oak barrels giving rise to a stronger oaky flavour than those wines just aged in oak barrels.

Big A wine full of flavour.

Biscuity A quality usually associated with the nose and palate of Champagne.

Bite The fresh flavour that acidity brings to a wine.

Bitterness The acid and tannin taste resulting from over-pressing grape-skins, pips or stalks.

Blanc de Blancs A French term for a white wine made using white grapes only. On a bottle of Champagne it would signify a wine made solely from Chardonnay.

Blanc de Noirs A French term for a white wine made using red grapes only, achieved by removing the skins from the must before any colour leaches out.

Blending Mixing together several batches of wine (either different grape varieties or different parcels of the same variety) to create a final wine that is hopefully greater than the sum of its parts.

Blind Tasting A tasting where the identity of the wine is unknown. The reference does not relate to the state of the tasters afterwards!

Blowsy A low acidity wine that appears too fruity and unbalanced.

Body The weight of a wine on the palate (light, medium or full).

Botrytis cinerea Usually shortened to botrytis, "noble rot" is an unwelcome fungus, unless you want to make sweet wines, in which case botrytis is your best friend. It attacks the bunches and lives off the water within the grapes, thus concentrating the sugar levels.

Bottle Shock A recently shipped (or recently bottled) wine that appears to be jet-lagged, and needs time to settle down.

Bouquet The smell, aroma or nose of a wine.

Brettanomyces (Brett) A curious yeast that gives rise to a peculiar "mousey" smell on a wine. Not unpleasant in small amounts, but it can become a wine fault if it dominates.

Briary A term used to indicate a mixed berry fruit flavour, coupled with spicy notes.

Brilliant Apart from the obvious explanation, this word is also used to describe a clear, bright colour of a wine.

Brut French for "dry".

Bush Vine A training system that makes the vine look like a goblet! The vines are free standing, without a trellis, with short trunks and the grapes grow on short arms resembling a little tree. Used in low vigour, hot climate vineyards and is common for Grenache in McLaren Vale and the Barossa Valley.

Capsule The covering protecting the cork in a bottle of wine.

Cassis French for "blackcurrant" – a Cab Sauv descriptor.

Cat's Pee Not being "cat-men" we cannot vouch for this term, but it's a popular description for the nose on a Sauvignon Blanc.

Cedarwood The nose on an oak aged Cabernet Sauvignon or Merlot, particularly found in fine clarets.

Chewy This refers to the palate of a richly textured, often high alcohol wine. The flavour is so dense you can almost "chew" it.

Chocolate Dark chocolate can be found on many big red wines, perhaps in the combination of aroma and texture.

Cigar-box Another classic red Bordeaux term for the aroma of oak and fruit combined.

Cleanskin Traditionally, a wine sold at a lower price without a label or any indication of its identity. In recent years, the addition of an alternative label has become common, revealing, more or less, the identity of the wine. Wines are cleared as cleanskins for a reason - you've been warned!

Closed A wine that is somewhat subdued, not giving away much in the way of aroma or flavour. It usually needs more time to age or more air in a decanter.

Cloudy A bad sign. A wine that has not been stabilised, exhibiting suspended yeast, bacteria or micro-organisms, or a result of sediment in a red wine being shaken up unwittingly.

Cloying Mouth-coating, usually referring to a sweet wine and often a sign of a wine lacking in balancing acidity.

Commercial Not a derogatory expression, but rather an indicator of a crowd-pleaser, and what can be better than that?

Complex The sign of a fine wine, having a multi-layered flavour. A wine that reveals different aromas and flavours every time you taste it. Winemakers aspire to making complex, balanced wines.

Confected Seemingly a "chemistry-set wine" that is "made" in the winery rather than "grown" in the vineyard. A wine reminiscent of confectionery.

Cooked A feeling that the fermentation was too hot and the wine ended up being "stewed", with high alcohol and lacking balance.

Corked(-y) A faulty wine spoiled by a tainted cork – which happens far too often, in our opinion. See also 'TCA'.

Crisp A white wine with refreshing levels of acidity.

Cuvée A catchall word for an individual barrel, a blend or a style.

Decanting The process of pouring a wine out of its bottle into a decanter or jug, for the purpose of removing its sediment or just letting it breathe.

Demi-Sec A French term meaning half dry, therefore medium dry.

Depth The concentration or richness of flavour.

Developed A term to indicate maturity, as in underdeveloped – too young; well developed – ready to drink; over-developed – too old.

Digestif A smart word for an after dinner drink, a fine curtain-call to finish off a good dinner.

Domaine A French word for a winery that owns it own vineyards and makes its own wine.

Double-decanting Pouring a wine into a decanter, then back into its original bottle after having washed out any sediment.

Dusty A palate sensation usually associated with highish tannin levels, almost as if there was a dusty coating to the wine.

Earthy Another dimension to the aroma and palate, coming from the soil. A welcome element in the complexity of a wine.

Elegant An even, lingering flavour, that is pleasing, refined and not too overblown.

En-Primeur Any wines that are offered for sale before they have been bottled, similar to buying a "future".

Eucalyptus Found on the nose, this distinctive smell often pops up on Coonawarra Cabernet Sauvignons.

Extract The "guts" of a wine, making up its body.

Fermentation The conversion of sugar to ethanol (alcohol) and carbon dioxide (CO_2) by the addition of yeast.

Filtration The straining of solid particles from a wine.

Fine There are two meanings to this. "Fine Wine" is a catchall term for expensive and possibly rare wine. "Fine" on its own, implies a degree of "class" and "complexity".

Finesse Often used in the same breathe as "elegance", this is another word used for a complex if slightly lighter-bodied wine. Nearly always mentioned in the context of expensive Champagne.

Fining The clarification and stabilisation of must or wine by the addition of a "fining agent" which coagulates or absorbs solids.

Finish The end flavour left on the palate (aftertaste), measured in terms of length.

Flabby A wine lacking in balancing acidity, one stage worse than blowsy.

Flinty A gunflint or smoky scent picked up on Loire Sauvignon Blancs, coming from the French word "fumer" – to smoke (as in Pouilly-Fumé).

Fortification The addition of alcohol (usually grape spirit) to a fermenting wine (or after fermentation in the case of sherry) to arrest further fermentation, by inhibiting the yeast's ability to convert sugar to alcohol. This results in a higher than normal alcohol wine known as a fortified wine.

Forward A wine that can be drunk earlier (in its lifetime) than expected.

Free-run juice The finest quality grape juice that runs out of the grapes even before the press has been started as a result of the crushing process.

Fresh A wine with perky acidity and a lively flavour.

Funky Not always complimentary, this term can mean that a wine is a touch faulty but not enough to detract from the overall impression of the wine.

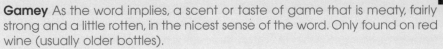

Gamey As the word implies, a scent or taste of game that is meaty, fairly strong and a little rotten, in the nicest sense of the word. Only found on red wine (usually older bottles).

Glugger A jokey word for a simple, undemanding, easy-to-drink wine that would please everybody's palate. Perfect for a party.

Grassy The "green" smell, often reminiscent of cut grass (cricket pitches), particularly in Sauvignon Blanc and Cabernet Franc.

Green An unripe smell and taste often found on thin Merlots and Cabernet Francs associated with an unripe crop resulting from overproduction or a bad vintage. Green wines tend to have "raw" acidity on the finish.

Grip The firm feeling on the back-palate brought about by dominant acidity or tannin. Essential in very ripe wines.

Hard Almost always followed by "tannins" i.e. too young to drink.

Harsh Another acidity and tannin adjective, suggesting a high degree of one or the other, or both.

Heady A dizzy-making feel to a wine. Not for quantity reasons, just alcohol levels.

Herbaceous Not to be confused with "green", this word conveys the scent of greenhouses or garden centres. Often a pleasant extra dimension to a wine.

Hot Wines with high alcohol.

Lanolin An oiliness found in some heavy white wines, particularly Semillon.

Late harvest Vines that are picked later than normal in the quest for extra ripe grapes with which to make intense dry white, very full-bodied reds and sweet wines.

Leathery Another superb descriptive word that conjures up new shoes, motorcycle gear, tack rooms and all manner of leather goods. Often found on Shiraz, Grenache and Cabernet blends.

Lees The dregs or sediment that settles at the bottom of a barrel or fermentation tank made up of dead yeast cells, grape-skin fragments, grape seeds and tartrates.

Legs The patterns made by wine sliding down the inside of a wine glass, as a result of its viscosity. Also known as "tears". Not a sign of quality, but simply of alcohol level.

Length The time that the wine's flavour lingers on the palate – the "finish".

Lively A reference to the keen acidity in a young wine.

Magnum Double-sized bottle (1.5L)

Malolactic Fermentation The chemical conversion of harsh malic acid to softer lactic acid, often shortened to "malo". White wines that have not been through malo often have punchier acidity. Cooler climate whites tend to go through malo to soften the overall impact of the acidity on the palate.

Meaty Always with reference to a huge red wine – you may need a knife and fork!

Mellow A character trait brought on by age, this usually means soft and smooth with a harmonious palate.

Méthode Traditionnelle Along with "Méthode Classique", the accepted terms for the finest process of sparkling wine production where the second fermentation occurs in the bottle in which the wine is sold. The old term was "Méthode Champenoise".

Mousse The fizz on the surface of a glass of sparkling wine or Champagne.

Mouth-feel A superb self-explanatory term referring to the sensation of a wine on the palate.

Musty A hygiene problem somewhere along the line leading to a stale aroma or taste. Usually disappears with aeration. If it doesn't, bin it!

New World This term refers to winemaking countries outside of Europe and the Mediterranean.

Nose The aroma, bouquet or smell of a wine.

Oak The wood used to make barrels in which wine is fermented and matured. French, American and Eastern European forests are the main sources of oak for wine barrels.

Oaky The smell and taste of oak barrels. Shouldn't be too intrusive.

Old World European and Mediterranean-bordering wine making countries.

Organic A wine made from grapes grown without the use of manmade chemical herbicides, pesticides or fertiliser.

Oxidised A wine spoiled by oxidation tends to be browning in colour and stale on the nose and palate.

Palate The flavour of a wine and also a word for your mouth.

Petrol Older Rieslings tend to have this unusual, pungent scent.

Press The grape squeezing apparatus.

Pungent Strongly scented.

Puttonyos The level of sweetness of Hungarian Tokaji (1-6).

Quaffing Drinking with purpose. See "glugger". This is what you would do with a case of gluggers!

Reductive A word associated with a "skunky" smell on a wine. This smell is of sulphur compounds such as hydrogen sulphide that should subside with aeration. Decant the wine and wave it around!

Residual sugar The remaining sugar in a wine that accounts for its degree of sweetness.

Rubber A sulphurous nose if too strong, but can actually be an attribute of some cheaper New World reds, or Italian Dolcettos.

Screw cap The closure of choice for any self-respecting winemaker who wants their product to make it to the consumer in exactly the way they put it into the bottle. Stelvin is one brand of screw cap.

Sediment The solids found at the bottom of some old red wines.

Sharp A term used for acidity beyond that of a balanced nature.

Short A disappointing "length" of aftertaste.

Silky Very smooth on the palate.

Sinewy A lack of juicy fruit character, exposing the acidity and tannin elements of a red.

Smoky In reds, smokiness can be found on a range of wines, particularly Shiraz, Nebbiolo, Mourvèdre and Grenache. In whites it is only really used for Pouilly-Fumé. See 'Flinty' above.

Spicy Regularly making it into our tasting notes, spicy means just that. Often countering a fruity flavour, a herbal spiciness on whites and a dried-spice character on reds is common and welcome.

Spittoon The correct term for the bucket that you spit into.

Spritz A gentle prickle of fizz on the palate. Found on young whites.

Structure The physical framework on which a wine's flavours are hung.

Sulphur Similar to the smell of a "struck-match", sulphur is detectable on the nose, but should disappear when the wine comes into contact with air.

Sulphur Dioxide (SO₂) Used as a preservative in finished wine and labelled as "Preservative 220 on the bottle."

Supple A lush, round style of wine with no obvious, hard acidity or tannin.

Tannin The bitter, astringent flavour that is found in grape skins, seed and stalks as well as oak barrels, that thankfully softens as red wines age. Tannins give rise to a "drying" sensation in the mouth and a harsh feel on the inside of the cheeks.

Tartrates The harmless crystals that are deposited during winemaking and occasionally form in bottles of wines. In our opinion, the appearance of tartrates in a white wine is a good sign as it means the wine has not been filtered – a process which means the wine inevitably loses some of its flavour.

TCA The full name is "2,4,6-trichloroanisole", the unpleasant, musty-smelling compound that gives rise to cork taint in wine.

Terroir A French word that rolls all of a particular vineyard's attributes such as micro-climate, soil, drainage, altitude, aspect, exposure and slope, into one beguiling term.

Toasty The nose associated with oak-aged wines, on account of the insides of the barrels being charred or toasted.

Tobacco See "Cigar-box".

Ullage The space between the top of the wine and the bottom of the cork in a bottle of wine.

Unctuous Intense, oily character usually associated with sweet wines.

Unfiltered Just that, a wine that is not filtered. More likely to throw a sediment and may, in time, require decanting.

Vanilla An aroma resulting from oak ageing, particularly in American oak.

Varietal A wine that displays textbook grape variety characteristics.

Vegetal A word that groups together various vegetable smells and tastes, mostly with reference to red wines. Not always derogatory.

Velvety The smoothest and most luxurious of textures on the palate. Merlot, Pinot Noir and other sensuous red varieties can attain this character if they are of the finest quality.

Vertical Tasting A wine tasting consisting of a number of different vintages of the same wine.

Vigneron A French vineyard worker.

Vintage The year in which a wine was produced.

Volatile Acidity (VA) Acetic acid, that in certain concentrations gives an off-putting vinegary smell. This is usually brought about as a result of shoddy winemaking.

Woody Over oaked, when you can't see the fruit for the trees!

Yeast The "agent" that transforms the sugar in grape juice into alcohol and CO_2 via the process of fermentation. Yeast is naturally found on grape skins or can be added by the winemaker in a process called "inoculation".

Yeasty The fresh-baked bread nose found on Champagne and other white wines mainly using Chardonnay.

Zesty A citrus taste associated with acidity and also with some white grape varieties like Sauvignon Blanc and Semillon.

We have not included "cheeky", "train-brakes", "frigid", "impudent", "wet park benches", "sweaty arm pits", "bashful", "precocious", "sex on the forest floor," or other such tasting terms. We'll leave it to you to figure these out!

index of food and wine

index of food + wine